NO MORE HEROES

Southern Literary Series
FRED HOBSON, SERIES EDITOR

NO MORE HEROES

NARRATIVE PERSPECTIVE AND MORALITY IN
CORMAC McCARTHY

LYDIA R. COOPER

LOUISIANA STATE UNIVERSITY PRESS)((BATON ROUGE

Published by Louisiana State University Press
Copyright © 2011 by Louisiana State University Press
All rights reserved
Manufactured in the United States of America
FIRST PRINTING

DESIGNER: Mandy McDonald Scallan
TYPEFACE: Whitman
PRINTER: McNaughton & Gunn, Inc.
BINDER: Dekker Bookbinding

Portions of chapter 3 first appeared, in somewhat different form, as "'Do you see this?': Meaning and Relationship in the Judeo-Christian Imagery of McCarthy's *Cities of the Plain*," *Journal of the American Studies Association of Texas* 36 (2004): 13–28, and are reprinted with permission. Chapter 4 first appeared, in somewhat different form, as "'He's a psychopathic killer, but so what?': Folklore and Morality in Cormac McCarthy's *No Country for Old Men*," *Papers on Language and Literature*, v. 45, no. 1, Winter 2009. Copyright © 2009 by The Board of Trustees, Southern Illinois University Edwardsville. Reprinted by permission.

Library of Congress Cataloging-in-Publication Data

Cooper, Lydia R., 1980–
  No more heroes : narrative perspective and morality in Cormac McCarthy / Lydia R. Cooper.
    p. cm. — (Southern literary series)
  Includes bibliographical references and index.
  ISBN 978-0-8071-3721-5 (cloth : alk. paper) 1. McCarthy, Cormac, 1933– —Criticism and interpretation. 2. McCarthy, Cormac, 1933– —Technique. 3. Narration (Rhetoric) 4. Heroes in literature. 5. Ethics in literature. 6. Empathy in literature. I. Title.
  PS3563.C337Z62 2011
  813'.54—dc22
                                                                                2010022280

The paper in this book meets the guidelines for permanence and durability of the Committee on Production Guidelines for Book Longevity of the Council on Library Resources. ∞

For my mum and dad

CONTENTS

ACKNOWLEDGMENTS IX
ABBREVIATIONS XI

INTRODUCTION
NARRATIVE PERSPECTIVE AND MORALITY IN McCARTHY'S NOVELS 1

1.
"WORD AND FLESH"
NARRATIVE AND MORALITY IN THE EARLY APPALACHIAN NOVELS 24

2.
"A DREAM OF SHRIVING"
EMPATHY AND THE AESTHETICS OF CONFESSION IN *SUTTREE* AND *BLOOD MERIDIAN* 52

3.
"PLEDGED IN BLOOD"
LINGUISTIC INTERIORITY AND REDEMPTION IN THE BORDER TRILOGY 76

4.
"HE'S A PSYCHOPATHIC KILLER BUT SO WHAT?"
MORAL STORYTELLING IN *NO COUNTRY FOR OLD MEN* 110

5.
"THERE IS NO GOD AND WE ARE HIS PROPHETS"
HEROISM AND PROPHETIC NARRATIVE IN *THE ROAD* 132

CONCLUSION
FINDING HEROISM THROUGH EMPATHY IN McCARTHY'S NOVELS 161

WORKS CITED 179
INDEX 183

ACKNOWLEDGMENTS

This book would not have been possible without the generous support of many wonderful people. The first debt of gratitude I owe is to Art Palacas at the University of Akron, in whose 2002 graduate course on linguistics I wrote my first paper on McCarthy. Palacas also offered me the opportunity to present this paper at the PALA (Poetics and Linguistics Association) conference at New York University during the summer of 2004. In addition to being a great linguist and teacher, he is an inspiring human being, sacrificially embodying the ethical principles he teaches.

At Baylor University, Joe Fulton deserves more thanks than I could ever give. He is an exemplary mentor and model of professorial excellence, such as when he proved a point by telling a rapt class about the time he cherry-bombed a church. Despite his terrorist inclinations as a child, however, his adulthood has shown him to be a great scholar who, even with multitudinous obligations, mentors graduate students with patience and care, making himself available for every step of the process.

Richard Russell is another exemplar of academic excellence. Unlike Fulton's, his childhood was blameless, although his graduate classes are extended experiments in sleep deprivation and the consumption of caffeinated beverages. Yet his thorough and inspirational teaching forges professors out of graduate students and writers out of dabblers, and I am inexpressibly grateful to him.

Mike Parrish, Luke Ferretter, and Greg Garrett at Baylor University also guided me skillfully through the early stages of writing this book. I would like to thank Garrett in particular for his seminar on religion and literature in which he taught *Blood Meridian* and *The Road* with special attention to Roman Catholic imagery and the sacramental. I had not previously considered either concept, but I now realize they are central to any reading of McCarthy's works. In addition, I would like to mention the students of that class. Of notable influence was Robert Hamilton, who voiced what I have long felt about McCarthy's writing but had not been able to articulate. According to Hamilton, McCarthy's prose is "the King James Bible on crack."

With sincerest thanks, I would like to express my gratitude to Fred Hobson for his work both on the Southern Literary Studies series of LSU Press and on this book project, and to John Easterly, who is the Platonic ideal of an executive editor in so many ways, not least of which is his meticulous attention to detail and his enthusiasm for the works that he sees through from primordial mess to finished project.

And, finally, I thank my parents for being wonderful parents, despite the fact that they have not yet read any novels by Cormac McCarthy, nor will they ever read this book. Love you both!

ABBREVIATIONS

All the Pretty Horses	ATPH
Blood Meridian	BM
Child of God	COG
Cities of the Plain	COTP
The Crossing	TC
No Country for Old Men	NCFOM
The Orchard Keeper	TOK
Outer Dark	OD
The Road	TR
The Stonemason: A Play in Five Acts	TS
The Sunset Limited: A Novel in Dramatic Form	TSL
Suttree	S

NO MORE HEROES

INTRODUCTION
NARRATIVE PERSPECTIVE AND MORALITY IN McCARTHY'S NOVELS

The arc of the moral universe is indeed long but it does bend toward justice.
—CORMAC MCCARTHY, *The Stonemason*

The naturalistic novel is therefore not so superficial or reductive as it implicitly appears to be in its conventional definition. It involves a belief that life on its lowest levels is not so simple as it seems to be from higher levels. It suggests that even the least significant human being can feel and strive powerfully and can suffer the extraordinary consequences of his emotions [...].
—DONALD PIZER, *Realism and Naturalism in Nineteenth-Century American Fiction*

IN *The Orchard Keeper* (1965), jailed bootlegger Marion Sylder criticizes the idealistic fervor of young John Wesley Rattner. "[Y]ou want to be some kind of goddamned hero," he tells the boy. "Well, I'll tell ye, they ain't no more heroes" (214). In general, Cormac McCarthy's bleak literary worlds, scarred by grotesque images of human squalor and depravity, lend credence to the bootlegger's claim. But despite the "nihilistic mood" that seems to brood over these brutal landscapes, the concept of heroism is not completely consigned to ancient history (Bell 1). Examples like the father's despairing yet self-sacrificial love for his son in *The Road* (2006) suggest instead that questions about the definition of heroism and goodness may be intrinsic to human nature. A complex dialectic between despair and idealism runs through McCarthy's corpus, making any attempt to identify a unifying worldview in the novels a challenging, if not impossible, task. However, the novels consistently illuminate the valiant inner struggles of men trying against all odds to be good. In these cases, the narrative shifts from McCarthy's typical mode, an omniscient third-person narrator, to a limited third- or even first-person perspective, permitting readers to engage empathetically with the character's moral thoughts, perceptions, or intentions. While McCarthy's literary cosmos may be creeping closer and closer to apocalyptic damnation, narrative shifts in point of view and brief yet provocative revelations of interior thought draw attention to those characters seeking community and justice—characters who, in other words, demonstrate a fragile heroism in the face of doom.

Of course, declaring that there may be merit in studying narrative perspective and its relationship to empathy and morality in McCarthy's novels raises an immediate objection: namely, that one of the most notable—and noted—narrative techniques McCarthy employs is his restriction of revealed internal thoughts and perceptions. Richard B. Woodward claims, for instance, that McCarthy is a "writer who renders the brutal actions of men in excruciating detail, seldom applying the anesthetic of psychology" (28). Jay Ellis likewise draws readers' attention to the "salient feature" of McCarthy's style, "the absence of regular psychologizing" (5), while James Bowers considers it "striking to find a contemporary writer of McCarthy's gifts that has so spurned the Joycean tradition of interiority" (14). Rick Wallach also points out that McCarthy's earliest published writings, his short stories, demonstrate a "descriptive distance from the character's center of consciousness [that] reaches its apogee in the mature works, [where it becomes] a key tenet of McCarthy's style" (20). Such critical concurrence reflects the almost overpowering impact of McCarthy's most typical narrative style, the objective, omniscient narrator so tonally distant and removed that readers feel as if they were watching the fictional events from the wrong end of a telescopic lens.

McCarthy's narrative style therefore seems to almost consciously reject the twentieth-century novel's attention to the important role of literary empathy. In *Empathy and the Novel*, Suzanne Keen claims that literary empathy, a reader's "vicarious, spontaneous sharing of affect" with a fictional character, has not always been perceived as a boon (4). From their birth in the early eighteenth century, novels were suspected of dangerously stirring up too many passions (37). It was only the "translation of *Einfuhlung* in the early twentieth century" that finally created a sea change in popular views on empathy, most notably captured by Virginia Woolf's radical assertion that empathy, rather than narrative, ought to be the driving force of fiction (59). Some contemporary theorists criticize such ethically motivated approaches to literature, worrying that overemphasizing empathy as a reason for reading may flatten or ignore the variances of human experience and expression. But Keen argues that a cross-cultural and universal concern about a human tendency to lack compassion for others actually drives the theoretical practice of reading empathetically: "[T]he presence of Golden Rule variants may show a near universal worry that humans tend not to treat others as they would themselves," she says (163). However, if the ubiquitous Golden Rule indicates a certain universal concern about self-serving behavior, McCarthy's novels demonstrate a rather more-than-usually severe pessimism about humanity's general aptitude for inhumanity.

At first glance, the very inhumanity practiced in McCarthy's novels might seem to suggest that his is a literary universe inhospitable to the practice of empathy. It is his pessimism about humanity, after all, that produces his characteristic narrative style in which an omniscient narrator alienates readers from fictional characters by relating the events of the story in a tonally objective and removed voice. Thus, a question arises: are McCarthy's novels merely nonempathetic depictions of inhumanity, capable only of showing readers what *not* to do, what *not* to be like? Martha Nussbaum suggests that the ethics of empathetic reading requires readers to maintain a discriminatory distance from texts. The reader holds a "conversation both with other readers and with the arguments of moral and political theory," so that, occasionally, readers must "reject some experiences of reading as deforming or pernicious" (10). In other words, she warns that the ethically minded reader may consider certain texts too dark, too resistant to any attempts at finding an edifying interpretation. Such texts, Nussbaum implies, may not merit the ethically minded theorist's efforts. McCarthy's literary universe is a blighted one, a place where rapists, cannibals, and blood cults wander unchecked, and such a damaged cosmos may cause readers to pause and consider whether such a world is, after all, "deforming" and "pernicious."

However, such a conclusion seems, against all expectation, too reductive for most of McCarthy's critics. For example, Edwin Arnold admits that *Blood Meridian,* in many ways McCarthy's most spectacularly nihilistic work, may be reduced to the argument that "life is infinitely fascinating but ultimately has no meaning other than that man imposes on it" (61). And yet the intuitive reader will discover, Arnold says, that even in the face of the novel's catastrophic ending, "moral choice remains" (63). Arnold's insistence that there must be some redemptive meaning in even the most diabolical novel is one that seems to undergird most criticism on McCarthy's controversial corpus. Voicing such an underlying assumption, Jay Ellis asserts that McCarthy's novels depict an ominously "darkening worldview," but despite his gloomy prognostication, Ellis castigates those few critics who "mis-read" McCarthy as a nihilist, comparing them to critics who reductively assert that Samuel Beckett is a nihilist (290). The reluctance of so many critics to write McCarthy off as a nihilist, despite their recognition of the unplumbed depths of depravity in his works, suggests that his novels present a rather complicated ethics. Reality itself can be rather dark, and perhaps McCarthy's complex, knotty ethical arguments demand attention precisely because they offer necessary insight into an increasingly complicated nonfictional world.

But even granting such an assertion, how can McCarthy's novels, so resistant to revelations of interior thought or emotion, justify an extended analysis of narrative perspective and empathy? After all, a cursory scrutiny of the novels reveals that McCarthy frequently fuses egregiously violent narrative events with an aesthetic style that emphasizes the implacability of a universe unconcerned with human life, a narrative style that often estranges the reader from the characters rather than encouraging empathetic connection. Yet this resistance to facile constructions of literary empathy suggests the critical importance of those moments that evoke, or even demand, the reader's empathy, moments that do indeed crop up throughout McCarthy's corpus. In *The Act of Reading*, Wolfgang Iser discusses the interplay between an aesthetic text and the reader's reception of that text, pointing out that artistic writing distances itself from realism, or from a sort of one-to-one transmission of an idea. Rather than merely trying to faithfully transmit an image or idea to the reader, the artistic text throws up impediments to the reader's reception of the image or idea, making that concept in some way surprising and alien. The result of this counterintuitive process, Iser says, is that readers read *and react* to the text, so that readers "comprehend the fictional text through the experience it makes us undergo" (189). If Iser is correct, then McCarthy's alienating narrative style may be constructing an engaged audience, one that is, subconsciously or not, already participating in what Nussbaum calls an active education in building the "capacity for humanity" (121).

Thus, examining McCarthy's aesthetic construction of empathy, a construction that prohibits readers' empathetic engagement with most characters while directing readers toward a more sympathetic encounter with other characters, reveals a consistent yet complex argument about the ethical necessity of imagination in human interaction. Before commencing an examination of the aesthetics of empathy in McCarthy's novels, however, it is important to recognize that his most eye-catching narrative style—one that refuses to reveal characters' internal thoughts and by so doing estranges readers from an empathetic engagement with the characters—is not ubiquitous. That is, while McCarthy does restrict revelations of characters' internal thought processes, he does not eradicate such revelations altogether. The almost exclusive critical focus on the novels' more dominant mode of narration has, for the most part, overlooked the crucial role played by those few revelations of interior thought.

Some of McCarthy's fiction actually does construct ordinary worlds peopled with sympathetic characters whose thoughts and emotions are described on a regular basis. For example, despite its apocalyptic narrative content, *The Road* (2006) portrays a father and son who share a tender, meaningful emotional bond and whose bond is described through narrative revelations of the father's emotions. This emotionally intimate narrative technique is not as unusual as it may seem. Nor is *The Road*'s focalization of a loving relationship unprecedented. McCarthy's first published short story, "Wake for Susan" (1959), consistently reveals the protagonist's thoughts and emotions, using most of the obvious stylistic means for doing so. Furthermore, the story constructs a rather pointed argument in favor of the ethical individual's obligation to practice empathy.

In order to explore how McCarthy's fiction constructs opportunities for readers to engage empathetically with characters, both traditionally and nontraditionally, it is important to first briefly examine how fictional texts in general reveal characters' interior worlds and draw readers into an empathetic engagement with those literary worlds. In *Language in Literature,* Michael Toolan claims that narratives often employ a variety of "discourse modes"—basically, literary techniques for revealing different characters' perspectives. The two primary modes are direct and indirect discourse, where direct discourse is the direct revelation of a character's speech or thought, often signaled by explicit speech or thought tags ("She wondered, 'Why did he do that?'"), while indirect discourse reveals such information indirectly ("she wondered why he had done that"). As Toolan points out, direct thought is "more versatile, dramatic, etc. [than indirect thought]," and also "tends to imply narratorial respect for a character" (107, 108). In "Wake for Susan," McCarthy relies on direct discourse, revealing his protagonist's emotions and thought processes through explicit thought tags (e.g., "He felt"), as well as using syntactic shifts that indicate directly represented (though not formally introduced) thought (3). For example, at one point the story's protagonist, a young man named Wes, picks up an old, spent rifle ball and examines it. The sentences following indicate Wes's thoughts through a syntactic deviation, an explicit tag, and a sentence framed by an evaluative adverb and an evaluative adjective:

> In the rain-washed red clay gulley he stooped and picked up a flattened hog-rifle ball. He scraped the mud from the oxidized lead and examined it. Well. Wes wondered when it had been fired, who had fired it, and at what, or whom? Perhaps some early settler or explorer had aimed it at a menacing Indian. (3)

In this passage, the syntactic fragment "Well" indicates that narration has given way to the presence of an evaluative consciousness; someone, upon observing the rifle ball, is preparing to draw some conclusions about what that spent ball means. The consciousness in this case cannot be attributed to the observing narrator but must belong to the story's protagonist, Wes. The next sentence explicitly attributes the evaluative tone to Wes: Wes "wondered" about the rifle ball. The following sentence is prefaced by an evaluative adverb ("perhaps") and ends with an evaluative adjective ("menacing"). The sentence's evaluative mode must once again be attributed to Wes, as he turns the ball over in his hand and muses about its historical significance and—as the story later explains—the role of death and the nature of what remains.

But of course the stylistic revelations of Wes's evaluative consciousness in this passage are by no means typical of McCarthy's novels. On the contrary, McCarthy's novels are, as mentioned previously, renowned for their implacable rejection of characters' interior thoughts. An obvious example is the punctuation-stripped prose, which lacks "unnecessary" commas and apostrophes and, most noticeably, all quotation marks. McCarthy also restricts the use of speech and thought tags. In general, the visual starkness of the text reflects an equal absence of subjectivity. The lack of commas, ellipses, and parentheses—all of which often indicate the presence of an evaluative consciousness—mirrors a syntactic refusal to acknowledge evaluative consciousnesses other than that of a distant, removed narrator. For example, in *Blood Meridian* (1985), the main character, an unnamed kid, is shot in a bar fight. Like the section from "Wake for Susan" examined earlier, the opening pages of *Blood Meridian* depict a scene involving a fired rifle and a question about the nature of death and the worth of human life in light of the ubiquity of death. The tone, however, is noticeably more distant, the boy's plight failing to dent the flinty objectivity of the narrator:

> On a certain night a Maltese boatswain shoots him in the back with a small pistol.
> Swinging to deal with the man he is shot again just below the heart. The man flees and he leans against the bar with the blood running out of his shirt. The others look away. After a while he sits on the floor. [. . .] Only now is the child finally divested of all that he has been. (4)

The syntactic patterns in this passage remain standard subject-verb-object constructions until the final sentence, unlike the passage in the short story, where syntactic fragments ("Well") indicate a shift from the narrator's perspective to the evaluation of the character. Finally, the last sentence in this example from *Blood Meridian* refers to the kid as "the child," a verbal infantilizing that the kid would, one presumes, fiercely resent. In other words, the larger metaphysical connections between the kid getting shot and the kid being stripped of his inherited identity must be attributed to the narrator rather than the kid.

This distant, nonempathetic narrative style typifies McCarthy's novels, it is true, but while *Blood Meridian* refuses to reveal its characters' thoughts, not all of McCarthy's other novels banish all revelations of characters' interior worlds in the same fashion—even when they *appear* to do so. In McCarthy's novels, shifts in point of view are rarely indicated through explicit direct or indirect discourse markers, but the absence of explicit thought tags should not be taken to mean that the narrative perspective has not shifted to the interior world of a character. Interiority—descriptions of the interior thoughts, intentions, and observations of a given character—can be revealed through many linguistic and stylistic devices. Occasionally, as in his short story "Wake for Susan," McCarthy's novels indicate interiority through explicit linguistic clues, such as "he thought." More commonly, his novels limit such explicit clues. In situations where the text seems relatively external, however, there are still occasions (a few) on which a text reveals a particular character's *perceptions* without explicitly describing that character's thought processes. These perceptions are revealed through shifts in narrative point of view. That is, a third-person omniscient narrator may describe an individual character's thoughts, but in those cases the interpretation and revelation of the thoughts must be attributed to the omniscient narrator. When the narrative shifts to a limited third-person style, however, the text often reveals the perceptions of the focal character in such a way that the reader may attribute the perceptions or evaluations in the text to that particular character rather than a distant narrator or the author. Typically, authors use explicit textual clues, such as "he thought," to indicate when an omniscient narrator is ceding point of view to the limited perceptions of a single character (the "he" doing the thinking). McCarthy's novels, of course, resist such explicit textual clues, but they do use some systematic linguistic clues to indicate a movement from omniscient to limited perspective.

Shifts in perspective from objective narration to subjective narration often appear as implicit linguistic clues—subtle directional words indicating a particular character's point of view or a variation in sentence styles—rather than more obvious textual clues. From a linguistic perspective, all words or phrases that indicate point of view express the perspective of the text and are therefore important clues in textual interpretation. Linguist Susumu Kuno, in *Functional Syntax: Anaphora, Discourse and Empathy*, claims that certain verbal expressions are by nature directional and that an examination of the directional expressions of a given sentence will indicate the perspective from which that sentence is presented. In his chapter "Empathy Perspective," Kuno says that directional expressions create a phenomenon he calls literary empathy. Literary empathy, for him, is based on the assumption that a reader automatically attempts to identify him- or herself with the speaker of a text or, in the absence of a clearly identified speaker, with the character whose point of view controls the narrative of a text (206). Kuno uses the term "speaker" to mean the person controlling a text's point of view. He claims that even in the absence of explicit indications of the person controlling a limited text's perceptions (such as "he thought"), texts contain some stylistic elements that point to the character whose mentality controls the text. He even says that "[s]peakers unconsciously make the same kind of decision that film directors make about where to place themselves with respect to the events and states that their sentences are intended to describe" (204). A text indicates point of view through words that demonstrate a particular perspective, such as the phrases "come up to" and "go up to." These phrases are directional and imply a primary or controlling point of view: "X *comes up to* Y [. . .] requires that the speaker describe the action from the camera angle of Y rather than X" (225). In other words, directional terms, and likewise deictic terms, terms such as "here" or "today," which require a contextual referent, indicate a particular point of view that "controls" a text, at least to the extent of controlling the "camera angles" that record the particular scene's actions and events. In McCarthy's novels, shifts in perspective are frequently delineated through such directional words and phrases and through changes in syntactic style from full sentences to fragments.

Suttree (1979), a semiautobiographical novel, demonstrates the significance of examining directional words and syntax shifts as key indicators of shifts in perspective, shifts from omniscient narration to the point of view of a single character. This novel thematically suggests that humanity is defined in terms of empathic connections and that without empathy, the human remains disconnected from virtue, self-knowledge, and community. Given this argument, it is not surprising that the novel frequently reveals the thoughts and emotions of the main character, Cornelius Suttree, encouraging readers to practice empathy for him even when he fails to practice the same for his friends and family. At times these revelations appear in the form of first-person passages from Suttree's point of view—the most obvious form of direct discourse—but at other times, the narrative shifts from the omniscient third person into the limited third person, from Suttree's point of view, without any of the obvious textual clues. For example, in the scene in which Suttree first meets and then defends the mentally slow Harrogate, the objective narrative shifts into Suttree's perspective without an explicit linguistic tag:

> Suttree looked at him [Harrogate]. He was not lovable. This adenoidal leptosome that crouched above his bed like a wizened bird, his razorous shoulderblades jutting in the thin cloth of his striped shirt. Sly, rat-faced, a convicted pervert with a botanical bent. Who would do worse when in the world again. Bet on it. But something in him so transparent, something vulnerable. (54).

In this scene, the narrative sentence ("Suttree looked at him") is followed by a modally evaluative sentence. "He was not lovable" is a judgment made on Harrogate, but to whom ought readers attribute that judgment? The narrator? Suttree? No explicit thought tag constrains readers to recognize Suttree as the consciousness making the evaluation, but the following sentence fragment indicates that Suttree's perspective controls the narrative at this point. The possessive pronoun "his" can refer to Harrogate or Suttree, since the antecedent is not clear. In the context of this passage, however, it seems that "his" refers to Suttree; Suttree has been woken by Harrogate's peering over the edge of his bunk into Suttree's. Three of the following four sentences in this passage are also syntactic fragments. The only other grammatically complete sentence in the passage, "Bet on it," is in the imperative, and its attribution is not ambiguous: the speaker must logically be Suttree addressing himself. Following the first narrative sentence, then, this entire passage must be understood to take place inside Suttree's mind. As Suttree watches Harrogate hovering over him, he evaluates the boy's physical and moral ugliness yet feels compassion for the boy, so the shift in perspective, indicated through such tenuous markers as a vague pronoun reference and a syntactic shift, illuminates a compelling moment of empathetic connection on Suttree's part.

McCarthy's novels most frequently indicate shifts in perspective through syntactic style shifts. His eye-catching virtuosic and pyrotechnic style shifts have captured critical attention from the beginning. Vereen Bell notes, for example, that one of the novelist's most distinguishing characteristics is his syntactic style, which "ranges amazingly from plainest human speech to a dense, polyphonic rhetoric" (xiii). Since Bell's groundbreaking work, many critics have noted the striking contrast between the two most prevalent literary styles in McCarthy's novels. The first style, a "stripped," Hemingwayesque narrative in which a basic Anglo-Saxon vocabulary predominates, often gives way to a dense, syntactically compounded style peppered with archaic or arcane vocabulary. This second style, of course, attracts the most critical attention, and responses to and interpretations of the style vary considerably.

Linguistic analyses of this second style suggest that the elevated diction "foregrounds" these dense passages, constraining readers to pay closer attention to them and to expect deeper meaning from them. Nancy Kreml's "Stylistic Variations and Cognitive Restraint in *All the Pretty Horses*" and Arthur Bingham's "Syntactic Complexity and Iconicity in Cormac McCarthy's *Blood Meridian*" are both insightful linguistic analyses of McCarthy's dense passages. Both authors suggest that style shifts may indicate perspective shifts, although they restrict their discussions to the specific texts on which they focus and make few remarks about larger interpretive themes throughout McCarthy's corpus. Kreml, on the one hand, argues that the "foregrounded" linguistically dense style in *All the Pretty Horses* "allow[s] the reader access [. . .] to the inner workings of the characters' minds" (37). Bingham, on the other hand, claims that the linguistically dense passages in *Blood Meridian* foreground scenes of violent action rather than characters' interior worlds. McCarthy's use of the "dense" literary style, Bingham says, is in direct contrast to his literary predecessor's use of that style; "Faulkner's complicated syntax was often used to depict a character's stream of consciousness," he points out, "but with the exception of Judge Holden, if McCarthy's characters in *Blood Meridian* have interior life the reader never learns of it" (20). And Judge Holden's interior life is revealed only through his spoken monologues, so that the reader has no more insight into the workings of Holden's twisted mind than do his companions. Thus Kreml and Bingham, two of the only critics to address the function of the two literary styles' interplay in McCarthy's novels, seem to arrive at two divergent conclusions. If these critics are right, then the foregrounded style in one novel functions differently than in the other novel.

A possible solution to this quandary is to note that the "foregrounded" passages in *All the Pretty Horses* differ syntactically from those in *Blood Meridian*. The *All the Pretty Horses* passages are often complex sentences or fragments ("Sweeter for the larceny of time and flesh, sweeter for the betrayal" [141]), while in *Blood Meridian*, they are usually compound narrative sentences ("In the neuter austerity of that terrain all phenomena were bequeathed a strange equality and no one thing nor spider nor stone nor blade of grass could put forth claim to precedence" [247]). In McCarthy's novels, complex or fragmented sentences almost always indicate a shift into a limited third-person perspective, but compounded syntax only sometimes indicates a shift in perspective. Most frequently, the dense, lyrical style produced by McCarthy's characteristic compounded sentences merely suggests the presence of the unnamed omniscient narrative voice that dictates most of McCarthy's novels. Robert Jarrett agrees with Kreml that the stylistically lyrical passages in *All the Pretty Horses* tend to reveal "interior" moments, but he conflates John Grady's revealed interiority with the lyrical passages in *Blood Meridian,* failing to distinguish between the disparate uses of the style in the two novels (Jarrett, *McCarthy* 122). For Jarrett, lyrical passages in all the novels indicate the presence of a "literary" character, a character who is literate and whose mental life is revealed textually. He proposes that

Judge Holden and Suttree are such characters and that both are "avatars" of the author, and so the revelations of interiority merely indicate that "[l]anguage's esthetic appeals can be wielded for good or for ill" (124). Judge Holden's flowery speeches are authorial and impressive, but they are *speeches,* not revelations of his mental life, which remains as hidden from view as any other character's in that primordially dark novel. Clearly, syntactic styles do function differently in different novels.

So shifts between narrative perspectives may be signaled by explicit discourse markers, or they may be signaled more subtly by shifts in syntax or the presence of directional words or phrases. Complicating this study even more, McCarthy uses almost every conceivable mode of narration, so that novels narrated by a distant third-person narrator occasionally undergo radical shifts from unintrusive to intrusive narration. For example, in *Child of God* (1973), the narrator deviates twice from an objective, third-person descriptive style to the imperative mood, directly addressing the audience by claiming that Lester Ballard is "[a] child of God much like yourself perhaps" and, later, adjuring the audience to "[s]ee him [Ballard]" (4, 156). *Blood Meridian* also commences with a narrative adjuration: "See the child" (3). At other times, however, intrusions into the objective narrative come from other consciousnesses in equally radical shifts from third to first person. In *Child of God,* whole sections are narrated in the first person by (unnamed) members of the community who watch Lester Ballard (e.g., 9, 17). *No Country for Old Men* (2005) also employs sections of first-person narrations that act as interpretive frames for narratives primarily viewed through the uninterpretive eyes of an omniscient narrator, while *Suttree* and *The Road* include brief interludes of first-person narration in texts that are primarily narrated in the limited third person.

What overarching conclusions, if any, can be drawn from these complex and seemingly inconsistent patterns of syntactic style and narrative point of view? An examination of narrative perspective—revealed explicitly by verbal thought tags or implicitly through syntactic style shifts—suggests that shifts in narrative point of view consistently draw attention to characters' instinctive movements toward "goodness," however vaguely that quality is defined. That is, while narrative point of view typically remains with an omniscient observer, occasionally the perspective changes to that of a particular character, or the omniscient narrator becomes an active character, evaluating and interpreting the text. These shifts in point of view can occur as subtly as a move from a panoramic description of landscape to the limited perception of a single human observer. They can also be as dramatic as a shift from third-person narration into first-person narration. But shifts in point of view are consistent in one respect: they draw attention to morality—a character's ethical impulses, for example, or a character's moral action.

Thus, in the three examples cited earlier, from "Wake for Susan," *Blood Meridian,* and *Suttree,* only two passages—from the short story and from *Suttree*—give any indication about the internal worlds of the characters. In both instances, the revelations of the characters' internal worlds suggest that they are sensitive to moral quandaries and possess an awareness of their own moral responsibility. So, for example, in the short story, Wes recognizes the metaphysical weight of death symbolized by a rifle ball. Later, he creates a fantasy love affair with a dead girl in order to grieve her death and the death of all people whose lives are lost in the shadow of history. In the section from *Suttree,* Suttree feels pity for Harrogate despite recognizing the boy's moral turpitude. This pity prompts Suttree to defend Harrogate from another inmate and become a surrogate father figure to the boy. *Blood Meridian*'s kid, however, draws no larger conclusions from his near-death experience, and his apathy toward human life—even his own—is mirrored by the narrative's refusal to grant him an active internal life.

The patterns set up by these three passages are consistent throughout McCarthy's corpus. Some of McCarthy's darker novels, such as *Blood Meridian,* are narrated by a mostly unintrusive, distant third-person narrator with no shifts in point of view. Other narratives follow more morally developed characters, such as Wes in "Wake for Susan," a young man prefiguring John Grady Cole in the Border Trilogy. As in the short story, the narrative mode in the two novels of the trilogy that follow John Grady often shifts into the limited third person in order to reveal his perceptions or thoughts. Finally, novels such as *Suttree* and *The Road* follow the main character so closely that the narrative often reveals the inner workings of the characters' minds, at times moving so close that the character's first-person voice actually takes over the narration. An examination of narrative perspective therefore suggests that McCarthy's novels systematically privilege the heroic moral attitudes and actions of characters populating horrific and violent literary worlds.

The significance of shifts in narrative perspective, it should be emphasized, lies in the fact that such shifts are departures from the normal narrative mode. McCarthy's bleak landscapes bear all the traditional literary markings of American naturalism, not least of which is a reliance on an omniscient third-person narrator who empirically examines the effects of outside forces on the narrative's main characters, who in turn are permitted little or no control over the text's point of view. And McCarthy's characters certainly demonstrate little or no internal thought processes or evaluative consciousness as they stumble around, buffeted by implacable natural forces and driven by insatiable primal urges. This tendency on McCarthy's part to avoid revelations of interiority is deeply ingrained. For example, "A Drowning Incident," the second of McCarthy's two short stories, follows the actions of a boy while remaining distant from his motivations and thoughts. As Wallach points out, the short story describes the boy's thought processes rather than the content of those thoughts, reflecting the same narrative "distance" that characterizes McCarthy's novels (20). Such narrative distance has led some critics, including James R. Giles, to assume that McCarthy's naturalism is unalleviated and unnuanced. Giles claims that McCarthy's deterministic universe denies characters agency and interior life, a technique that is typical of naturalistic writers; but, according to Giles, while most naturalistic writers suggest that society can be redeemed, McCarthy denies all such potential for social amelioration (5). Such a bleak evaluation is hardly warranted, however. Throughout McCarthy's corpus, some characters distinguish themselves from the herd of unthinking human creatures, and these characters are undeniably more likely to make conscious choices indicating an ethical commitment or a sense of internal rectitude.

The existence of a few such unusually moral characters does not indicate that McCarthy is not a naturalistic writer. Quite the contrary. Donald Pizer, in *Realism and Naturalism in Nineteenth-Century American Fiction*, claims that there is often a tension at the heart of naturalistic novels between an authorial recognition of the primal, destructive nature of humankind and a conflicting "desire to find some meaning [. . .] which reasserts the validity of the human enterprise" (11). In Pizer's view, naturalism as a literary movement is far more complex than many critics recognize. In focusing on the social outcasts of corrupt societies, naturalism essentially reasserts an "ethical conception of life, for it asserts the value of all life by endowing the lowest character with emotion and defeat and moral ambiguity, no matter how poor or ignoble he may seem" (12). Morality in McCarthy's novels is a function of human nature as much as violence and depravity are, if a less common function. The novels privilege those rare moral choices, portraying them as beautiful and courageous precisely because they so often crumple under the implacable destructive force of nature. But these moral characters nevertheless exist in a naturalistic world. A character's moral choices should not be interpreted as indicating his or her internal growth or maturation, which would be more common to realistic novels than naturalistic ones. The fact that McCarthy's characters are not entirely devoid of interior life, in the end, draws attention to a life- and meaning-affirming quality made all the more precious for being so rare.

It is also important to note that shifts in narrative perspective illuminate many different levels of morality, from vaguely moral inclinations to strongly ethical behavior. While McCarthy's moral characters may be identified as such by their lack of actively *bad* behavior—they do not, for instance, scalp people, rape children, or eat babies, as some of the bad characters do—their morality is sometimes faint enough that it fails to show up in their actions. For example, Sylder fails to verbally reinforce John Wesley's desire to be a hero. In McCarthy's universe, morality, in some situations at least, must be defined as different from merely "good" external behavior. Suttree, for instance, is a problematic example of a moral character because, although he grapples with moral questions, he usually fails to live up to his own moral standards. He is, as one character puts it, a "fourteen carat gold plated son of a bitch" (*S* 156). In the end, Suttree is moral only because he contends internally with his own immorality. McCarthy's novels thus suggest that morality is an internal state, a struggle against the despair of a meaningless world, as much as it is a set of external behaviors. An examination of those few revelations of interior consciousness, then, reveals their significant role in McCarthy's corpus. In his stage play *The Sunset Limited,* the street preacher Black defends his attempt to stop White from committing suicide by claiming that he has an ethical obligation to save others. When White questions the source of this obligation, Black says that he gets all of his ideas from his religious beliefs: "The first thing you got to understand," he says, "is that I aint got a original thought in my head. If it aint got the lingerin scent of divinity to it then I aint interested" (13). McCarthy's literary landscapes are in general very hellish places, but rare glimpses of compassion and hope suggest that these human qualities bring a "lingerin[g] scent of divinity" to an otherwise morally rancid universe.

Given that these novels are populated by the nastiest sludge of the human species, from incestuous hillbillies to pedophiles, genocidal maniacs, and cannibals, and given that even the most moral characters seem to have internalized, to some extent, the rampant misogyny, misanthropy, and misery of their worlds, a statement should perhaps be made at this point about the nature of moral behavior in McCarthy's novels. After all, moments in which any characters display emotions or thoughts deserving of readers' empathy are few and far between. Yet the scarcity of such moments does not correlate with their impact on readers. As Keen points out, "*empathy for fictional characters may require only minimal elements of identity, situation, and feeling, not necessarily complex or realistic characterization*" (69, italics hers). Yet even more than the encouragement of empathy by minimal literary "elements," the denial of empathy is an effective tool underscoring the significance of that literary function. Iser claims that literary negation—the denial of a reader's expectation—frequently intensifies the underlying message of a text as readers are forced to construct the implicit message left by the negation. That is, what the text denies or deletes contrary to a reader's expectation draws attention to that missing thing, so that "[n]egation is therefore an active force which stimulates the reader into building up its implicit but unformulated cause as an imaginary object" (213). Iser uses William Faulkner's *The Sound and the Fury* as an example of a text that, through its multiple perspectives, "gives rise to a pattern of expectations which the reader has to abandon from one account to the next" (219). In a similar pattern, McCarthy frequently sets up characters and then denies readers access to those characters' minds and emotions, violating readers' expectations of the normative modern literary experience. Often in these cases, what is left in the blank void when empathy fails, the reader realizes, is an utter lack of humanity. In other cases, McCarthy's novels demonstrate a complicated pattern of negation and limitation. Empathy is at times utterly denied, as in *Blood Meridian*, and at times is reduced to its most minimal expressions, as in *All the Pretty Horses*. Yet these reductions and denials in fact stimulate readers to recognize the link between empathy and humanity. And, against all expectations, readers practice more empathetic engagement with the novels than they are consciously aware of doing.

Even more significantly, the virtue exhibited by McCarthy's few decent, civilized characters is not necessarily either constrained or diminished by their more obvious moral flaws. In *Reading Lolita in Tehran*, Azar Nafisi claims that the reading of fiction is inherently ethical, that "[i]t is only through literature that one can put oneself in someone else's shoes and understand the other's different and contradictory sides and refrain from becoming too ruthless. Outside the sphere of literature only one aspect of individuals is revealed. But if you understand their different dimensions you cannot easily murder them" (118). This idealistic description of the power of literary empathy seems initially to have little to do with McCarthy's violent, murderous texts—until one notes that Nafisi bases her argument for the ethical clout of literary empathy on Vladimir Nabokov's *Lolita*, a novel that invites readers to empathetically engage with one of the most morally reprehensible characters in literature, the child-rapist and murderer Humbert Humbert. The ethics of empathy does not derive from the goodness of the character with whom readers empathize, then, but rather from readers' ability to understand the humanity of even the most despicable human beings—to understand that evil as well as virtue are human potentialities.

Like Nabokov, McCarthy seems interested in asking readers to engage with morally uncomfortable perspectives, perspectives that draw readers' attention to the darkest, bleakest depths of human depravity. But maybe that is precisely the point of literary empathy. McCarthy's fictional worlds are—intentionally or not—filled with ethical landmines. For example, Nell Sullivan points out that Rinthy Holme, one of the few good characters in *Outer Dark*, is not permitted any narrative authority. The text never shifts into her perspective, thereby valorizing her virtue; Rinthy, Sullivan concludes, is a victim of McCarthy's characteristic misogyny, her "doll-like" portrayal symptomatic of a general objectification of women (68). McCarthy's novels depict few women, it is true, and the women who do appear are often either corpses or on their way to becoming corpses. Of course, men are just as likely to be objectified, turned into corpses, or more explicitly dehumanized by being described exclusively in bestial terms. *Suttree*'s Harrogate, for example, is a relatively innocent if disgusting young man, introduced in derogatory terms as "a slavering nightshade" and later described as "rat-faced" (*S* 34, 54). These two examples of textual dehumanization are problematic enough, but McCarthy's depictions of minorities are often even more ethically troubling. Alejandra, a blue-eyed Mexican girl with a European education, is John Grady Cole's love interest in *All the Pretty Horses,* while swarthier Mexicans constitute the dangerous element in the novel, guarding and populating the prison. This example is just one indication of the consistent association of the ethnic "other" with evil. In *No Country for Old Men*, Anton Chigurh may be blue-eyed, but he is "exotic"—his evil is explicitly associated with his ethnic alterity (112).

Despite McCarthy's misogynistic silencing of women, the dehumanizing descriptive terms leveled at already-marginalized characters like Harrogate, or the stigmatizing of the ethnic other, however, narrative intrusions or shifts in perspective warn readers against practicing a similar lack of empathy. Suttree, for example, mimics the narrator in applying dehumanizing adjectives to Harrogate; he finds him an "adenoidal leptosome," making him sound more like a biological specimen than a thin, runny-nosed boy. But Suttree nevertheless learns to feel compassion for the young man, a compassion illuminated by the novel's revelation of Suttree's mental life (54). In McCarthy's fiction, all people, both men and women, are often subjected to descriptions associating their human qualities with bestial or inanimate images and terms. Nevertheless, revelations of interiority rehumanize these characters, who would otherwise be no more than faintly animate beasts.

In fact, the dehumanized and marginalized characters are often perceived by other characters, or by the novel's narrators, as symbols of the root cause of inhumanity: a fundamental alienation, an incurable loneliness. While Sullivan has a point in arguing that Susan, Wes's dead object of desire in McCarthy's earliest short story, has some resemblance to dead women like Magdalena in *Cities of the Plain* (1998), she does not fully explore the symbolic nature of this fantasy love affair, and it is as a symbol that Susan speaks most profoundly to Wes of the need for humans to be—ironically enough—more than merely symbols. McCarthy's first story is stylistically juvenile compared to the rest of his fiction, and the central metaphor is so blatant that it seems to beg for more nuanced readings, such as Sullivan's. However, as embarrassingly as it is presented, the metaphor should perhaps be permitted to stand on its own. In the story, Wes's imagined affair has very little to do with Susan as a woman. His fantasy is predicated upon his feeling that "Susan should have a lover" (4). Susan represents for Wes not *women* specifically, but rather the less specific "dead" of humankind—she is "all the lost Susans, [. . .] all the people; so beautiful, so pathetic, so lost and wasted and ungrieved" (6). Wes's love affair is not with a corpse so much as it is an affirmation of a mysterious spiritual interconnectedness of humanity throughout history.

McCarthy's second story, "A Drowning Incident" (1960), returns to this theme of the necessity of grief over death as a validation of life. Stylistically far more advanced, this story follows an unnamed boy who discovers a sack of drowned puppies. Apparently believing that the puppies were born to his hound dog Suzy and drowned by his father, the boy takes one of the drowned puppies—a crawfish has burrowed into the puppy's stomach and its entrails are "green" and "oozing"—and places the rotting corpse beside his sleeping baby sister. He then waits for his father to return home (4). In this story, in contrast to "Wake for Susan," McCarthy restricts interiority. The narrator informs readers that the boy "had [. . .] a great hollow feeling which [. . .] gave way to a slow mounting sense of outrage," but the central action of the story is related with no indication of the boy's mental life, no explanation of his intentions, and no description of his feelings upon the completion of his act (4). By restricting revelations of interiority, McCarthy requires the audience to construe the boy's rationalization and intentions, and as Iser's theory of aesthetic negation predicts, this narrative device is far more effective than the somewhat forced metaphor of the earlier story. "A Drowning Incident" ends with the boy "waiting for him [the father] to come home," and this cryptic narrative sentence pushes the internally and externally silenced waiting into bold relief (4). What is missing draws attention to itself. In this instance, the absence of descriptions of the boy's emotions draws attention to the vital necessity of those emotions. Restricted interiority and the final static description of the boy sitting and waiting thus heighten the story's energy, stylistically mimicking the boy's act by insisting that the father—and the audience—read into the silence all the rage and grief that death ought to incur.

In the dark worlds of McCarthy's corpus, human affinity is always endangered if not practically extinct, but it is also the source of human hope. The urge toward connectedness with others becomes absolutely primal in these novels. When a character's internal thoughts and motivations are revealed, such revelations almost always serve to emphasize that character's visceral need for others. Even the narrative events underscore the importance of connection. Rinthy's search for her child, Billy's search for his pregnant she-wolf in *The Crossing*, the father's love for his son in *The Road*, and so many of McCarthy's characters' despairing search for an extant God all suggest that these characters are implacably drawn toward some elusive sense of connection. Even radically disconnected characters such as Lester Ballard express desires for affinity through perverted and grotesque sexual desires. Ballard cannot function within society, but he seeks warped versions of connection through his necrophilia and through his affinity for womblike caves (he first emerges from his recently discovered caves "slick with red mud" and later, trapped in the caves, has "cause to wish for some brute midwife" [107, 189]). McCarthy's novels do not construct nuanced arguments about ethics and morality. Instead, they focus on stripping away all signs of humanity in order to examine the tiniest seed of what it means to be good. In the novels, what it means to be good, essentially, is to recognize at some instinctive level the need one has for others. Morality may appear as nothing more significant than a visceral desire for community or connection. But that most primitive empathic impulse haunts the otherwise inhumane worlds with a devastating "scent of divinity" (*TSL* 13).

McCarthy's repeated iterations of the craving for intimacy and connectedness present in even the most malformed soul draw attention to the importance of ethical readings of the texts. In stripping away the veneer of civilization, McCarthy reveals the uncivilized horrors in humankind's dark heart, but the darkest of hearts possesses an equally present yearning for companionship, respect, and love. Readers are encouraged to empathize with these instinctive desires and thus to recognize the shared bond between all humans. At the same time, however, the more typical removed third-person narrator permits readers to remain morally distant from the often corrupt and sometimes completely deranged characters. In McCarthy's universe, empathy almost never extends to the evocation of sympathy. Instead, the narrative style encourages readers to maintain a firm grip on their critical capacity; readers are primed to execute judgment even as they recognize their shared humanity with the characters they judge. Empathy in these novels is therefore deeply affective, even if it does not provoke the level of emotion readers may expect from twentieth-century novels. Nussbaum claims that empathy can be disconcerting when practiced in conjunction with judgment, because such critical empathy encourages the reader to recognize both shared humanity and shared inhumanity. Critical empathy "exacts a frequently painful confrontation with one's own thoughts and intentions" (5). Examining the aesthetic constructions of empathy in McCarthy's novels therefore draws attention to the uncomfortable realization that the absolute and self-sacrificial love depicted in *The Road* springs from the same source as Ballard's necrophilia. The different paths such desires for connection take are determined, perhaps, by the smallest of ethical margins.

So, although the narrative techniques in all of McCarthy's novels are complicated and function differently in different works, the moral urgency of narration remains a driving force through all the novels. Chapter 1 will examine the systematic narrative shifts that valorize moral behavior in McCarthy's three early Appalachian novels, from the narrator's problematic exhortations to pity Ballard in *Child of God* to systematic shifts in narrative perspective that privilege moral behavior in *Outer Dark*. Chapter 2 considers the aesthetics of confessional and anticonfessional genre patterns in *Suttree* and *Blood Meridian* in order to study the link between revealed interiority and penitence. Chapter 3 looks at revealed interiority in the Border Trilogy. *All the Pretty Horses* and *Cities of the Plain*, the two novels in which John Grady Cole appears, reveal John Grady's interior world at key moments in the narrative—moments of moral ambiguity, ambition, or guilt. *The Crossing* and *Cities of the Plain*, however, do not reveal the interior world of the second protagonist, Billy Parham, who is an equally moral character (even, some might argue, a less problematically moral character). Billy's role places him as the narrator and interpreter of John Grady's self-sacrificial death, and because Billy interprets John Grady's death, he himself is interpreted through an observing narrator. The role of narration is interwoven with the text's patterned revelations of interiority, creating a complex landscape upon which play out the valiant struggles of two ethical men in a world so damaged that it is threatened by encroaching apocalypse. Chapter 4 suggests that Chigurh and Sheriff Bell in *No Country for Old Men* are depicted as fairy-tale "devil" and "prophet" archetypes, and the foregrounded fairy-tale elements in the novel play out that text's argument about the creative nature of narrative in a destructive world. Chapter 5 examines revelations of the father's thought processes in *The Road*, processes that draw attention to his role as a prophet and guide to his son, who is imagined as an incarnation of human goodness. These readings demonstrate that the value of human life is inextricably tied to the value of words in McCarthy's dark but sublime fictional world. In the novels, stories construct meaning and instruct in empathy and as such form a bulwark against the overwhelming tide of human degeneracy.

In general, McCarthy's moral characters tend to recognize—and often agonize over—the fragility of their belief in the worth of their own choices. Ben, in McCarthy's play *The Stonemason*, claims that "nothing is finally understood" but notes that he has chosen nevertheless to bear witness to the "small acts of valor [that] may be all that is visible of great movements of courage within" (131). These small acts he imagines to be represented by his father's work-hardened hands, the craft of stonemasonry being symbolic of his father's belief in constructive meaning. It is an image that, for Ben, holds the possibility of a greater redemptive meaning. But Ben also recognizes the possibility that this image holds no redemptive meaning; his choice to bear witness is made despite his awareness of the devastating possibility that all images are meaningless, that there is no God to bear witness and so the human capacity to bear witness is also meaningless. Ben's fear reflects White's conviction of ultimate meaninglessness in *The Sunset Limited*, but unlike White, Ben holds onto a tenuous belief in spite of an undermining despair.

McCarthy's novels avoid reductive conclusions about the meaningfulness of morality, since the characters who demonstrate heroic qualities and who fiercely hold to the value of moral acts are, in the end, only a few characters stumbling around in a world seemingly contrary to their redemptive visions. At the same time, the novels place the reader in the position of the one who finally bears witness, like Ben, to the otherwise hidden struggles of these characters. McCarthy's few narrative revelations of the "courage within" thus illuminate and privilege those small acts of valor (*TS* 131). Ellis at one point notes that McCarthy seems to value deed more than word, that he "prefers the hand to the mouth" (60). On the one hand, at some level this statement is doubtless true, since the deed predominates over the word so comprehensively. On the other hand, McCarthy's novels suggest that even though the deed may count for more than the spoken word, the internal thought process, the moment of a single choice, may in the end be the most significant measure of the human condition. However much an apocalyptic despair seems to brood over the novels' blasted landscapes, interior revelations of morality suggest that hope may be a defining characteristic of humanity. And since narrative is the means by which these interior moral commitments are valorized, the novels suggest that heroism and narrative are inseparable from each other and, by extrapolation, from human existence.

Narrative is thus a vehicle for bearing witness to moral courage, and at times narrative is the only means by which morality is recognized. It is telling, for instance, that Marion Sylder's criticism of his idealistic acolyte's belief in the value of just and ethical behavior is verbal. He attempts to crush the boy's idealism by telling him that "they ain't no more heroes" (*TOK* 214). The boy looks back at Sylder with a disillusioned gaze, and faced with the disillusioned child's countenance, Sylder half-rises and thinks, "*That's not true what I said. It was a damned lie ever word*" (214, italics his). Sylder "takes back" his verbal statement inside his head, so the boy never hears it. Readers, however, are privy to Sylder's recognition of his own verbal failure. In the next scene, the boy leaves Sylder and goes out to return a bounty that he won for killing a hawk, demonstrating a stubborn refusal to relinquish his belief that life matters and cannot be reduced to monetary value. Sylder may be correct that heroism itself is futile, but the boy's physical act reiterates Sylder's mental self-correction. Readers, unlike the characters in the novel, are permitted to connect the boy's physical action and Sylder's mental one, indicating that thought processes play a vital role in interpreting the troubling worldview of McCarthy's corpus. McCarthy's novels foreground the most extravagant catastrophes of human evil, like the test atomic bomb exploding at the end of *The Crossing* or the frenzied drug-related murders in *No Country for Old Men*. But through this horrific tapestry of violence, careful readers find woven throughout slender threads of hope in the form of a few individuals who recognize and practice the saving graces of love and imagination in a world set on destroying those very qualities. A systematic examination of shifts in the novels' narrative perspective, from the omniscient third-person narrator to the perspective of a single individual, thus provides sufficient evidence to conclude that it is indeed a "damned lie" that there are not still heroes in McCarthy's dark and decaying literary world.

1
"WORD AND FLESH"
NARRATIVE AND MORALITY IN THE EARLY APPALACHIAN NOVELS

Black: I see a different truth. Settin right across the table from me.
White: Which is?
Black: That you must love your brother or die.
White: I don't know what that means. That's another world from anything I know.
— CORMAC MCCARTHY, *The Sunset Limited*

A T the end of *Outer Dark* (1968), Culla Holme meets a blind prophet figure who tells him, "It's all plain enough. Word and flesh" (240). The blind man's enigmatic assertion reflects the tension that runs through McCarthy's fiction, a tension between competing views on the meaningfulness of life expressed through their rejection of language as a means of effecting empathetic connection. In *Outer Dark*, this tension comes to a head in a confrontation between the blind prophet and Culla, in which the blind man suggests an intrinsic link between life (flesh) and language (word). Culla, however, rejects both word and flesh when he refuses to speak and warn the blind man away from a nearby bog. Culla thus sentences the stranger to death through his refusal to speak, an action committed not out of malice but rather out of Culla's radical lack of empathy, his complete disconnection with other humans. Just previously, Culla has met the bearded maniac whose band of ruffians later kills and eats Culla's son. The maniac asks Culla to guess his identity, and Culla responds sullenly, "You ain't nothing to me" (234). Culla's refusal to show interest in this man whose followers devour human flesh is reminiscent of the same disaffection shown by the kid in *Blood Meridian* (1985), who tells the Judge who will (rape?) and murder him, "You aint nothing" (331). This cross-textual similarity suggests that Culla and the kid are similar characters marked by their disaffection with the worth of human life, men who verbally deny the significance of evil men and consequently deny the importance of the flesh they mutilate. In *The Sunset Limited* (2006), Black claims that words are meaningful because flesh (human life) is inherently meaningful; he says, appropriating Auden's famous assertion, "[Y]ou must love your brother or die" (121). White, however, claims that "forms"—by which he means symbolic language, which he pictures as hung human cadavers—"no longer have any content" (139). The contention between White and Black elucidates the tension between Culla's view of the world and the blind prophet's: language is meaningful only if human life also has meaning. McCarthy's three earliest Appalachian novels, *The Orchard Keeper* (1965), *Outer Dark*, and *Child of God* (1973), all follow the tortuous paths of characters who have in some way rejected humankind. Consistently throughout McCarthy's corpus, the rejection of humanity is inextricably tied to a rejection of linguistic power, in particular the power to control narrative interpretation through point of view. And in these early novels, word and flesh are so interwoven that characters who deny the significance of the latter are textually denied access to the former.

In *The Achievement of Cormac McCarthy*, Vereen Bell somewhat misleadingly claims that McCarthy's first three Appalachian novels present a consistent fictional world, one in which "meaning does not prevail over narrative," a condition resulting from the fact that the novels' main characters are "for the most part solitary and unsocialized" (5). Bell's descriptions of these early novels portray them as almost monolithically dark, chaotic, and peopled by wandering misfits in the murderous and deranged vein of Flannery O'Connor's famous Misfit in "A Good Man Is Hard to Find." However, as Barbara Brickman points out, the grotesque and spectacular violence of *Child of God*, which follows a deranged, necrophiliac killer named Lester Ballard, and *Outer Dark*, in which a man and his sister look for their child, incestuously begotten and abandoned for dead by the violent brother, tend to eclipse *The Orchard Keeper*'s comparatively ordinary and moral world (57). In *The Orchard Keeper*, a young boy, John Wesley Rattner, looks to an itinerant moonshine-runner, Marion Sylder, as a father figure, neither of them realizing that Sylder has killed John Wesley's real father. Although speckled with violence and predicated on murder, *The Orchard Keeper*'s bildungsroman story line wends its way through eruptions of violence and social decay while keeping its attention fixed, albeit anxiously, on moral certainties, such as definitions of heroism and goodness in a viciously corrupt world. While these three novels are often classed together—both for convenience and because of their similarities in setting relative to the rest of McCarthy's corpus—the nuances among them ought not to be overlooked. The three novels display worlds of varying chaos and carnage, and they also present different narrative techniques weaving together those variously disordered worlds. An examination of the use of narrative point of view illuminates the subtle variations in these novels and suggests that they by no means present monolithic worldviews. Rather, although each novel explores themes of the human quest for meaning and for connection, the various novels explore these themes from different perspectives, arrive at different conclusions, and employ different stylistic techniques to play out the different approaches.

There are important differences among these novels to consider, but first the thematic similarities need to be recapitulated. Consistent and crucial themes can be seen throughout McCarthy's corpus and crop up as early as his two short stories, published during his college years. In both "Wake for Susan" (1959) and "A Drowning Incident" (1960), the protagonists are faced with an image of death—a tombstone and a drowned sack of pups, respectively—and the subsequent narratives depict their reactions. Wes in "Wake for Susan" responds to the tombstone engraving by creating a vivid fantasy life that attempts to resurrect a long-dead girl, or at least to resurrect a fresh grief over her death. The boy in the second story more problematically brings a decaying corpse of a puppy home and places it next to his sleeping sister, suggesting his rage at his father's drowning a litter of dogs. The short stories address themes of death and degeneration, but death functions as the definitive calibration of the value of life. If death, in the final analysis, is meaningless—something not to be grieved or even remarked upon—then life is also meaningless. Death remains constant in all of McCarthy's works. What differs is characters' reactions to and interpretations of the meaningfulness of death. So while a fundamental darkness pervades McCarthy's corpus, darkness is not the final—or even the most important—word. Bell claims that McCarthy's preliterate, antisocial characters and the elusive transcendence that exists outside their peripheries suggest that "existence precedes essence," that people exist without meaning but that some characters "dream" of meaning, an act of hope that "impose[s] some human rule upon their otherwise bereft lives and change[s] mere living into being" (115). Bell spends little time elaborating on these transcendence-seeking "dreamers," but his point is well taken: in McCarthy's literary worlds, death is the single known absolute. But death, while absolute, is not the final answer to the deeper mysteries that haunt these texts and the few characters who actively seek transcendence.

Transcendence, of course, is also a tricky country to navigate in McCarthy's corpus. Very few characters achieve enlightenment of any sort; in McCarthy's novels, the act of seeking seems to be an end in itself. Courage lies in the capacity to seek community, to recognize and adhere to archaic moral obligations, and to practice hope (however agnostic) in the face of the known absolute, death. In his early short stories, McCarthy describes the immeasurable value of life through a boy's love affair with a dead girl and another boy's horrifying revenge for a drowned puppy's death. His earliest published writing, in other words, demonstrates some of the same dysfunctional relationships that crop up in his later work, but those dysfunctional relationships also foreshadow later works' consistent themes of humanity's search for meaning. The stories also foreshadow McCarthy's development of one of his most important stylistic devices, restricted interiority. The three early Appalachian novels demonstrate varying degrees of restricted interiority just as they also explore varying "takes" on the themes of death, grief, and the incurable ache for human connection. Also, just as McCarthy's short stories demonstrate a mature shift from the more abstract *idea* of a dead woman to a tangible *image* of a crawfish-infested dead puppy, the three early novels pay increasing attention to the physical world rather than the more ephemeral world of human thought and emotion. However, as "A Drowning Incident" suggests, narratives that focus on action and on physical bodies (a puppy corpse placed in a baby's crib) nevertheless point to larger metaphysical questions about the nature of death and morality.

McCarthy's first novel actually demonstrates more explicit descriptions of interiority ("he thought," and so forth) than most of his later novels. Furthermore, *The Orchard Keeper*'s attention-grabbing use of italicized memory and thought suggests that interiority in all its forms is less restricted in this novel than in many later works. *The Orchard Keeper* tends to get overshadowed by the much more explicitly vicious worlds of *Child of God* and *Outer Dark*, a critical oversight that fails to recognize this novel's attention to the persistent nature of hope. As Brickman points out in "Imposition and Resistance in *The Orchard Keeper*," the novel's central themes deal with questions of moral codes and standards, themes that "become problematic" in the two later novels, leading too many critics to ignore those themes altogether in this novel, even though later novels, such as the Border Trilogy, focus on these very themes (57). Arthur Ownby's and John Wesley's struggles in *The Orchard Keeper* are consistent with struggles of characters searching for a moral code in a chaotic, codeless world in *All the Pretty Horses* (1992) and *The Crossing* (1994). In *The Orchard Keeper,* for instance, young John Wesley traps and kills a hawk for bounty money and later learns to regret his action, a minor plotline in this novel that parallels the major plotline in *The Crossing,* where Billy Parham traps a she-wolf and then journeys to Mexico to right his wrong (*TOK* 77). In fact, it is possible to argue that *The Orchard Keeper*'s central argument is posed by Marion Sylder when he tells John Wesley that "they ain't no more heroes" in the world (214). The boy's minor heroisms, however—saving a hound and attempting to repay the bounty he earned for the hawk—suggest that Sylder is right in finding his argument to be, in the final analysis, a "damned lie." Heroism in this novel, as in so many of McCarthy's novels, is mostly futile. But the fact of it remains: heroes may not be able to *right* the wrongs of the world—to bring back the dead or stop death from happening—but even failed attempts at salvation are evidence of some human instinct for life and hope.

James Bowers, in a brief discussion of McCarthy's narrative techniques, points out that *The Orchard Keeper*'s italicized sections play out the novel's narrative themes of heroism. These sections "interrupt the main narrative to reveal a series of Arthur Ownby's memories," including an estranged wife, his discovery of Rattner's corpse, and so forth (141). These italicized memories indicate that Ownby possesses a moral consciousness, unlike the more dubiously moral Sylder. More importantly, Ownby's capacity to recall anything makes him an unusual character. Bowers does not explore at length the significance of this power, but he asserts that "[a]lthough the italicized passages diminish as we proceed chronologically through the fiction, the significance of the first-person tales increases" (141). What Bowers means here is that memories related in the third person earlier in the novel give way at the end of the novel to directly represented, first-person memories. The sections revealing Ownby's directly represented thoughts toward the end of the novel offer explicit interpretive devices; the old man's moral quandaries suggest that he is aware of a sort of primal obligation toward his fellow man and toward nature. When the boy attempts to return the bounty he earned for the hawk in the following scene, readers interpret the boy's actions in light of Ownby's internal monologue in which he concludes that it is immoral to benefit from another creature's suffering (TOK 229).

Bowers feels that Ownby's memories hold interpretive weight, but these directly represented memories and thoughts are not the same narrative technique employed in *Suttree* (1979). In that novel, Suttree's thoughts are revealed through "free indirect narrative, abandoning the use of italics save in the long prolegomenon" (Bowers 141). The important distinction between the use of directly represented thought in *Suttree* and *The Road* (2006) and that in *The Orchard Keeper* is that Ownby's thoughts are represented in his dialect. The only two characters whose thoughts are represented directly are Sylder and Ownby, and both of them "think" in their Appalachian dialect. Sylder thinks that what he said was "*a damned lie ever word,*" and Ownby thinks that "*Ever man loves peace and a old man best of all*" (214, 229). The elimination of unstressed end syllables, like the dropped "y" in "every," represents their accents, so that the recorded thoughts are kept as close to the actual *sound* of the men's voices as possible. These dialectic representations are not present in third-person indirectly recorded memories. For example, in the last italicized section of the novel, Ownby is being examined by a doctor, whose questions about Ownby's scars prompt the old man's flight of memory. In that memory, Ownby is seated "*in decorous rectitude*" (230). Another indirectly recorded memory—the first recorded memory in the novel—represents the thoughts of a minor character, the barman Cabe, who recalls an "incident" in which the bar's porch collapsed into a ravine. In that memory, Cabe recollects that "[t]*he* [bar's] *rear door* [. . .] *once g[ave] onto a porch*" (23). The linguistic sophistication of both of these memories, consistent with the diction of indirectly recorded memories throughout the novel, indicates that the memories being recalled are dictated by a narrator, since neither man would describe the scenes in his *own* voice using such phrases as "decorous rectitude" or "giving onto." In contrast, both *Suttree* and *The Road* often use such archaic and elevated diction and vocabulary in directly recorded thought, where the diction must be attributed to the character himself. Suttree, for instance, remembers his grandfather dying and thinks, "He wheezed my name, his grip belied the frailty of him" (*S* 13). And in *The Road*, the father thinks, "On this road there are no godspoke men. [. . .] Query: How does the never to be differ from the never that was?" (27). Both passages are recorded in the first person and thus must be attributed to the respective "speakers," Suttree and the father, who apparently are capable of using vocabulary like "belied" and "query" and ornate diction that separates possessive phrases ("frailty of him") and creates new vocabulary ("godspoke") in order to explore metaphysical questions of the nature of death and the eschatological end of humanity. The narrative points of view in *Suttree* and *The Road* clearly are more closely tied to the main characters, Suttree and the father, both through limited close third-person narration and first-person narrative sections, unlike the points of view in *The Orchard Keeper*, where the omniscient narrator's voice is kept distinct from the voices of the characters whose mental worlds are revealed.

The narrative shifts between points of view rapidly in *The Orchard Keeper*. Because of the shifting perspective and the different men's memories that pepper the narrative, there cannot be any clearly identifiable "protagonist" in *The Orchard Keeper* (in contrast to *Suttree* or *The Road*, both of which focus on one clearly identified protagonist). Additionally, as *The Orchard Keeper*'s narrative shifts into more than one character's perspective, again contrasting with *Suttree* or *The Road*, the narrative fragments the novel's overarching questions about the role of morality in a morally ambiguous world. For example, Ownby's directly represented thoughts concern his musings on morality, but, just as Sylder's somewhat positive thoughts are never communicated in speech, the old man's musings on morality are also never put into speech. In fact, the old man's moral musings appear only at the very end of the novel, after he has been incarcerated in an insane asylum, relegating his interior world to the ramblings of an unhinged and aged man. However, his internal monologues demonstrate a rigid moral code: he will not benefit from another's suffering—a moral code that the boy, John Wesley, later adopts and practices. But because Sylder's and Ownby's directly represented thought is represented in the dialect of the speaker, the thoughts remain clearly distinct from the narrative itself.

Given that *The Orchard Keeper* isolates interior thought, representing that thought in dialect, the novel's argument about heroism ultimately remains somewhat ambiguous. However, because for McCarthy indirectly recorded memories and directly recorded thought are always associated with moral characters or with characters struggling with moral questions, the novel finally suggests that although the world may have lost its legendary "heroes," it cannot fully escape an innate desire for heroism. Furthermore, through shifts in point of view, readers are encouraged to empathize with characters such as the boy who demonstrate a commitment to behaving heroically, or at least to believing in heroism despite harboring sincere doubts on the viability of such an archaic concept. For the most part, the narrative remains distant, dictating the lives and actions of the characters. When the narrative point of view does shift to the viewpoint of a particular character, that character is always engaged in some sort of moral struggle. For example, Sylder is introduced as a man who is part of a world where landscape is as animate as the primordial creatures thereon; Sylder is born in a region where the mountains "contort the outgoing roads to their liking," but Sylder himself is stripped of agency by a narrator who dictates the relevant information of his life—his birth in 1913 and so forth:

> It [Red Branch, a small community in eastern Tennessee] was a very much different place in 1913 when Marion Sylder was born there, or in 1929 when he left school to work briefly as a carpenter's apprentice for Increase Tipton, patriarch of a clan whose affluence extended to a dozen jerrybuilt shacks [. . .]. (11)

The facts of Sylder's life are consistently subordinated (in this case, in literal syntactic subordination, as well as semantic subordination) to the facts of the natural and political landscape around him.

The narrative remains far removed from Sylder until he walks into a bar. Once in the bar, the narrative point of view narrows suddenly to the perspective of Cabe, the barman, who watches Sylder and slowly recognizes the long-absent man:

> Sylder eyed the coins briefly, then looked up.
> Come on, Cabe, he said. We drinkin or not?
> Yessir, Cabe said, clambering down from his stool. Then he thought: Cabe. He studied the man again. Wraithlike the face of the lost boy grew in the features of the man standing at the bar. (14)

Narrative action (Sylder's eyeing the coins then lifting his gaze) gives way to description of internal action with the explicit verbal tag, "he thought." The thought ("Cabe") is not explicated; the single word indicates that Cabe is reflecting on the fact that a seeming stranger knows his name, and that reflection causes him to look a second time at Sylder, upon which a descriptive sentence ("Wraithlike the face of the lost boy [. . .]") depicts Cabe's mental perception. Cabe, however, is not necessarily moral; he is a minor character who intrudes upon the novel's action little enough that his morality is beside the point. But as Cabe watches the arrival of Sylder and, shortly after, the arrival of Kenneth Rattner, the narrative remains close to his perceptions. These two men are described as nondescript members of the moiling masses clustered at the bar, but their faces nevertheless prompt Cabe's memory. He recalls the bar's porch collapsing, and in Cabe's memory, men and timber are sucked down "*with wild cries into the pit below*" (25). Cabe's recollection of the porch collapse resembles nothing so much as Michelangelo's Sistine Chapel painting of souls being sucked down to hell at the apocalypse. Sylder, a lying bootlegger, and Rattner, a murderous lunatic, are only semispecified examples of this damned mass of humanity. Cabe's memory indicates his primal recognition of the innate depravity of the two men sitting before him at the bar.

Cabe's memory offers an interpretive device for understanding the role Sylder and Rattner play in *The Orchard Keeper*'s narrative; significantly, Rattner is always observed, and Sylder is almost always observed—either by the omniscient third-person narrator or by other characters in the novel. Their lives may be interpreted, but they do not possess the capacity to interpret their own lives. In other words, the omniscient narrative style observes and objectifies Sylder and Rattner, just as Cabe's memory symbolically imagines them in their apocalyptic damnation. This omniscient narrative style shifts dramatically, however, in its introduction of Arthur Ownby, an old man whose moral philosophy inspires John Wesley to believe in the possibility of heroism in the corrupt contemporary world. Ownby is introduced by name, much like Sylder, but the narrative swoops down almost immediately into his finite perceptions. He sits on his porch watching the rain, "[r]ain falling now from a faultless sky," and the next sentence, a descriptive fragment, "A girl's laugh on the road," is clearly meant to be a flicker of Ownby's directly represented sensation: he hears a fragment of laughter from a girl in the present, and the sound triggers a memory of his own wife. The following sentence, "He remembered," verbally introduces his memory and describes Ownby's association of rain and a girl's laughter with an image of his wife as a young girl riding by on a wagon (21). Ownby and the boy, John Wesley Rattner, are both introduced and permitted narrative agency; they can imagine, perceive, and remember, unlike Sylder and Rattner, who generally move, speak, and behave without any indications of thought or intentionality.

Most scenes with Ownby and John Wesley are narrated from the perspective of one or the other. At one point John Wesley and his young friends sit around listening to "Uncle Ather's" stories. The scene begins in a removed narrative voice; the boys are described as "troglodytes gathered in some firelit cave" (150). Once the old man commences his story, however, John Wesley's perceptions control the "camera angles" of the text:

> Caught him with my bare hands, and I got the scars to prove it. Here he [Ownby] extended a leathery thumb for inspection. The boy [John Wesley] slid from his chair and bent studiously over it. Right here, the old man said, pointing to a place on the inside just above the web. See?
> Yes, he said. The skin was wrinkled like an old purse; in that myriad cross-hatching any line could have been a scar. (151)

According to Kuno, "subjects are most likely to be regarded as discourse topics," and thus the subject noun phrase provides the "empathy focus in sentences where the first subject-verb-object clause is an unmarked one" (222–23). The first place to look for an empathy focus, then, is the subject of a sentence. The narrative throughout the verbal exchange in the above passage, however, suggests that the empathy angle remains distant, fixed, with a removed, observing, omniscient third-person narrator. The subjects are variously described as "[t]he boy" and "the old man" (*TOK* 151). The same voice that described the boys as "troglodytes" here depicts John Wesley as a "boy" and Ownby as an "old man," both blanket age categorizations that suggest an empathetic distance. However, when the old man points to a scar on his thumb, the following sentence describes the boy looking, but the subject is the unadorned third-person singular pronoun "he." The controlled focus of the gaze suggests that the description of Ownby's skin—and the evaluation made on it, that it is so "cross-hatched" that any particular scar is unidentifiable—must be John Wesley's particular gaze. In this scene, Ownby tells a story about the scar, a story that describes a mythic, unkillable mountain lion. The boy seems taken by the story of the mountain lion, a story described from his perception, and his rapt attention reflects his consistent empathy with animals.

Earlier in the novel, John Wesley is given a hound dog. Sylder, a surrogate father figure to the boy (though a problematic one, given that he has killed the boy's biological father), takes John Wesley hunting with the dog. When the dog falls into a river in pursuit of a raccoon, John Wesley jumps into the river to rescue the dog. John Wesley's point of view also controls the narrative during his dramatic rescue of the hound dog, one of the climactic scenes in the novel. The section begins, "He never even felt the water," and the entire scene continues to be narrated from the perceptions, feelings, and thoughts of John Wesley (123). After he pulls the dog from the river, the narrative continues in his perception:

> They came with the light and Sylder looked at him huddled in the willows, still holding the dog. He didn't say anything, just disappeared into the woods, returning in a few minutes with a pile of brush and dead limbs.
> One of the men was kneeling with him and stroking the dog, examining her. She looks all right, he said, don't she son?
> He couldn't get his mouth open so he just nodded. He was beyond cold now, paralyzed. (124).

As in the previous scene, the nondescriptive third-person pronoun "he" anchors the text inside John Wesley's perceptions. At first the attribution is ambiguous; "Sylder looked at him" may suggest either Sylder or "him" as the one controlling the text. But the text's directional verbs are all relative to John Wesley's physical positioning. Sylder and the other hunters "come" and Sylder "returns" from the woods: both "coming" and "returning" are directional verbs with a "deictic constraint" (Kuno 226). That is, "coming" and "returning" necessitate a source, in this case John Wesley on the river bank. The penultimate sentence in this passage is controlled by a modal verb, "couldn't," making it more interior than any previous sentences in the passage. McCarthy's characteristic restraint, refusing to depict the intentions or internal workings of a character's mind, in this case disappears since the important information in the sentence, the boy nodding, is followed by an explanation of *why* he nods: he is "beyond cold." This stylistic departure draws attention to the boy's self-sacrificial heroism in saving a dog, a compassion that reflects John Wesley's innate commitment to the natural world but also reflects similar commitments in later McCarthy characters, such as Billy Parham, who risks his life repeatedly to save a she-wolf in *The Crossing*. In other words, John Wesley's heroic dive is related through his point of view, and Arthur's revealed thoughts and perceptions indicate a man concerned with an archaic moral code that necessitates an ethical relationship between men and nature.

While Ownby and John Wesley's thoughts dominate the novel's revelations of interiority, the morally problematic Marion Sylder intriguingly gets his share of narrative point of view and revealed interiority as well. For example, the scene where Sylder kills Kenneth Rattner is narrated from Sylder's point of view, not narrated by an omniscient third-person narrator as are most of the passages following Sylder. This section shifts into Sylder's point of view when he sees himself "hollow-eyed and sinister" in the mirror above a bar, the same bar where he meets Rattner (32). The narrative remains close to Sylder's perspective and is liberally scattered with indirect discourse markers, such as "[H]e wonder[ed] vaguely as he stepped into the air again why he had come here and where he thought he was going" (32). Although he recognizes his own "sinister" nature, the audience is informed that he senses even more strongly *Rattner's* nature. Sylder, upon seeing Rattner, is filled with "a profound and unshakable knowledge of the presence of evil" (33). This description of Sylder's internal thought process is one of a very few indications of internal evaluation in McCarthy's oeuvre. It seems at odds with the rest of McCarthy's novels, but its purpose here seems to be to isolate Rattner's evil as a deeper and more inexplicable type of evil than Sylder's own vaguely dispossessed and disinterested badness. When Rattner attacks him, Sylder fights back and kills the man, and the narrative descriptions throughout reveal Sylder's internal world both through his perceptions and through indirect discourse markers like "he thought" (39). Throughout the novel, Sylder never fully commits to moral action, but his unusual level of interiority during the fight scene indicates that he recognizes on some level that there is a dark force at work in his world. Later in the novel, he tells John Wesley that "they ain't no more heroes," but the following italicized internal thought explains that even he does not quite believe this statement; Sylder warns John Wesley not be a "hero" and go after the corrupt Gifford, but, having sent the boy away, Sylder thinks that Gifford is "*a rogue and a outlaw [. . .] and it's few lie deep in the pit, that far beyond the pale*" (214). Sylder attempts to live in a morally ambiguous way (as a bootlegger), but his few connections to pure evil, with Rattner and Gifford, respectively, suggest to him that evil does in fact exist, and if evil exists, then those men who stand against it, like John Wesley, may indeed be worthy of the archaic epithet "hero." *The Orchard Keeper*'s use of point of view and interiority, then, presents a rather nuanced view of morality. John Wesley tries to believe that morality has meaning and purpose, but he is shaken by doubts about the efficacy of moral actions in a corrupt world. Sylder doubts that morality has meaning, but unlike John Wesley, Sylder is shaken by a tremulous certainty that morality *matters*.

Commencing with a woman giving birth to a child begotten upon her by her own brother, *Outer Dark* presents a significantly more deranged and villainous fictional world than does *The Orchard Keeper*. Not insignificantly, *Outer Dark* has no first-person narrative passages, nor does it have any intrusive direct-address comments from the removed and distant third-person narrator explicating a particular means of interpretation. In fact, the protagonists, Culla and Rinthy Holme, are such opaque characters that Denis Donoghue has described them as "like recently arrived primates, each possessing a spinal column but little or no capacity of mind or consciousness." Although Donoghue acknowledges that a few minor characters, such as the doctor and the shopkeeper, who pity Rinthy, are "ethically precocious," he does not further explore those minor characters ("Teaching *Blood Meridian*" 260). Yet the novel's coldly objective, observing narrative shifts point of view briefly for each of these ethically precocious minor characters, drawing attention to their perceptions of Rinthy and thus offering an indication of their motivations for such kindly behavior. For example, at one point, Rinthy climbs a hill to look for a sign of the tinker who has stolen her baby. The narrator describes her as "[t]he watcher on the hill" and narrates her actions. She finally stands up, walks down into town, and enters a shop. The omniscient, removed third-person narrator describes the shopkeeper, but the point of view suddenly narrows to the limited perspective of that shopkeeper. Rinthy looks at him, and "he [sees] that she must [be] ill" (54). The shopkeeper's perception of the ill girl precipitates his sympathetic response to her. He offers her water and asks her about herself, demonstrating a willingness not only to listen but to understand. When Rinthy enigmatically tells him, "I'd hate for you to know what all else he [Culla] done," the shopkeeper starts to smile and then stops. (56). His abrupt cessation suggests that he has deduced at least something of Culla's crimes, which Rinthy has not in any way described. Thus the novel underscores the shopkeeper's empathetic response to the "ill" girl by limiting the narrative point of view to his own subjective and sympathetic one for as long as Rinthy remains within his sight. Even so slight a shift in narrative point of view highlights the "ethically precocious" characters' morality by demonstrating their pity for the pity-deserving Rinthy.

Perhaps more than most McCarthy novels, *Outer Dark* is a novel wrought from ancient materials. The heavy use of allegory and biblical allusion in the novel has led critics to regard the text as presenting a sort of revisionist Christian fable, but what the book actually *does* with its spiritual and literary underpinnings poses problems for critics, who have proposed interpretations that range from fancifully positive, as in Christopher Metress's study, to devastatingly negative, as in James R. Giles's study of naturalism in the novel. At its most basic level, *Outer Dark* is, as Richard B. Woodward points out, a "twisted Nativity story" (30). A brother, Culla Holme, impregnates his sister, Rinthy, and then abandons the baby in the woods. A tinker rescues the child, and Rinthy takes off after the tinker in an attempt to reclaim her child. Culla meanwhile pursues his sister, for no apparent reason. Flitting through the landscape are three wild men, a "grim triune" inexplicably dedicated to killing and cannibalizing (*OD* 129). Metress claims that Culla's confrontation with the blind pilgrim at the end of the novel shows "a distinction that McCarthy wants explicitly clear, a difference, if you will, between the blind man's *via negativa* and Culla's *via nihilo*" (152). However, if the two men present competing theological views, the novel seems to undercut the apophatic redemption Metress finds embodied by the pilgrim (Metress 154). Culla, in the end, watches the pilgrim wander off and wonders if the blind man knows that the road ends in a bog. "Someone should tell the blind man," Culla thinks, but he makes no effort to warn him (*OD* 242). The novel ends with an expectation of grotesque hilarity—a blind man floundering to death while an inbred Appalachian hillbilly watches in bemusement.

Giles, by contrast, finds this dark ending indicative of the fact that "[t]he world of *Outer Dark* is so fallen, so depraved, so plagued by violence that it exists outside the possibility of change or reform" (5). He considers this spiritual and physical wasteland "perhaps even more depraved than T. S. Eliot's" (6). However, Giles's analysis is also suspect, if for no other reason than that Eliot's "The Wasteland" does not depict the human condition as one of unnuanced depravity. Like Eliot's poem, *Outer Dark* cannot be read as presenting an argument for total human corruption without risking a gross oversimplification of the novel's nuances. Rinthy, for instance, is not immoral at all, and readers who overlook her purity and love are guilty of a blindness that even the minor characters in the novel overcome. Yet Rinthy's quest is thwarted in the end, just as the blind prophet shambles off toward his death, so it is not possible to argue that the novel offers images of redemption. Instead, *Outer Dark* describes a crazed and vicious world teetering on the edge of biblical hellfire but haunted by equally bizarre yet agonizingly beautiful glimpses of love and tenderness. Through its restricted descriptions of characters' interior thoughts or motivations, the novel draws attention to the opacity of immoral characters, but through brief moments of shifts in narrative perspective, *Outer Dark* illuminates a few instances of compassion. Thus, although the novel describes a bleak view of the human condition, it nevertheless suggests that no dark is absolute.

In the opening scene, a description of Rinthy giving birth to her child, the narrative voice remains close to Culla's perspective but retains an interpretive capacity that suggests Culla does not, in fact, control the empathetic perspective of the text. So, for example, the narrative relates Culla's actions and, to some extent, indicates his vatic grudges, desires, and fears, but because the objective, omniscient narrative voice retains a subtle tone of evaluation, the camera angles remain firmly planted beyond Culla, observing him, recognizing some animalistic drives that the audience may, reluctantly, recognize as common to humanity. The narrative voice retains a judgmental tone, though, refusing to allow empathy to devolve into sympathy. After waking from a dream, Culla gets up and goes outside the cabin at the sound of a tinker's bell:

> There had been no one to the cabin for some three months, he himself coming harried and manic into the glade to wave away whoever by chance or obscure purpose should visit so remote a place, he himself slogging through the new spring mud four miles to the store and back once a week for such few things as they needed. Cornmeal and coaloil. And candy for her. (6)

In this passage, Culla's actions—walking outside to meet (and head off) the tinker—give way to some depiction of his motivations. The twice-repeated reflexive structure "he himself" indicates an intensity of feeling that cannot be attributed to the narrator. That is, the narrator does not care whether or not Culla has maintained an isolated home in which his impregnated sister can bring her child to term without the outside world recognizing Culla's crime. According to Kuno, "picture noun reflexives are expressions which require the speaker to enter into their referents' internal feeling" (238). In this case, the picture noun reflexives (reflexives following the noun they modify, as in "he himself") indicate Culla's somewhat resentful recognition that he maintains his isolation but pays for it. The sentence fragments "Cornmeal and coaloil. And candy for her," like most sentence fragments in McCarthy's stylistic universe, indicate a level of interiority, in this case a grocery list of supplies Culla has brought back to the cabin. Once again, the second fragment, "candy for her," suggests a level of resentment that becomes apparent later when Rinthy asks for cocoa and Culla refuses to go ask the tinker for any, and then again when Rinthy asks for a midwife and Culla refuses to fetch her (9, 10). Yet, while the text provides some indication of Culla's feelings—indications bolstered by his later dialogues with Rinthy—it nevertheless retains a narrative distance. Culla is described as "harried and manic," and later he is "like some witless paraclete" (18). These descriptions indicate that the power of perspective and, therefore, the power of interpretation rest with the omniscient and removed narrator, a narrator who is willing to permit indications of Culla's motivations but who nevertheless presents Culla in distinctly unsympathetic terms.

The omniscient narrative voice permits a few indications of Culla's motivations without justifying or empathizing with those emotions, but shifts in narrative perspective indicate that the narrator's negative interpretation of Culla differs from the narrator's more charitable interpretation of Rinthy. For example, the first time Culla enters a store, a clerk watches him, but the perspective remains outside both the clerk and Culla. The clerk is described as "looking up out of the shabby and ludicrous propriety of his celluloid collar and winecolored cravat," a narrative description that plants the scene's camera outside of the clerk's perspective (38). Shortly after this description, Culla stands looking at items behind a glass counter, "[h]is gray eyes [moving] over the tiered wares with vague wonder" (39). The description of Culla's eye color emphasizes that the camera is outside of Culla's perspective as well as the clerk's. When Rinthy later approaches the store, the narrative perspective begins observing both Rinthy, with her "dead yellow hair" and "smile all bland and burdenless as a child's," and the clerk, "a dark lean German of middle years" (53, 54). Yet when the clerk looks at Rinthy, the camera angle shifts; the clerk sees "that she must be ill," and this observation prompts him to later "notic[e]" her sweaty clothes and "wait[. . .]" for her to explain her situation (54, 55). After listening to her vague prevarications, the man says, "Come back," proffering the abandoned girl some gesture of welcome (57). The distant narrator of *Outer Dark* never indicates explicit approval or disapproval, but through a refusal to adjudicate sympathy to Culla, the narrator strips Culla of any power to elicit readers' pity. Rinthy, on the other hand, is met by several shopkeepers and random kindly folk whose perspectival gazes notice her and sympathize with her, leading readers to do the same.

Slight indications of the perspective shifting to the storekeeper's gaze give way to more poignant and explicit shifts in perspective later in the novel. Twice characters accuse Rinthy of lying about her devotion to her child, but the narrative then shifts into the perceptions of those characters. As the narrative "camera" views the suffering girl from the points of view of these characters, the reader, watching along with them, is invited to mimic their transformations from skepticism to sympathy. The first of these examples occurs in the scene where Rinthy visits a doctor. Initially the narrative descriptions are situated firmly in the perspective of an outside observer. Rinthy's and the doctor's actions are observed and described equally as they begin their verbal exchange. As their dialogue progresses, the doctor—who does not seem to have been enraptured with the image of the filthy girl in the first place—becomes more antagonistic toward Rinthy. At one point, he tells her, "You're lying to me" (153). Yet as the doctor gets ready to throw her out, he is struck suddenly by an empathetic awareness of her plight. He begins to speak, and then "something half wild in her look stop[s] him" (155). It is only after this moment of awareness that he helps her. Later, Rinthy finds the tinker and cajoles him to return her child. The tinker rejects her request and abandons her, but as he leaves her, Rinthy begins to cry, and the tinker "c[an] hear it a long way down the road" (194). The haunting sound of Rinthy's crying stays with the tinker even after he has traveled too far for her voice to carry to him (194). *Outer Dark*'s respective journeys, then, represent two types of attitude toward human connection: Rinthy's desperate desire for nurture and for love and Culla's apathetic inability to fully quit either his sister or his son, no matter how little he cares for either. Of those attitudes, only one is justified in terms of physical survival. Culla, with his bestial opacity and lack of empathy, survives seemingly unaffected, while Rinthy is left weeping by her dead child. Yet of the two narratives, only Rinthy's is followed by a sympathetic gaze.

If *The Orchard Keeper* teases out the ambiguous nature of heroism through a complex pattern of shifting points of view, and if *Outer Dark*'s even more austerely omniscient narration depicts a world almost—but never entirely—devoid of compassion or empathy, *Child of God* employs a more direct yet equally compelling narrative technique to express that novel's questions of human depravity and the need for connection. *Child of God*'s narrative follows Lester Ballard but rarely descends to his point of view. The most noticeable narrative techniques in this novel are the italicized first-person sections of text narrated by townsfolk attempting to explain Ballard. Perhaps equally eye-catching and thematically more compelling, however, the main text's omniscient third-person narrator at times directly addresses the audience, much as the narrator does who commences the prologue to *Suttree* by addressing the audience as "Dear friend," or the narrator who, as *Blood Meridian* opens, commands the audience, "See the child" (*S* 3, *BM* 3). Bowers claims that McCarthy's rare moments of "intrusive narrative commentary [. . .] situate McCarthy's narrator in the role of tale-teller" (126). The metatextual role of this narrative technique, then, draws attention to the interpretive function of narration. So, for example, the "intrusive" narrative voice in *Blood Meridian* ironically refuses to offer interpretations of the narrative events, providing endless fodder for critics trying to interpret that novel. In contrast, the narrative voice in *Child of God* seems intent on making the point that the reader ought to interpret Ballard as a sympathetic, or at least pathetic, man—an interpretation that grows increasingly absurd as Ballard's depravity sinks to new depths, literally and metaphorically.

The narrative voice intrudes first when it suggests that readers perceive Ballard as "like yourself" (5). Ballard is, at the time, urinating onto a pile of straw in a barn. The "small, unclean, unshaven" man is immediately associated with scatological and primitive desires, instincts, and urges. He is "of Saxon and Celtic bloods," and so he scuttles around performing basic Anglo-Saxon acts: "pissing," "shitting," "eating," and "fucking" (5, 13, 15, 88). Although the narrator adjures the audience to empathize with Ballard, Ballard himself resists empathy. This resistance plays out in his depraved behavior, in his lack of interior thoughts, and in the inability of the observing townsfolk to interpret or empathize with him. Throughout the novel, sections of text are narrated by unnamed and random townspeople who observe and describe Ballard but, in the end, fail comprehensively to interpret him, finding him instead essentially unfathomable. Although these narrators recognize Ballard's few talents, such as his accuracy with a rifle, and acknowledge that his father's hanging and the loss of his ancestral property may have further unhinged his already disordered mind, the narrators are nevertheless careful to paint a picture of a man already beyond the pale of civilization. In the last such section, the narrator says, "They wasn't none of em [the Ballards] any account," and tells a story of one who left Sevier County and was hanged in Mississippi. "Goes to show it ain't just the place," the narrator says. "He'd of been hanged no matter where he lived" (80–81). Ballard's essential "badness" requires his death, a death isolated from other humans in an insane asylum, uninterpreted, unpitied, and utterly alone.

However, while all the narrators—the novel's narrator and the different townsfolk—fail to *interpret* Ballard, they all struggle to find some way of empathizing with him. One of the Sevierville townsfolk narrators recalls a time when, as a child, Ballard, seemingly unprovoked, punched another child in the face. The narrator says, "I felt, I felt . . . I don't know what it was. We just felt real bad," indicating that Ballard's behavior was so far beyond normal that it evoked in all the onlookers a disquieting sense of the depths of atavistic brutality to which Ballard would one day descend. However, the narrator suddenly concludes his memory with an isolated, unexplained sentence seemingly at odds with the rest of the story: "He never done nothing to me" (18). Even when describing Ballard's essential vice, this narrator emphasizes both Ballard's uniqueness—how he demonstrated unprovoked and disproportionate violence—and his *non*-uniqueness. This narrator is part of a community that has absolutely rejected Ballard, evicting him from his ancestral home and refusing him even an abandoned shack for lodging. This is a communal rejection that occurs even though, according to this particular narrator, "he never done nothing to me." This narrator thus describes Ballard's extraordinary behavior while recognizing in a bald statement that Ballard's unprovoked violence is, in many ways, only an extreme version of that which all humanity is capable of committing.

Thematically, *Child of God* poses a troubling theological question. If Ballard is just as much a "child of God" as the novel's audience, then the line that separates the "civilized" from the sociopaths like Ballard is very fine and is held in place by the tenuous and seemingly arbitrary grace of a problematically absent God. In *Outer Dark*, the blind prophet asks, rhetorically, "And who did Jesus love, friends?" and answers himself, "The lame the halt and the blind, that's who" (226). Likewise, in *The Orchard Keeper*, an unkempt and disreputable Kenneth Rattner castigates a driver who refuses to pick him up as he hitchhikes outside of Knoxville. "You wouldn't pick up Jesus Christ, would you," he shouts after the disappearing car (8). *Child of God*'s narrator thus seems to be expounding on a "least of these" theology referenced in these other early Appalachian novels, a theology that associates God's attention and care with social outcasts, in particular with those people who are physically and, more important, morally handicapped. Crucially, while the narrator of *Child of God* never requires that readers sympathize with Ballard's *actions,* the narrator nevertheless demands a pity that would extend, if nothing else, to a lift in a car or a glass of water (the storekeeper gives Rinthy a drink of water in *Outer Dark*)—minor actions that demonstrate a theology convinced of nothing but that it is only the arbitrary grace of God that separates Ballard from the rest of humanity.

Throughout the novel, Ballard's demonic actions are disturbingly mitigated by a narrative voice intent on demonstrating this strange theology. In one of the most horrifying scenes of the novel, Ballard shoots a girl and her mentally deficient child and then rapes the girl's corpse (118–120). This scene, however, is preceded by two scenes that depict, first, the girl shaming Ballard, and, second, the belittling of Ballard's prowess with a gun. Ballard, an inarticulate and uneducated man, comes to the girl's house to talk with her father, and she embarrasses him by intentionally mishearing his promise to "owe" her as a promise to "blow" her (29). In a later scene, Ballard wins a shooting game at a fair so many times that the game's owner chases him off. Ballard, clutching his stuffed animals, wanders alone and isolated through the laughing crowds. A little girl sees him and "she edge[s] closer to the girl by her side" (65). Ballard's savagery, then, is precipitated by verbal rejection and public shaming. The coincidence of social rejection and Ballard's rage is underscored by the narrator. When Ballard is fleeing for his life from the sheriff, he falls into a river and starts to drown. But, the narrator says, he could not drown; "his wrath seemed to buoy him up" (156). The narrator at this point stops narrating in order to directly address Ballard's wrath and his audience's complicity in that wrath. "See him," the narrator says. "You could say that he's sustained by his fellow men, like you" (156). A society that rejects "the maimed and the crazed," the narrator suggests, is a society that sustains the savagery enacted by those very deranged souls (156).

The narrative voice in *Child of God* does, at times, move into Ballard's point of view. While the point of view is only loosely controlled by Ballard's mind—the shift is always described in explicit cues like "he thought"—it is notable, not least because Ballard at no time demonstrates any sort of moral consciousness. However, each instance in which the narrative point of view is associated with Ballard humanizes him, even when it demonstrates that he is truly a despicable human being. For example, at one point, Ballard is thrown into prison. The narrative shifts into Ballard's point of view with a description of his perception of the jail: "Ballard thought the fare not bad. He even liked the coffee" (53). After this explicit shift, the narrative says, "They had a nigger in the cell opposite" (53). Kuno's explanation of the use of directional phrases indicates that this description—and the passage following—must be interpreted through the perspective of Ballard. The cell is merely "opposite"—opposite *what*, readers are not told, and that information is superfluous if the source of the directional adverb is Ballard. If Ballard's cell and Ballard himself are the location from which "opposite" is measured, then "they" and "nigger" must be measured from Ballard's perspective as well. "They"—the nameless, faceless—represent the police in Ballard's world; "they" are the ultimate "other" to Ballard, ironically, since he forms a sort of connection to "the nigger" when the man tells Ballard, "White pussy is nothin but trouble" (53). This shift into Ballard's point of view, then, reveals a man who forms tenuous connections (connections not strong enough to deter derogatory racial terms) based on a shared misogyny.

Earlier in the novel, the narrator describes Ballard as a "loveless simian shape," and the narrator's dehumanizing descriptions reflect a fascinating retaliatory nature of descriptions throughout the novel (20). Ballard dehumanizes women, the police, and the man in the cell "opposite," but the audience is reminded that Ballard has been dehumanized by a community and the narrator who observes him. The retaliatory nature of descriptions is made explicit at one point in the novel, when Ballard shoots a cow but fails to kill it. The injured cow hustles away from Ballard "holding its head at an odd angle" (34). A townsperson recalls once when Ballard was set upon by a man who hit him with an axe. "Lester Ballard never could hold his head right after that," the narrator says. "It must of thowed his neck out someway or another" (9). Ballard, attacked and injured, reenacts that savagery on another living creature, turning it into a bestial image of himself.

In the same way, the novel insists on a sort of natural retaliation for crimes; Ballard, in the end, is "flayed, eviscerated, dissected" by science students just as he mutilated corpses for his own pleasure (194). Ballard's crimes are neither diminished nor excused. But the novel is equally insistent that Ballard's brutality reflects an extreme and concentrated form of social brutality—whether in the more socially acceptable form of racial slurs, the exclusion of the "maimed and crazed," or the more fundamental failure of society to recognize itself in the demented face of Lester Ballard. The novel ultimately suggests that readers' refusal to acknowledge Ballard as a child of God much like themselves is a failure that sustains savage retaliation like his. If Ballard is permitted any semblance of interiority, it is only to make the point that he only *seems* inexplicable. All humans, the narrator seems to argue, are inexplicably vicious creatures. All humans are likewise haunted by the same desires for respect, for connection, for love. Critics who ignore the interior revelations in this novel are therefore implicated by the novel's thematic argument. For example, at one point, Ballard stares at the stars and wonders "what stuff the stars [are] made of, or himself" (141). This scene presents the only evidence of Ballard's capacity for higher mental thought, reminding readers of the essential and mysterious likeness of all physical things, from stars to humans. To deny that mystery is to choose blindness. To acknowledge that mystery is to admit a terrifying connection between "ordinary" people and Ballard.

The link between interiority and morality in McCarthy's corpus suggests that "words and flesh" are conjoined, and to devalue the one is to devalue the other. *Child of God* even suggests that human life has such significance that any human being—even one as corrupt as Ballard—deserves recognition and empathy. Empathy requires some elemental sense of connection, and this ephemeral sense of connection often plays out in complex narrative shifts into the perceptions and interior worlds of moral characters, although in novels like *Outer Dark*, interiority is restricted to the point of being on the brink of extinction. If there is a common thematic thread weaving these three Appalachian novels together, then, it is their attention to the critical recognition of human responsibility toward others. That responsibility is portrayed through aesthetic language, narrative styles in which the reader's imagination is engaged as the reader is required to recognize some likeness with a fictional person through imaginatively empathizing with the character. Empathy, in other words, is described as the key to moral and meaningful life, and the reverse—a denial of the humanity or specific value of another person—is the root of absolute and horrific dehumanization.

These novels' linguistic affirmation of life is mirrored thematically through the symbolic action of naming. That is, in all three novels, when a character names another human, that action signals respect and ethical behavior. By contrast, refusing to name another person automatically devalues the other and signals a deeply unethical worldview. Through the metaphor of naming, the three novels establish a clear connection between the capacity of language to spark imaginative connection and, subsequently, the ethical exigency of practicing imaginative language. For example, at the end of *The Orchard Keeper,* John Wesley Rattner visits his mother's tombstone and stops to read the inscription, a verse from the book of Exodus, spoken by God: "If thou afflict them in any wise,<th>/<th>And they cry at all unto me,<th>/<th>I will surely hear their cry" (245). In this text, God warns those who are evilly inclined to be wary of harming others, because any harm done to a human being is an affront to the God who knows and cares for those people. Upon reading this inscription and its message, John Wesley reaches out and "pat[s] the stone softly, a gesture, as if perhaps to conjure up some image, evoke again some allegiance with a name, a place, hallucinated recollections in which faces merge[. . .] inextricably, and yet true and fixed" (245). In this way, the narrative reiterates the argument at the heart of McCarthy's short story "A Wake for Susan," namely, that the act of mourning or remembering the dead is inherently ethical, that it reflects a fundamental recognition of the inherent connectedness of human beings. Even more importantly, the *fact* of that recognition, the hallowing of human connection, is a moral choice. John Wesley's hand touching the words carved on the stone prompts his imaginative flight of fancy, enabling him to mentally revivify his love for his mother until "he no longer care[s] to tell which were things done and which dreamt" (245). The connection between imagination and reality—his memory of his mother versus the reality of their estrangement—suggests that, in the end, reality is and ought to be subordinated to imagination. Sparked by his mother's name and a biblical passage inscribed on stone, John Wesley constructs an imaginative connection to the woman who bore him, demonstrating the link between written language and ethical attitudes toward others. Words, *The Orchard Keeper* suggests, are inextricable from humanity's capacity to connect with each other. As long as a boy recalls his mother's face and his connection to her—an action prompted by written words that describe an act of speech as a sacred act of faith—their love exists and has meaning. After all, as God tells his people in the verse from Exodus, the root of help—meaningful human aid—lies in the act of language, tongues "cry[ing] unto me" (245).

John Wesley's imaginative leap, of course, contrasts dramatically with the blatant dearth of imagination and empathy in the later two Appalachian novels. *Outer Dark* draws explicit attention to the capacity of naming to create the possibility for empathetic encounters through repeated demonstrations of the alternatively devastating effects wrought by a refusal to name or empathize with another. For example, at one point Culla comes upon the three wild men sitting around a fire—his first encounter with the "grim triune" who later devour his child in front of him (129)—and Culla asks the men for sustenance, warmth, and food. They allow him to eat their meat, a strange type of flesh he has never tasted before. He asks, "What kind is it?" but the men refuse to answer (171). They then ask his name, and at first he refuses to tell them, although he later admits that his name is "Holme" (174). Upon his reluctance to give his own name, the bearded leader of the wild group commences a lengthy speech about how some things, some people, do not need names. Culla has refused to name his own child, of course; while Rinthy humanizes the infant by calling him "her chap," Culla never even refers to the child. At the conclusion of his speech about naming, the bearded man says, "I wouldn't name him because if you cain't name somethin you cain't claim it. You cain't talk about it even. You cain't say what it is" (177). The "him" to whom the bearded man refers is one of his tawdry band of miscreants, but this philosophy about naming explains Culla's refusal to name his son—a son that the three men later eat.

In that later scene, Culla comes upon the three wild men again, and they, having killed the tinker, have the deformed child who, the bearded man susses out, belongs to Culla, although Culla vehemently denies their relationship (132–33). When the bearded man asks Culla to bring the child to him, Culla agrees, handing the child over to the man who will murder him. Culla wants to know what the bearded man will do with the child, but the man replies that he wants "nothing. No more than you do" to do with the child (135). Then the man asks Culla what the child's name is, and Culla says, "I don't know" (236). The bearded man nods and reasserts that the child has no name, for "names die with the namers. A dead man's dog ain't got no name" (236). In this scene, which ends with the unnamed member of the perverse triumvirate slicing the child's throat and drinking his blood, the catastrophic results of Culla's refusal to name and claim his son are depicted in (literally and figuratively) eviscerating precision. Just as the men refused to name the mystery meat at their first fireside encounter, so Culla refuses to name his son and the child is killed and cannibalized. This novel graphically asserts an extreme end result to Culla's persistent lack of imaginative empathy. In denying his relationship to the boy, refusing to acknowledge that relationship at all or the deed that gave birth to the child, Culla tries to deny his complicity in his sister's suffering or the child's very existence. Yet denial does not remove responsibility. Instead, it damns

Culla to complicity in the consumption of his child and, afterward, damns him to wandering in an "outer dark" without end and without human love or connection.

Just after the scene in which the child is killed, *Outer Dark*'s narrative switches to following Rinthy as she wanders into the now-abandoned glade and finds the remnants of her child. Her search for her son is a quest born from a yearning for affinity, a desire to be reconnected to the child taken from her, and the depth of that yearning for connection is poignantly manifested through her constantly leaking breasts, which continue to produce milk even six months after her child disappears. Culla's search for his sister, of course, does not demonstrate that same desire for human connection. He seems instead to search for her out of a strange inability to separate himself from her. He has impregnated her, but he shows her no affection. If anything, their relationship seems to be based on proximity. The point here is that, while shifts in the narrative's point of view focus readers' attention on characters who demonstrate a marked capacity for compassion, the novel thematically suggests that all people feel a desire for human connection, but the choice to embrace or reject that desire is the root of ethical engagement with the world.

So, at the end of *Outer Dark*, Rinthy sits near the fire and waits "all through the blue twilight and into the dark" (237). In this novel, the narrator does not even indicate what Rinthy waits *for*, but her waiting near the charred remains of her child evokes the boy's waiting near his sleeping sister and the dead puppy in "A Drowning Incident." As in the short story, the restriction of interiority forces the action itself into bold relief. That static image waits for, expects, and demands interpretation. Rinthy lies down beside the burned-out fire and the charred bones and, mimicking her calling the child her "little chap" throughout the novel, the narrator here informs readers that "little sister" sleeps beside the bones of her infant (238). In other words, Rinthy, like the unnamed baby beside whom she lies, has been divested of her name and identity by her brother, the tinker, and those other cruel humans who deny the necessity of human empathy and compassion. But the narrator refuses to permit readers to join Culla and the others in denying Rinthy's humanity and need for familial love. Culla may lie about his relationship with his sister and his child, but the novel's narrator insists that readers counteract Culla's denial. In this way, although Rinthy suffers the same fate as the unnamed, dehumanized child—the reader is left to assume that she dies in the glade, because at least in terms of the narrative, she ceases to exist—she is nevertheless bound to the reader by a familial relationship, an imaginative yet undeniable rehumanizing; she is the reader's "little sister" even if she belongs to no one else.

The narrator's insistence on Rinthy's shared humanity—even a familial bond—with the reader contrasts with Culla's denial of such bonds of affection. At the end of the novel, Culla meets a blind man who heads for a bog, and he thinks that "someone should tell" the man about his impending doom, but of course Culla, who has little respect for human life and who consistently denies his responsibility to others, does not speak a word (241). Thus, the refusal to name or to speak results in death, as in the devouring of the child and the abandonment of Rinthy and the blind man to their fates. But Culla's silence is visited upon him as well. The novel begins, after all, with Culla's nightmare in which a preacher who cannot heal him casts him off, and Culla is terrified. At the end of the novel, the blind man tells Culla that he, the blind man, once met a preacher who could not heal a man whose affliction he could not name. The preacher, confronted with his own failure, wandered away. The blind man says that he "wants to tell" the preacher—presumably that he is still worthy as a preacher even if he fails to heal—because, without such assurance, the preacher would "never have no rest" (241). Culla refuses to speak to save the blind man, and the novel ends with Culla wandering off into a darkness in which he will, one assumes, "never have no rest." *Outer Dark* thus suggests that the refusal to name others and to acknowledge shared humanity is a fundamentally vicious crime. Without recognizing one's connection to another and one's consequent responsibility toward that other, no meaningful connection is possible. In the darkest of all possible worlds, such a denial results in a fatal lack of imagination that becomes a figurative blindness, a metaphorical damnation to a world where people neither speak nor find salvation.

Child of God likewise emphasizes the connection between speaking and imagination through depicting the damning results of a lack of imaginative empathy. The novel ends with Ballard dying in an insane asylum where "he ha[s] nothing to say to a crazy man" who has been interred in the asylum for eating the brains of his victims who has "long since gone mute with the enormity of his crimes" (192). In this, Ballard's final prison, he is joined by other destroyers of human flesh like himself, where they coexist without meaningful connection in mute helplessness. After Ballard's death, four medical students dissect him, and the narrator compares the students poring over Ballard's intestines to "haruspices of old" who see "monsters worse to come in their configurations" (194). Thus, Ballard's torn, spilled flesh prophesies further mutilations. Throughout the novel, Ballard is consistently rejected by fellow Sevierville townsfolk. For example, when Ballard tries in his violent, inarticulate way to have sex with a living woman, she screams at him (understandably enough), and when he grabs her gown and leaves with it, she calls "various names after him, none his" (43). When he goes into the house of a girl whom he will kill, she taunts him, claiming that he "ain't even a man. You're just a crazy thing" (117). Such consistent dehumanization, specifically dehumanizing Ballard by unnaming him, stands in bold contradiction to the narrator's consistent naming of Ballard, calling him first "a child of God" (4) and then calling him by name, "Ballard," even when he is reduced to viscera and skeletal fragments (194). The novel thus underscores the violence inherent in unnaming a person, in denying the individual her or his identity and by so doing denying one's shared humanity with that person. According to Culla Holme and the bearded maniac of *Outer Dark,* if a person does not name someone else, that person is not responsible for the other. While the narrative of *Outer Dark* suggests that such an attitude is reprehensible, *Child of God* questions whether such an attitude is even tenable. A person as deranged and bizarre as Ballard, the narrator of *Child of God* suggests, is in the end the responsibility of those who condemn him. If he shares common human traits—a desire for love, respect, and a home—with more reasonable humans, then those ordinary folk have a responsibility toward him, if only to recognize him as "like" themselves.

All three early Appalachian novels thus suggest that the desire for a meaningful connection with another is not just an intrinsic human attribute—for there are individuals like Culla Holme who feel such instincts yet deny them—but such an attitude is in fact an ethical obligation to act. Taken together, the three novels are vivid, often gory, depictions of lost souls and broken societies. And given their emphasis on depravity and darkness, it is no surprise that the novels are often categorized as unremittingly dark examples of American naturalism. In some cases, the trajectory of the narrative seems to outpace the actual events, as in *Child of God,* where the sheriff who pursues Ballard is named Fate, a name as subtle as the character names in medieval morality plays (44, 162). This novel tells the story of a man doomed by his tainted blood and chased by Fate, and the narrative follows a predictable downward course. The dream- and presentiment-laden world of *Outer Dark* likewise follows the inevitable wandering of its characters away from any semblance of civilization into a damnation of biblical proportions. Even the nuanced naturalism of *The Orchard Keeper* devolves into realms of broken fences and dying light. However, the naturalism of these novels is more complex than many critics have acknowledged. For example, Duane R. Carr claims that McCarthy's Appalachian novels take place in a "Hobbesian world," where "survival does not depend on thought processes but rather on the instinctual drive to overpower one's fellow creatures" (10). After the more noticeably moral worlds of McCarthy's later novels, critics have been less likely to describe the early novels in such narrow and dark terms, but critics still generally categorize these Appalachian novels as, at best, darkly naturalistic.

However, an examination of the novels' patterned shifts in point of view and their thematic emphasis upon recognizing human interconnection through the act of naming indicates that these novels do not describe gloom for its own sake. Rather, they create dark canvases against which the few feeble gestures toward morality or human affinity stand out. The descriptive energy of McCarthy's writing burns in his most lifeless images, from the diseased puppy's flesh to the charred flesh of the child next to whom Rinthy interminably waits. Through those images, the literary word bears mute witness to the immeasurable significance of flesh. Because literary techniques—shifts in perspective and the association of naming with imaginative empathy—are used to illuminate characters' recognition of their need for each other, it is, in the end, the narrative word that insists on the value of human flesh. And this connection between narrative and humanity, the novels suggest, is "plain enough" (*OD* 240).

2
"A DREAM OF SHRIVING"
EMPATHY AND THE AESTHETICS OF CONFESSION IN *SUTTREE* AND *BLOOD MERIDIAN*

The priest gave a little smile, lightly touched with censure, remonstrance gentled. God's house is not exactly the place to take a nap, he said.
   It's not God's house.
   I beg your pardon?
   It's not God's house.
—CORMAC MCCARTHY, *Suttree*

The saint however has his church with him and in him at all places. He goes and stands, he lies down and he sits, in his church. [. . .] The Holy Spirit preaches to him out of each creature; in everything that he sees, he sees God's preacher.
—JACOB BOEHME, *The Way to Christ*

NEAR the beginning of Cormac McCarthy's semiautobiographical novel *Suttree* (1979), the eponymous Cornelius Suttree, a failed father and an absconded scion of a Knoxville lawyer, gets drunk at a bar and, after proclaiming to a nearby wall, "I'm an asshole," collapses to the floor, where "[a] dream of shriving c[omes] to him" (77, 78). In other words, following a rather tepid confession of sin—that he is "an asshole"—Suttree is visited by a dream of the Roman Catholic rite of reconciliation and forgiveness. This rite of forgiveness provides brief counterpoints of hope to Suttree's tragic, fuguelike peregrinations through the slums of Knoxville's McAnally Flats. Vereen Bell claims that this novel is "one of detranscendence," that Suttree "detranscends, so to speak, in order to discover a meaningful form of transcendence" (73). Bell's creative oxymoron captures the strangely luminous quality of Suttree's dark wanderings in which redemption ultimately remains elusive but, paradoxically, the search for redemption seems to be itself a sanctifying journey. But if Suttree is haunted by his desire to find absolution for his sins, the characters of McCarthy's subsequent novel, *Blood Meridian* (1985), seem to exist in a state of absolute disinterest in questions of redemption or reconciliation with God or their fellow creatures. *Suttree* also reveals the interior life of its protagonist more than does any other McCarthy novel, a striking contrast to the narrative style of *Blood Meridian*, which reveals no interior mental activity on the part of its vehemently unpenitent characters, making it to date the novel least revelatory of characters' interior lives in McCarthy's corpus. An examination of these two novels' contrasting stylistic depictions and denials of interior life suggests that the novels assume an aesthetic link between confession, empathy, and forgiveness. *Suttree*, through stylistic revelations of the protagonist's recognition of his own sin and need for redemption, permits its audience to find some measure of forgiveness for this lost soul, whereas *Blood Meridian*'s narrative refuses its characters any redemption by insisting that they neither acknowledge their sins nor recognize their need for forgiveness.

Despite their obvious aesthetic and thematic differences, *Suttree* and *Blood Meridian* both emphasize the critical role of genuine penitence in permitting even the slightest possibility of redemption. *Blood Meridian* constructs a primitive, ferocious world in which characters behave brutishly, without thought or reflection. Indeed, the epilogue points to the critical absence of any internal "light" and the subsequent pointlessness of any external signs of penitence. In the novel's final italicized section, unnamed men follow a fire-starter who goes about striking light in the darkness. These unnamed men follow the light, but they "*appear restrained by a prudence or reflectiveness which has no inner reality*" (337). The narrator critiques the empty appearance of wisdom or "*reflectiveness*" without a corresponding "*inner reality*" in a way that evokes Suttree's similar critique of religious forms that are devoid of an internal reality. For example, in *Blood Meridian*, the unnamed kid is "divested" of his inherited identity, his "origins [. . .] remote as is his destiny" (4). But the kid, having shucked off the trappings of his genetic inheritance, never finds another identity to replace the one he has lost. *Blood Meridian*'s kid seems to make a journey that is a dark antithesis to the traditional pattern of the bildungsroman, in which a young man leaves his father's identity and home and ventures into his own future and fortune. This initiating action, the young man's departure, commences the kid's unenlightening journey and in fact seems to pick up or mimic the final narrative event in *Suttree,* in which Suttree realizes that he needs to let "everything fall away from him. Until there [i]s nothing left of him to shed" (468). Suttree's own "divesting" carries the same implications as the kid's: he is a man about to embark on a journey from Tennessee into the trackless unknown, and in order to commence his journey, he divorces himself from his patrilineal heritage. But unlike the kid, in place of the paraphernalia of his heritage, Suttree "take[s] for talisman the simple human heart within him" (468). That is, Suttree gets rid of the external manifestations and signs of his father's family and his Roman Catholic faith and instead embraces a genuine internal recognition of his need for others and his connection to the world around him.

The critical distinction between the kid's journey and Suttree's journey, then, has little to do with external narrative events. Physically, both protagonists quit their fathers' houses in order to wander aimlessly in search of some undefined telos. Yet the thematic significance of their journeys is strikingly different. While the kid ambles into an unredeemed world of cannibalism, rape, crucifixion, and mutilation, Suttree finds glimpses of grace through moments of warmth expressed in his relationships with other inhabitants of the slums. Suttree's final encounters bring him first to a kindhearted transvestite who offers "genuine solicitude" (468), then to a boy carrying a jug of water who smiles and offers Suttree a drink in a sacramental reenactment of the Eucharist (470–71), and last to a stranger who stops his car to give Suttree a lift even though Suttree has "not lifted a hand" (471). These brief benedictions contrast with the kid's apocalyptic encounter with his nemesis, Judge Holden, at the end of *Blood Meridian.* When the judge sees the kid at a bar, a chance meeting years after the main events of the narrative, the judge immediately says to him, "This night thy soul may be required of thee" (327). *Suttree* and *Blood Meridian* trace narratives with potentially similar narrative arcs—the doomed wanderings of inherently flawed sons fleeing the religion and identity of their fathers—but the novels impose upon these two potentially similar protagonists utterly dissimilar fates. Suttree and the kid receive, respectively, grace and death.

As Jay Ellis points out, McCarthy is a novelist who pays much explicit attention to the physical—actions, spoken words, natural landscape—and limited attention to the internal life of the mind (60). But even a cursory comparison of *Suttree* and *Blood Meridian* suggests that the life of the mind must play a significant role in the redemption, or at least the redeemability, of a character. In fact, the key distinction between the forms of the two novels seems to be that *Suttree* makes specific and vital use of revelations of the protagonist's internal world—his thoughts, intentions, fears, and despair—while *Blood Meridian*'s protagonist does not seem to possess an internal life at all. Such a distinction makes sense because both novels center around ideas of crime and forgiveness; therefore, the presence or absence of penitence must play a significant role in determining readers' interpretations. So, for instance, *Blood Meridian*, the "consummate revisionist western," points to the American heart of darkness—a darkness that the epigraphs from Paul Valéry and Jacob Boehme suggest derives from evil acts committed without "sorrowing" and "as if they were irresistible" (Bowers 8). Acts so committed demonstrate the perpetrator's lack of reflection and refusal to take responsibility. And without sincere penitence, such a creed implies, the act of shriving is an empty performance. Yet *Suttree* suggests that the corollary may also be true: with genuine penitence, it may be possible to flee the "slaverous and wild" hounds of hell—symbolically, the overwhelming loneliness of death—and find instead meaningful reconciliation and communion with others (471).

This emphasis upon the necessity of penitence in restoring meaningful communion is consistent with traditional Roman Catholic teaching. According to the *Catechism of the Catholic Church*, the only qualifications necessary for a person to achieve forgiveness are, first, confession of sins and, second, true penitence (*CCC* XI.1480). And indeed, Boehme, the Lutheran mystic McCarthy quotes in an epigraph for *Blood Meridian*, contends that the unsaved man is a "[h]ellish worm or abominable beast" who is "eternally in horrid darkness" (29). Boehme's description of the realm and condition of those who reject God's forgiveness evokes the "*terra damnata*" of *Blood Meridian* (Bowers 8). The only escape from such despair, Boehme claims, is "[w]ith downcast eyes [. . . to] begin to confess [. . .] sin" (34). Regardless of his other more heretical teachings, Boehme's focalization on the role of confession in the attainment of forgiveness is consistent with Catholic orthodoxy, in which "[p]ersonal confession is thus the form most expressive of reconciliation with God and with the Church" (*CCC* XI.1484). Significantly, both Boehme and the *Catechism of the Catholic Church* foreground the *recognition* of sin as the all-important first step toward contrition. Boehme calls such a recognition a "hunger for sorrow" (31), an attitude that the *Catechism* calls "sorrow for and abhorrence of sins committed" (*CCC* XI.1490).

Suttree, of course, embodies at least this step in the penitential process when he expresses grief incurred by his recognition of his own culpability. For example, at his son's funeral, Suttree rejects the accusations from his wife and the priest, but when the priest says his name, which is also his child's name, during the ceremony, "everything bec[omes] quite clear. He [Suttree] turn[s] and la[ys] his head against the tree, choked with a sorrow he ha[s] never known" (153). Suttree's recognition of his sin, his failure to love his son, contrasts with the kid's rejection of such filial and paternal responsibility. Near the end of *Blood Meridian,* a wandering group of "violent children orphaned by war" finds the kid, now a grown man, at his campfire (322). In a reenactment—and foretelling—of his bizarre pseudofilial relationship with the judge, the kid calls one of the boys "son," a term to which the boy strenuously objects (321). Later, the now-grown kid shoots the boy, and the boy's companions bear his body into the desert. Watching them leave, the narrator claims, "Out there was nothing. They were simply bearing the body off over the bonestrewn waste toward a naked horizon" (323). The flattened, inimical horizon seems to bear the inner characteristics of its world, a world in which father figures and children act without bearing any moral responsibility toward each other, and a world in which there is neither recognition of crimes committed nor grief expressed for them.

The revelations of penitence in *Suttree* and the contrasting lack of penitence in *Blood Meridian* suggest the role that the concept of confession plays in the ethical landscape of both novels. In order to examine the function of confession in the two novels, however, it may be helpful at this point to pause and establish some critical aspects of the confessional narrative genre. A confessional text reveals the intimate thoughts of the speaker to examine the speaker's intentions and motivations and on those bases evaluate them. In traditional confessional texts, such as Saint Augustine's *Confessions* or Leo Tolstoy's *A Confession,* the speaker addresses the text to the divine, encouraging the audience to read the confessional text as a devotional, a pattern of the spiritual discipline of confession from which the reader can learn and upon which the reader can then model his or her own confession. The distinction between fiction and memoir, in this case, is that if the primary audience of a confession like Saint Augustine's is the divine, the primary audience for a confessional novel is the human reader. Consequently, a fictional confession relies heavily on literary empathy as the text's speaker reveals her or his own tarnished humanity and readers are encouraged to evaluate themselves in light of such confessions.

Thus, confession, in literary terms, promotes the reader's empathetic engagement with the text, a view that is endorsed by Edith Stein, who explains that the practice of empathy requires a conscious imaginative leap in which the empathizer draws on personal emotional experiences in order to *assume* the emotional reality of the other (17). Because empathy is a conscious decision, an act of will, Stein believes that it is an ethical act and part of what enables humans to become better people. "By empathy with differently composed personal structures," she says, "we become clear on what we are not, what we are more or less than others. Thus, together with self knowledge, we also have an important aid to self evaluation" (105). Confessional literature fulfills the same purposes that Stein lays out, namely, to draw the audience into imaginative engagement in order to provoke a response in which the reader likens his or her own experiences to those of the text's speaker in order to comprehend the emotional truth content of the speaker's experience. A confessional text uses empathy to direct the reader toward the next step, a critical evaluation of the morality or ethical value of both the speaker's and the reader's motivations. And, the *Catechism* assures believers, this is also the purpose of spiritual confession, to open the door to penitence and, through penitence, provide the way to redemption. And so the grace that touches Suttree at the end of *Suttree* illuminates the ethical significance of the confessional text, especially when *Suttree* is juxtaposed with the nonconfessional and perniciously hopeless *Blood Meridian*.

Yet the fact that Suttree's narrative draws attention to the beatific qualities of empathy does not necessarily indicate that the novel ought to be read as a confessional text—or even can be. After all, confessional novels are narrated in the first person, and *Suttree,* like all of McCarthy's texts, is narrated in the third person. Thus the novel cannot be uncomplicatedly categorized as "confessional." However, in structure the novel is markedly different from most of McCarthy's other texts, not least in the manner in which the voice of the protagonist seems to mimic and at times eclipse the voice of the narrator. Although *Suttree* in its entirety cannot be classified as a confession, the novel's revelations of its protagonist's thoughts, feelings, and motivations can be broken down into distinct categories, each category playing a specific role in the development of the character's—and the reader's—recognition of sin, experience of grief, and penitential recognition of the need for both judgment and mercy. As such, the novel plays with the central tenets of confessional literature, and at times the narrative takes on the aesthetic forms of the confessional genre.

The narrative style of *Suttree* is consistently more intimate than that of most of McCarthy's novels, especially *Blood Meridian*. For example, the narrative voice is typically in the limited third person, describing Suttree's actions and external world from his point of view, such as in the opening scene, in which Suttree "put one forearm to his eyes. He could hear the river talking softly beneath him" (8). The third-person narrator admits images and impressions *through* Suttree's senses (he, not the narrator, "could hear the river"). Furthermore, this narrator frequently explains Suttree's emotions in response to an event, such as when Suttree faces down Byrd, an inmate who has been threatening the mentally slow watermelon rapist, Gene Harrogate. Suttree "could see himself twinned in [Byrd's] cool brown eyes and he didn't like what he saw" (52). Clearly, such revelations belong to a narrative voice much more concerned with the inner workings of a character's mind than the narrator of *Blood Meridian,* who, in describing the kid's fateful first encounter with the judge, indicates that both characters feel some connection but refuses to explicate what that feeling is: "As the kid rode past the judge turned and watched him [. . .]. When the kid looked back the judge smiled" (14). Such actions—the kid checking over his shoulder and the judge smiling—are sufficient indications that this contact has been momentous. But beyond depicting the men's actions, *Blood Meridian*'s narrator reveals nothing.

Suttree as a whole is more attuned to the interior world of its protagonist than most other McCarthy novels. And the most unusual function of this novel's third-person narration is its revelations of Suttree's intentions or feelings when those particular feelings stand in direct contrast to his actions. Suttree as a character is not particularly likable. But his most morally reprehensible actions—his rejection of his mother's love or his violent attack on his mother-in-law—are complicated by the third-person narrator's revelations of his concurrent grief, fear, and yearning to take back or to rectify his terrible behavior (61, 151). For example, the Flannery O'Connor–esque mayhem that erupts when Suttree arrives at his ex-wife's home to ask when the funeral for their son will take place is framed by narrative descriptions of Suttree's emotions that seem to conflict with his egregiously bad behavior. Before arriving at the house, the narrator explains Suttree's deeply conflicted state of mind:

> Remorse lodged in his gorge like a great salt cinder [1].
> What will she say? [2]
> What will her mother say?
> Her father. [...]
> All night he'd tried [3] to see the child's face in his mind but he could not. (150)

When he makes the decision to attend the funeral, the third-person narrator first describes Suttree's emotional response to his child's death, "Remorse," then shifts to a direct representation of his thoughts [2], with a series of rhetorical questions demonstrating his despairing desire to connect to his broken family in emotionally appropriate ways, and finally returns to the third-person mode to explain Suttree's ultimate failure, his inability to remember his child's face [3]. When Suttree arrives at his wife's family's house, an altercation erupts and concludes with Suttree "fetch[ing]" his mother-in-law "a kick in the side of her head" and then fleeing the premises ignominiously (151). This entire scene is narrated without any indications of Suttree's mental state. But after the scene, as Suttree walks toward his son's funeral, the narrator explains that Suttree felt a "dread in his heart" (152). The narrator thus seems intent on describing Suttree's more appalling actions in excruciating detail, inviting the reader's judgment. But the framing revelations of the man's internal angst suggest that, at the very least, his actions are not inexplicable; they are profoundly corrupt but utterly human. Such descriptions of Suttree's feelings are key elements to the novel's capacity to draw on readers' empathy, but an empathy that is nevertheless quite critical. In so doing, *Suttree* evokes the all-important first step in the confessional process in which the person confessing acknowledges his sin without offering self-justification while simultaneously inviting forgiveness.

One of the most important functions of *Suttree*'s close third-person narrative mode lies in those moments that reveal Suttree's intentions when they are at odds with his behavior. For example, when he visits his Aunt Martha, he recalls his childhood, an act that violates his recent attempts to alienate himself from his family, both his wife and child and his paternal household. Yet the old woman's kindness kindles a spark of guilt in him as he begins to recognize that, even if his family is part of a corrupt wealthy class and his blood heritage is tainted, in abandoning his family he also has committed a crime. When he stands to leave his aunt's house, he "almost reached down to touch her" (132). In terms of physical action, nothing happens. But the narrative's revelation of Suttree's desire to make a human connection, to show through physical touch that he feels connection and love toward his aunt, permits the reader to see Suttree as a more conflicted character than his behavior suggests.

In one of the most poignant instances of such narrative revelation, Suttree returns from his trek into the mountains, a flight from human companionship following his son's death, and he walks into a store to ask directions to the nearest bus stop. The man behind the counter responds unkindly to his query ("Where you left it, I reckon") and "Suttree suddenly beg[ins] to cry" (294). The narrative then explains the action—his inexplicable tears—by underscoring their very inexplicability:

> He didn't know that he was going to [start crying] and he was ashamed. The counterman looked away. Suttree turned and went out. [. . .] Walking along the mean little streets in his rags convulsed with sobs, half blind with a sorrow for which there was neither name nor help. (294)

The narrator stresses Suttree's humiliation over his public display of grief, a pathos-inspiring response to which the reader would otherwise not be privy, as well as pointing out explicitly that the man's grief is both unnamed and unfixable. And the source of the grief seems to be alienation and loss—the death of his son and the coldness of a storekeeper put off by Suttree's rags. Thus, the third-person narrator of this novel breaks the opaque description of physical actions and expressions typical of McCarthy's novels in order to take note of Suttree's grief as well as his guilt, permitting the reader to empathize and perhaps even feel some measure of sympathy for him; consequently the reader is not precisely placed in the role of confessor to this misbegotten wanderer but rather is encouraged to behave as a fellow penitent, able to recognize in this unlovely soul some common humanity.

Of course, in *Suttree,* the most striking departures from the normative modes of McCarthy's narratives are in fact the loci of the novel's most critical confessional mode: the passages in which the third-person text shifts into the first-person, either with a first-person pronoun ("I") or through self-directed interrogatives ("What is this roaring? Who is this otherbody? I am no otherbody") (449). These passages delivered in a first-person voice from Suttree's perspective are syntactically fused with the close third-person voice that predominates throughout the narrative, so that as a result most of the novel's prose that does not include the actual first-person pronoun cannot be clearly identified as *not* being narrated "in" Suttree's voice. For example, at one point Suttree wanders through the wasteland of Knoxville's slums during a lightning storm, contemplating death, suicide, his current feckless existence, and his moral obligations to the living. The narrative is at times in the third person and at times in the first without clear distinction between semantic attributions:

> It cracked and boomed about and he pointed out the darkened heart within him and cried for light. If there be any art in the weathers of this earth. Or char these bones to coal. If you can, if you can.
> A blackened rag in the rain.
> He sat with his back to a tree and watched the storm move on over the city. Am I a monster, are there monsters in me? (366)

Suttree's existential angst merges with the frenetic violence of the natural world so that the narrative is never fully removed from his mind. Any observations or interpretations in the narrative cannot be unambiguously attributed to an omniscient narrator for the simple reason that all descriptions of the physical world, such as the "cracked" lightning-shorn sky, are translated by Suttree into symbols for his own internal corruption.

These first-person passages are significant not just because they are unusual in McCarthy's corpus and thus suggestive, but also because all of these passages, including the example cited above, share a thematic commonality. In particular, these passages explicitly reveal Suttree's recognition of guilt, or his sorrow over his actions, or his recognition of the immanence of death and his fear of that death—qualities that characterize confessional literature. Thus, in the previous example, Suttree's exilic wanderings suggest his internal anguish, but the source of that anguish is named only when the text shifts into the first person while Suttree acknowledges that he just may be "a monster" (366).

There are twelve such first-person passages in the novel, some as brief as the one cited above, all of them syntactically intertwined with the third-person narrative while remaining quite obviously distinct from it (13–14, 29, 61, 80, 86, 113, 129, 154, 291, 366, 449, 471). These direct revelations of Suttree's interior life permit audiences to see, unmediated by a narrator,

Suttree's evaluation of his own moral turpitude and, more importantly, his penitence and his desire to be something better, someone capable of meaningful human connection. So, for instance, when Suttree's mother visits him in jail, the text shifts into first-person narrative that reveals Suttree's recognition of his own moral corruption:

> Her lower chin began to dimple and quiver. Buddy, she said. Buddy . . .
> But the son she addressed was hardly there at all. Numbly he watched himself fold his hands on the table. He heard his voice, remote, adrift. Please dont start crying, he said.
> See the hand that nursed the serpent. [. . .] That raised the once child's heart of her to agonies of passion before I was. (61)

Suttree's behavior is related in the third person ("Numbly he watched"), but the sudden shift into the imperative mood ("See the hand") indicates a shift into his perspective, and that shift illuminates Suttree's bitter (yet well-deserved) self-recriminations.

These first-person passages spoken in Suttree's voice are distinct from the third-person narrator, but they are also distinguished from two first-person references that must be attributed to the third-person narrator or to someone other than Suttree. The first of these two first-person speakers is, of course, the one who commences the italicized prologue with "*Dear friend*" (3). This section, narrated in the same mode as the first-person narration of *Child of God* and *Blood Meridian,* begins the text, but the intrusive narrative style does not reappear in the main body of *Suttree,* in contrast to those other two novels. The second instance is the most bizarre in terms of its unique status in the novel. This instance appears in the second chapter, which departs from Suttree's story in order to introduce Harrogate. Here the narrative remains in the objective third-person mode for the entire section and then abruptly shifts to a more subjective tone at the end. Two men carrying shotguns catch Harrogate, "a slavering nightshade," as the boy is violating watermelons. Although one of the men yells to Harrogate to "[h]old it right there, old buddy," Harrogate, childlike, flees with his overalls unhooked. He trips and falls, the man fires his shotgun, and the pellets strike Harrogate, who begins to scream. The narrative voice at that moment shifts into the first person:

> He [Harrogate] caught up the bib of his overalls in both hands and turned to run. [. . .] The train bawled twice out there in the darkness. Now beg God's mercy, lecher. Unnatural. [. . .] Smooth choked oiled pipe pointing judgment and guilt. Done in a burst of flame. Could I call back that skeltering lead. (35)

In this section, the narrative voice relating actions breaks suddenly as it describes the farmer firing his rifle. An imperative voice—clearly not the Appalachian-accented voice of the farmer ("He aint mounted") calls to Harrogate using an elegant term, "lecher," in contrast to the farmer's spoken epithet, "old buddy" (35). This same voice, in a series of syntactic fragments, relates the frenzied firing of a gun that is "judgment and guilt"— the firing of the rifle, in other words, an instinctive act of "judgment" for Harrogate's outrageous "guilt." At the same time, however, the source of that "guilt" is ambiguous. Immediately after firing the gun, a first-person speaker expresses anguish at having shot a frightened teenager, "Could I call back that skeltering lead." This expression of guilt suggests that the first-person voice here must be attributed, oddly enough, to the Appalachian-accented farmer, who speaks out loud to express that anguish as he "fling[s] the gun away" and falls to his knees beside Harrogate, exclaiming, "Aw shit" and "Hush now" (35). The significance of the first-person narration in this section is that it gives a profoundly literate and articulate voice to a farmer at the precise moment that he recognizes and expresses sorrow over a wrongdoing. This brief moment, unique in the novel, suggests that perhaps the other sections of text that reveal Suttree's first-person voice do so not because Suttree is the protagonist but instead because Suttree feels sorrow. In other words, the revelations of a character's mind in this novel seem to be employed precisely because they illuminate an attitude of grief and penitence.

Such a narrative emphasis on guilt, using first-person passages to reveal characters' recognition of their crimes, suggests that *Suttree* is a novel interested in encouraging an empathetic connection between reader and fictional character for the express purpose of recognizing, naming, and sorrowing over inhumanity. In fact, at times the narrative style shifts from the typical tone of vulnerability, describing Suttree's thoughts and emotions even when not revealing them directly through his perspective, into a more distant third-person narrative voice that mocks or censures Suttree. This voice often uses grandiose syntax that suggests the biblical-sounding narrator of *Blood Meridian*, but unlike *Blood Meridian*'s narrator, the narrator in *Suttree* consistently draws readers' attention to Suttree's guilt, encouraging the reader to evaluate and censure the immorality of the character's actions. For example, at one point Suttree is ejected from a trolley for not having the coin necessary to ride. He consequently tramps through the streets, one foot in the gutter, a literal and metaphorical statement to the universe. The narrator describes him, parodying Robert Frost's "Stopping by Woods on a Snowy Evening": "Suttree with his miles to go kept his eyes on the ground, maudlin and muddlesome in the bitter chill, under the lonely lamplight" (179). The narrator's interpretation of Suttree's behavior—that he is "maudlin and muddlesome"—is rather censorious. And the playful, heavy-handed use of alliteration ("maudlin and muddlesome" and "lonely lamplight"), along with the oblique reference to Frost, undermines any emotional veracity in the scene. Suttree, the narrator informs the reader, does not currently deserve pity; he is, rather, being pathetic.

At another moment, the mocking tone of the distant third-person narrator takes up a positively epic, even biblical, resonance. When Suttree and his lesbian-prostitute girlfriend begin to dissolve their relationship, the narrative voice leaps away from the close third-person mode into the omniscient observing voice more typical in McCarthy's "epic" novels such as *Blood Meridian*:

> Follow now days of drunkenness and small drama, of cheap tears and recrimination and half-so testaments of love renewed. [. . .] For there were days this man so wanted for some end to things that he'd have taken up his membership among the dead, all souls that ever were, eyes bound with night. (405)

In this case the narrator distances himself from the novel's protagonist but does so in order to draw readers' attention to Suttree's hopelessness and suicidal ideation, a far more serious note than the one struck by the distant, omniscient third-person narrative style in the earlier example. Revelations of Suttree's thoughts, either through a close, limited third-person narrator or through the first-person voice, thus serve two functions: first, they reveal the character's thoughts and intentions in order to nuance the reader's interpretation of his behavior, permitting empathetic engagement with even the most despicable actions; and second, they permit audiences to witness

Suttree's anguished, often self-flagellating musings. The addition of a first-person revelation of a guilt-ridden farmer suggests that penitence is a vital theme in the novel and that true penitence can best be expressed in the first person, encouraging audiences to enter into a confessional attitude. Even the distant, omniscient third-person narrator does not settle for merely relating Suttree's actions but instead urges readers to judge Suttree, to recognize his limitations even when he fails to do so. The narrative modes thus construct a rather complicated character who provokes empathy even when he does not deserve sympathy.

Such complicated narrative modes emphasize the importance of penitence, the first step toward contrition and forgiveness. A traditional confession, of course, is spoken in hope of finding forgiveness from and reconciliation with God, a trajectory that perhaps seems at odds with Suttree's truculent agnosticism. But in fact, just as the novel practices a rather secular version of the confessional genre, so also Suttree's communion, earned when he learns penitence, is a human communion, not a religious one. At the end of the novel, as Suttree lies sick, he concludes that "the stink of the unshriven dead is a dire stench rising to affront the nostrils of God," a dark reference to last rites, the Catholic sacrament in which a dying soul is forgiven the evil deeds committed during life (455). As Suttree begins to imagine the "unshriven dead," he realizes that all of his friends and companions, the liars, thieves, and prostitutes with whom he has found companionship, are among these wicked hordes. And then, in his delirium, Suttree imagines himself called to confess before God, the "archetypal patriarch," and upon his confession, God unlocks the gates of hell and Suttree and all his friends, the "simmering sinners," pour forth and they "carry the Logos itself from the tabernacle and bear it through the streets" (458). The sinners escaping with the word of God—a reference to the Johannine description of Christ (John 1:1)—are swamped by the "prebarbaric mathematic" that erases them in oblivion (458). The conflict between the "oblivion" of the scientific certainty of death and the vibrancy of human life, in all its squalor, despair, and hope, makes Suttree finally realize that his primary sin has been his "[h]is subtle obsession with uniqueness" (113). His rejection of his family for their moral decadence and his obsession with his dead twin are just manifestations of a pride that has resulted in his being blind to the importance of human community. Recanting his obsession, Suttree proclaims in his delirium, "I know all souls are one and all souls lonely (459). *Suttree* thus seems to demonstrate what Stein considers the purpose of literary empathy: the capacity to construct a character whose vices and desires encourage readers to evaluate their own lives and behavior. Ethical behavior, the novel seems to argue, is born in one's recognition of guilt and the confession of that guilt in hope of reconciliation.

The significance of Suttree's ephemeral epiphany that redemption is found only in human community is perhaps best exemplified by a negative comparison, the novel so blatantly lacking any hint of penitence, and indeed humanity, *Blood Meridian*. In *Blood Meridian,* the omniscient narrator remains so far removed from the individual characters that there are never shifts into the perspective of any single character. The novel permits no empathetic engagement between reader and text, and, as one might expect, the characters themselves demonstrate a complete lack of empathy for others. Even a limited examination of this novel demonstrates the critical link between revealed interiority and morality throughout McCarthy's corpus. The inexorable immorality in *Blood Meridian* is exacerbated by its omniscient narrator, whose style of narration forcibly denies interpretation and so refuses to mitigate the violence of the story.

Moral depravity is so profound in *Blood Meridian* that, according to Steven Shaviro, "[i]t is useless to look for ulterior, redemptive meanings" in the novel, because the kid "keeps his distance from the claims both of destiny and of agency" (146, 149). The almost complete absence of any indications of the kid's thoughts or motivations reinforces the reader's impression that the kid cannot control his destiny. The kid does not seem to be conscious of his ability (if he even possesses it) to determine his own reactions to an inexorable fate, and thus he cannot interpret his own life. Even more provocative than the kid's lack of interpretive agency, however, is the absence of interpretive action on the part of the narrator. Because the novel's elegant descriptions of violence are coupled with such a flat refusal to interpret that violence, critics have generally found the novel almost inexplicably dark. Denis Donoghue points out that the narrative style, what he (mimicking McCarthy) calls "neuter austerity," subsumes questions of ethics within larger, cosmic perspectives in which human interactions seem puny and futile at best ("Teaching *Blood Meridian*" 267, 277). Of course, Donoghue points out, it would be a mistake to assume that this "neuter" narrator's voice is McCarthy's; "Nietzsche," Donoghue says, "is Judge Holden's philosopher, not McCarthy's" (277). The distant narrator, then, controls the interpretive possibilities inherent in the text, sometimes warding off ethical interpretations in order to present a visceral world of chaos stripped of any civilizing veneer of analysis or sense-giving interpretation. James Bowers provides what is possibly the most hopeful interpretation of *Blood Meridian*'s brutal narrative, claiming that the novel is "*the* consummate revisionist Western, [and] McCarthy's achievement is no less than a reimagining of history and the Western novel in an effort to lay bare national myths through the ethnic, racial, and social tensions of 1850s America" (8). Of course, laying bare those national myths does not necessarily lay them to rest. Tim Parrish points out that *Blood Meridian*'s devastating depiction of the American soul reveals that "the American's acts of self-expression are committed from within a terrible emptiness" (49).

The chaotic darkness of *Blood Meridian* derives much of its horror from its inexplicability. Like the kid, the novel itself seems to refuse to name or to face the darkness within its pages. In his linguistic analysis of the novel, Arthur Bingham discovers that the violent passages are stylistically foregrounded. These passages display a temporal immediacy achieved through a high density of active verbs and through parataxis, numerous clauses strung together with "and" conjunctions. The syntactic style of these violent passages creates a breathless and ruthless pace, but Bingham's project does not extend to any claims about *why* the violent passages are made all the more shocking through their frenetic linguistic style. While critics who study the novel's literary themes are apt to point out that its violence is significant, the point of that violence is challenging to pin down, since the novel so carefully eludes any indications of interior life, either on the part of its characters or on the part of its narrator. Mark Eaton, however, claims that this narrative opacity is precisely the point. A progression through increasingly horrifying violence, "*Blood Meridian* is a record of forgotten atrocities committed in the name of nationhood" (159). Eaton's argument is borne out through the novel's narrative refusal to interpret or to expiate the violence of the events or the crimes of the characters.

The novel begins with a brief description of the life of an unnamed child until his sixteenth year when, in 1849, he rides a mule south from Tennessee to Texas. In this section, the verbs are in the present tense and the narrative style indicates the presence of a narrator, both through a narrative intrusion in the first sentence ("See the child") and through inverted syntactic structures that seem to suggest an evaluative process (*BM* 4). For example, the final paragraph of the introductory passage reads: "He works in a sawmill, he works in a diphtheria pesthouse. He takes as pay from a farmer an aged mule and aback this animal in the spring of the year eighteen and forty nine he rides up through the latterday republic of Fredonia into the town of Nacogdoches" (5). The intricate syntactic and lexical patterns in this passage render the prose almost poetic; it is easier to imagine the narrator as a Homeric bard than as a man seated at an Olivetti typewriter. While the sonic quality of the passage is impressive enough, the ornate diction and syntax are perhaps even more compelling, and such unusual sentences lead readers to actively imagine a narrator—and, by implication, a narrative voice that both relates and interprets the passage's events.

The reader's sense of a narrative "presence" in this text is explained by Noam Chomsky's revolutionary linguistic study of transformational grammar. Using Chomsky's proposals, literary linguist Roger Fowler claims that a text's syntactic transformations have a direct impact upon the reader's interpretation of that text. The study of transformational grammar claims that the core or "deep structure" of a sentence can be transformed in such a way that the proposition of the sentence remains the same but the connotations of the sentence change. So, for instance, "John broke the window" and "The window was broken by John" contain the same core proposition—that, due to John's action, a window broke. But the sentences' two transformations focus readers' attention on different aspects of meaning. In the first sentence, the agent, John, is focalized, suggesting that he is fully responsible for the action, while the second sentence focalizes the window and its changed condition, mitigating John's responsibility in the reader's eyes. Fowler argues that sentence transformations "powerfully affect *perspective* upon meaning, by directing our attention on the content and the structure of the depicted world of a fiction in one way or another" (21). The final sentence in the passage from *Blood Meridian* quoted previously contains several transformations. The deep structure of the first clause of the second sentence would read as follows: "The farmer gives him an aged mule as pay." The fronted "he" and "as pay" draw attention to two aspects of the core sentence: the boy and the mule. The mule is more obliquely foregrounded than the boy by its unusual introduction ("as pay . . . an aged mule"). The second clause in this sentence more explicitly fronts the mule: "and aback this animal." In this prepositional phrase, the archaic "aback" infuses the already-contorted syntax with a style reminiscent of oral storytelling, a style of archaic syntactic structures more suited to fairy tales, such as "and in this house there lived an old woman." The transformations of *Blood Meridian*'s syntax thus suggest a very conscious literary style and indicate the presence of a *teller*. And because most readers are trained from childhood to recognize the moralizing habits of fairy tales, such a clear "tale telling" voice automatically causes readers to expect an element of interpretation. The events are portentous, and readers expect the narrator to explain in just what manner these events affect both the text and the outside world. Ironically, however, this passage and others like it that crop up through the rest of the novel never carry through with their implicit promise to impose meaning on the events of the text.

The passage to which Donoghue alludes in his description of *Blood Meridian*'s prose style is perhaps the most striking of these passages that purport to instruct readers in how they might pull some redemptive, or at least meaningful, insight from the narrative events. This passage is a description of the physical landscape Glanton's gang finds as they journey toward the Colorado River. The scene opens with the often-repeated, refrainlike phrase "They rode on":

> They rode on. The horses trudged sullenly the alien ground and the round earth rolled beneath them silently milling the greater void wherein they were contained. In the neuter austerity of that terrain all phenomena were bequeathed a strange equality and no one thing nor spider nor stone nor blade of grass could put forth claim to precedence. (247)

In this scene, the narrative voice inverts the object phrase and adverb ("The horses trudged the alien ground sullenly" becomes "The horses trudged sullenly the alien ground") and in so doing conjures a chanting quality, a strong iambic and anapestic meter rather than the prosaic meter the "core" syntax displays. Once again, the narrative voice is tonally "austere," even as the landscape is, but that austerity is nevertheless indicative of a vibrant presence. The poetic inversions tell readers, if nothing else, that a teller is spinning this tale. Yet the teller explicitly refuses to carry through with the implicit promise of such a narrative mode: the "strange equality" of the landscape carries the same characteristics of the narrator, in that it denies the rational mind's desire to arrange information in a sense-making hierarchy.

This narrative refusal to adjudicate meaning or preference is picked up thematically in this passage and is linked to the confessional failure that sits like a canker at the heart of the novel. Observing the bleak landscape, Judge

Holden claims that the blistering sun leaching them of color and life ought to be recognized as a symbol for one's need to "purg[e] oneself of those things that lay claim to a man" (248). That is, the judge here sets himself up as a confessor. He points out the men's need to confess and be freed of sin, and he suggests that the agonizing sun doubles as penitential suffering, capable of cleansing their unrighteousness. However, the men reject both the judge's assumption of the role of confessor and his assertion that they in fact are in need of forgiveness. The men believe that they are "well done with any claims at all," suggesting that they fail absolutely to differentiate between their physical state—which is malnourished and impoverished—and their spiritual state. Because they have no physical accoutrements that they can discard, they assume that they have also no spiritual taints that need to be purged. Thus, the "austerity" of the landscape suggests an equal mental austerity, an incapacity to identify sin even in the most blatant violations of human ethics. These scalp-hunting murderers listen to a call to purge themselves of vice and feel no need to heed that call. An important note is that Judge Holden's desire to play confessor should not be confused with a willingness on his part to recognize the need for forgiveness. In the scene directly following this one, the men sit around a campfire and discuss the nature of war and human corruption. In this scene, Judge Holden claims that he believes "[m]oral law is an invention of mankind for the disenfranchisement of the powerful in favor of the weak" (250). He calls on the priest to refute the violence and implied blasphemy of this claim, but the priest shrugs off the call by arguing that he was after all no real priest but only a "novitiate" (250). In this case, Holden draws out the priest's confession of complicity in the murderous commitments of the band of bloodthirsty men, but that "confession" is not a verbal recognition of sin but rather a verbal denial of sin. In other words, Judge Holden plays confessor to Glanton's gang, but only to make the point that all the men, both in their actions and in their testimonies, agree with his appalling devotion to a creed of brutality and bloodshed and furthermore do not perceive this violent creed to be worthy of confession.

Passages in *Blood Meridian* that carry a strong narrative presence refuse to interpret the events of the story, in other words, just as the characters in the novel refuse to face their guilt, to name it, or to recognize their need for forgiveness. As he demonstrates through aping the role of confessor, Judge Holden also provides the novel with lengthy monologues that ostensibly interpret the world of the narrative and the actions of the men involved, but as so many critics have pointed out, these "interpretations" are typically loquacious and erudite-sounding denials of interpretation. Even his bombastically evil speeches, like the one cited previously that castigates "moral law" and that seems to be the worldview begetting the actions in the text, are difficult to interpret, since the judge enjoys playing mind games with his audience, posing ambiguous questions and offering even more ambiguous answers and contradicting himself. Readers are given no indication how Holden thinks, and no other character's thoughts are revealed in the entire novel. The few indications of thought in the text, upon closer scrutiny, are not descriptions of thought (the content of a character's thinking) so much as they are indications *that* a character is thinking. For example, when the ex-priest Tobin warns the kid that there is a mysterious divine presence that gives all life meaning, the text indicates some thought process on the kid's part:

> For let it go how it will, he [Tobin] said, God speaks in the least of creatures.
> The kid thought him to mean birds or things that crawl but the expriest, watching, his head slightly cocked, said: No man is give leave of that voice.
> The kid spat into the fire and bent to his work.
> I aint heard no voice, he said. (124)

The verb "thought" in this passage is followed by an indication that the kid has misunderstood the ex-priest, but the description of Tobin watching the kid carefully and then elucidating his comment suggests that the kid's "thought" may in fact have been only a physical movement, a head tipping, observed by Tobin and interpreted as evidence that the kid misunderstood his claim.

Ultimately, the novel's stylistic choices—indicating the presence of a narrator yet refusing to permit the narrator interpretive powers and indicating the presence of thought yet refusing to show or interpret that thought—suggest that such mental opacity is in fact the whole point. In his seminal article on historical sources for *Blood Meridian*, John Emil Sepich lists various original texts, including Jeremiah Clemens's *Bernard Lile* and Samuel Chamberlain's *My Confession*, which describe in eyewitness accounts the atrocities McCarthy lightly fictionalizes in his novel (122). While he adeptly lays out the source texts for the novel, Sepich does not extend his analysis in this article to McCarthy's stylistic choices in changing or reinterpreting his source texts, except for a brief description of the evolution of McCarthy's terrifying Judge Holden (Sepich 126). A brief comparison of two passages, one from Chamberlain's *My Confession* and one from *Blood Meridian,* indicates that McCarthy's novel picks up a troubling lack of evaluation or self-awareness in Chamberlain's narrative and turns it into a fictional catastrophe of interior failure.

Chamberlain's "confessional" narrative is, of course, anything but confessional. Chamberlain describes his "derring-do" with aplomb and with only scant references to his reluctance at times to participate in the mass rape and slaughter of American Indian and Mexican peoples. However, as Holden's unprovoked violence escalates, Chamberlain describes his companions' cooling favor toward the judge. Eventually, they tie the judge out in the desert and leave him. Chamberlain, however, depicts his rescue of the condemned judge in heroic terms:

> We rode on in moody silence for several miles, when we halted and looked back. We could see him in the distance—a small dark spot on the desert. I could not stand it. "He is a white man, and no doggone 'greaser' or buck, and I'll be d—d if he shall go under in that fashion!" I cried out, and without waiting for answer I started back. (293)

Showing more pity for Holden (a "white man") than for the victims of Glanton's gang, Chamberlain's "confession" conspicuously lacks an expected level of penitence. Although he indicates that he decries the barbarism of scalp hunting, he nevertheless joins Glanton's gang knowing full well what he will be required to do. His accounts of the savagery they inflict on their victims is, at best, conflicted. At one point, he describes Glanton executing wounded Apache prisoners and claims, "All felt sad and guilty" (281), but just previously, Chamberlain has described the raid that resulted in those wounded prisoners as "most glorious" (280). Chamberlain's moral responses, then, are problematic on two fronts. His contrition for murder seems halfhearted at best, while his pity for Holden—a man he (somewhat respectfully) describes as a "cool[. . .] blooded villain"—seems remarkably genuine (271).

In a scene in *Blood Meridian* evocative of the one described by Chamberlain, the ex-priest Tobin tells the kid to shoot Holden. The kid twice sets up his rifle but refuses to pull the trigger. When Tobin remonstrates with him, the kid rejects the idea that he ought to kill Holden:

> The kid spoke to him. He aint nothin. You told me so yourself. Men are made of the dust of the earth. You said it was no pair . . . pair . . .
> Parable.
> No parable. That it was a naked fact and the judge was a man like all men. (297)

In this instance, the kid refuses to kill Holden not out of any sense of pity, and not because Holden is a white man (as Chamberlain gives for his reasoning), but rather because he does not identify Holden as evil enough to warrant killing. In this scene, the kid's childlike qualities are played up in his stumbling over the multisyllabic word "parable." Yet his childishness is curiously void of innocence, because the kid has a record of senseless killing to support the notion that his refusal to kill Holden reflects his own sense of kinship with the man rather than his distaste for killing itself. The kid's repeated refusal to acknowledge his unspoken tie with the judge reaches a climax in the final scene, where the kid once again says that the judge "aint nothing," and the judge finally kills the kid in an outhouse (331, 333). In other words, the kid's refusal to admit that he is essentially the same as the judge becomes a ritualized litany of denial, a litany that suggests *Blood Meridian* is nothing so much as an explicitly anticonfessional account of savagery. The kid confesses nothing, the ex-priest forgives nothing, and the narrator interprets nothing. While Chamberlain maintains a facade of penitence, McCarthy strips that facade away, depicting an affectless kid refusing to acknowledge, name, or stand against the brutally unapologetic judge. McCarthy draws attention, then, to what is neither in the novel, nor in Chamberlain's original text, nor in the official texts of American national memory: a true confession.

Comparing the anticonfessional *Blood Meridian* with the confessional aspects of *Suttree* thus reveals the importance of penitence and the role of narrative styles in permitting readers to witness and share in penitential acts. In *Suttree*, the interior perspective illuminates Suttree's isolation, but also his humanity, his sorrowing, and all the good that he wants to do but does not do, so that the reader recognizes Suttree's utter failure while also understanding that he is at least *capable* of penitence. *Blood Meridian* possesses no confessional qualities because no character is granted an interior world, and confession begins with repentance—a changed heart, which Boehme calls the "internal hearer" (163). For Boehme, actions, not sacraments, and attitude, not rites, are redemptive. He claims "there is no removal of sin in the sacraments, nor through them forgiveness" (161–62). Instead, Boehme says, there should be no distinction made between the religious person and the nonreligious person. The only just distinction should be between the holy and the profane. Thus, "[t]he saint has his church with him and in him at all places. [. . .] The Holy Spirit preaches to him out of each creature" (162). The saint experiences the mystical infusion of the divine into the ordinary because he sees the work of God wherever he goes and the work of God in him is manifested as "good [. . .] works" (164). Boehme's mystical privileging of intention over action illuminates Suttree's rather profane epiphany. When he wanders into a church, at one point, Suttree falls asleep. The priest wakes him and chastises him for sleeping in the house of God. Suttree, risking sacrilege, claims, "It's not God's house" (255). The narrative interprets Suttree's cryptic comment by describing Suttree's flight of fancy as he imagines his broken community performing secular sacraments, such as Suttree's "serving early Mass," stale bread and booze, with his friend J-Bone (254). In this scene, Suttree rejects the priest's offer of confession and gets up and walks out to the streets, where, as a wandering, agnostic mystic, he will confess his sins to his readers and find his communion with the penitent.

Depictions of Suttree's interior mental life therefore encourage readers to practice empathy, that is, to actively engage with the text, constructing an imaginative bond with an external (fictional) person. By contrast, *Blood Meridian* avoids any potential for empathy as it narrates actions but not motivations, portraying violence unmediated by reflection. The novel also denies readers any cathartic or redemptive experience. Readers, after all, may recognize the overwhelming guilt of the characters in the novel—a guilt that the readers, as fellow Americans and fellow inheritors of the rhetoric of Manifest Destiny, may share—but it is a guilt that the characters in the novel do not admit to and which readers therefore cannot empathetically "confess." The novel thus denies readers any sense of ethical assurance. As Donoghue points out, "Most of the events of the novel are barbarous, but they seem to be protected from any ethical comment" ("Teaching *Blood Meridian*" 264). A text in which the reader is not permitted any insight into the characters' motivations or intentions renders the reader capable of judgment but incapable of mercy. *Suttree*'s narrative describes a character in many ways as morally corrupt as the characters in *Blood Meridian*, but the mental intimacy of the narrative style and the text's confessional modes permit readers to practice both judgment and mercy, so readers may experience reconciliation with the character at the end of his journey. *Suttree*, in other words, achieves some measure of literary shriving. In conjunction these two novels seem to propose that the act of empathy is the key to ethical engagement with the world and is in many ways the aesthetic sine qua non of literary ethics, without which there can be "*no inner reality*" (*BM* 337).

3
"PLEDGED IN BLOOD"
LINGUISTIC INTERIORITY AND REDEMPTION IN THE BORDER TRILOGY

Where are the others? Where are the others. Oh I've had time in great abundance to reflect upon that terrible question. Because we cannot save ourselves unless we save all ourselves.
—CORMAC MCCARTHY, *The Stonemason*

If writing is not a tearing of the self toward the other within a confession of infinite separation, if it is a delectation of itself, the pleasure of writing for its own sake, the satisfaction of the artist, then it destroys itself.
—JACQUES DERRIDA, *Writing and Difference*

In one of the opening scenes of *All the Pretty Horses* (1992), John Grady Cole walks out into the night and remembers "a dream of the past" in which a band of American Indian warriors rode down from the north, "all of them pledged in blood and redeemable in blood only" (5). By the end of the novel, John Grady has killed and seen killing and is himself "pledged in blood." Like *Blood Meridian* (1985), McCarthy's earlier western novel, catastrophic violence scars the landscape of all the novels of the Border Trilogy. However, unlike the vicious, amoral kid in *Blood Meridian*, John Grady Cole is youthful, idealistic, and heroic, an "all-american cowboy," as Billy Parham says (*COTP* 4). The first two novels of the trilogy, *All the Pretty Horses* and *The Crossing* (1994), are more companion novels than sequenced novels, telling the stories of two different boys, John Grady Cole and Billy Parham, respectively. Both novels begin with the boys' attempts to fulfill archaic roles, a ranchero (John Grady) and a trapper (Billy). These archaic roles require a "pledging" in blood as both boys commit acts of violence called for by their occupations (breaking horses and trapping a wolf). Following these acts, the boys embark on redemptive quests, to save horses and she-wolves and, later, prostitutes and brothers. Yet both boys fail in their attempts at salvation, defeated by inescapable violence, the literal and metaphorical blood in which they have been pledged. However, through repeated Christian imagery—leading up to the climactic depiction of John Grady's sacrificial death as a pietà in *Cities of the Plain* (1998)—the novels pose a wrenching question about the possibility of redemption from guilt caused by bloodshed through meaningful empathetic and compassionate interaction with others. Through systematic shifts into John Grady's interior world, *All the Pretty Horses* and *Cities of the Plain* depict his search for redemption. Billy's narrative, however, is observed by an omniscient, removed third-person narrator. *The Crossing* and *Cities of the Plain* do not reveal his thoughts or permit him the level of interior life that John Grady possesses. In *Cities of the Plain*, the rationale for such a difference in revelations of the two characters' internal worlds becomes clear. Billy acts as a witness to John Grady's attempts at heroism, and Billy's grief over John Grady's death draws readers' empathetic attention to his valorous intentions, regardless of his actions' efficacy, thereby elevating his death from a meaningless act to a potentially redemptive, even Christological sacrifice. Likewise, the narrator who observes Billy's grief illuminates the significance of his grief. Therefore, just as Billy's sorrow validates John Grady's moral acts, the narrator's observation of Billy validates his morality.

The entire Border Trilogy strikes many critics as an oddly idealistic and optimistic exception to McCarthy's otherwise morally diseased universe. Edwin Arnold, for example, claims that *All the Pretty Horses* is "certainly a more reassuring tale than its dark double *Blood Meridian*" (64), and Gail Morrison says, "By contrast to McCarthy's other protagonists, John Grady is clearly more hero than anti-hero" (176). Jacqueline Scoones acknowledges the traditional McCarthian darkness of the Border novels but takes their equally evident heroism and morality to mean that the novels pose the possibility for both the destructive and the healing potential of humankind: "The hands of humans into which the world has been delivered entire—either through a god's creation or man's creation of atomic weapons—can," she says, "in fact, attend to the things of the world with care" (151). Some critics ignore altogether the pall of doubt cast over the trilogy by its catastrophic conclusion. Kim McMurtry claims that John Grady and Billy, although matured and sobered, quit their narratives with some faith in a provident God intact, and thus the "biblical truth of redemption through Jesus Christ is developed throughout these novels, becoming clearest in the most recent *Cities of the Plain*" (156).

But for other critics, the momentary lightness of these novels, personified in their seemingly moral protagonists, flickers and fades against the overwhelming darkness of McCarthy's body of work. David Holloway, for example, finds John Grady to be nothing more than a "Don Quixote for the commodity age" who "eventually becomes little more than a hollow pastiche of the character he so much wants to be" (20). And Jay Ellis claims that the religious imagery in *Cities of the Plain* may suggest the necessity of human empathy or hope, but that "that [imagery] runs beyond the proportion and force of imagery in these novels," because "[w]ithin these novels, death outpaces any resurrections" (289). Given that all three novels conclude with the protagonists having failed comprehensively in their respective quests, it is hard to deny that, despite the heroic protagonists, the cosmos of the Border Trilogy is bleak. The trilogy problematically presents good people coming to sticky ends, good people committing bad deeds, and good people dying abandoned in shacks, much as a very bad person, the kid, dies in an outhouse in *Blood Meridian*. The novels thus seem to suggest that morality is a puny and futile force at best and, at worst, a completely pointless endeavor. However, the narrative events—the deeds and deaths of the novels—are not the only litmus test for interpreting the significance of morality.

Through revelations of John Grady's interior struggles, and through the symbolically weighted narrative in *Cities of the Plain,* the Border Trilogy draws attention to the interior aspect of morality. In a world ruled by arbitrary fates as this literary universe seems to be, these novels propose that personal responsibility and ethical intentions may be the only effective measure of a man's morality. Not surprisingly, then, *All the Pretty Horses* foregrounds the role of personal responsibility more than any novel since *The Orchard Keeper.* Both a western and a bildungsroman, *All the Pretty Horses* tells the story of John Grady Cole, a cowboy who loses his ranch in 1948 and heads down to Mexico, the new "paradise" for cowhands. Even in Mexico, however, he gets caught in a conflict of old and new worlds colliding. John Grady falls in love with the daughter of a Mexican rancher. Although they know there are severe consequences for their relationship, they become lovers. When their relationship is discovered, John Grady is thrown in prison, where he ends up killing another prisoner in a knife fight. At the end of the book, he relates his story to an American judge, describing his "innocent" love that betrayed the man he worked for and a self-defensive moment that resulted in a stranger's death. The judge asks John Grady whether he had bad intentions, could have avoided the knife fight, or would do any of them again, to which John Grady answers no. The judge suggests that the matter is less serious than John Grady takes it to be, and John Grady replies, "But that dont make it right" (293). Just as the judge immediately questions John Grady's intent in order to make a judgment on his morality, readers must understand the intent of his character if they are to come to any conclusions about the novel's morality. If John Grady's acts of violence and social disruption are random, then morality is a random and meaningless idea in the novel. However, if his intentions are clear and moral, the failure of his actions to live up to his intentions cannot fully eradicate his moral potential. That potential may be limited by consistent failure but is nevertheless a striking capacity that marks John Grady out from many of McCarthy's other characters, who seem deprived of either agency or the desire to "do right."

Cities of the Plain revisits John Grady's moral dilemma but adds the character of Billy, who is not caught up in John Grady's epistemological and ontological crises. Billy's simpler quest is to keep John Grady, who plays the illusive role of a younger brother, alive. In the end, both boys fail. John Grady fails to save his prostitute and dies in a revenge fight, forcing Billy to bury his younger-brother stand-in just as he buried his actual younger brother in *The Crossing*. But after burying the failed hero, Billy continues to grapple with the significance of death. The Border Trilogy, in other words, presents failed external morality and failed external salvation, but the haunting question of internal redemption remains. John Grady's *attempts* at morality suggest his belief that internal morality matters existentially, regardless of the efficacy of the external action. And Billy's grief over John Grady's death suggests that a single human life has the capacity to matter mysteriously, existentially, despite the ubiquitous death haunting all human endeavors.

The argument about the existential value of human life posed in *Cities of the Plain* is elucidated by McCarthy's play *The Stonemason* (1994), in which Ben reflects that "[t]he world was before man was and it will be again when he is gone. But it was not this world nor will it be, for where man lives is in this world only" (104–5). Ben suggests that human existence is so interconnected that nothing existing outside of the human ken can be comprehended, and if it cannot be understood, then all that matters is the fact of human existence. With that premise, Ben concludes that ethical obligations are the only litmus test for a well-constructed life. He imagines himself standing before a judging God whose sole question is not how excellent a worker Ben has been, but merely, "Where are the others?" Ben understands, in his vision-dream, that "we cannot save ourselves unless we save all ourselves" (113). John Grady and Billy enact Ben's moral philosophy, desperately pitching themselves into quest after quest to save brothers, prostitutes, wolves, and horses. The quests fail, but failure is not necessarily an indication of value. Moral responsibility is prized in the Border Trilogy even though—or because—it is threatened by the incipient collapse of the human race. The problem, in these novels, is the dilemma of humankind's need to behave valorously and to bear witness to acts of valor in a world where ultimate meaning is unknown and perhaps unknowable.

The need to commit moral actions is problematic in the play as in the trilogy. If, as Ben suggests, salvation is impossible without "saving all ourselves," then surely any possibility for redemption is nullified. And in *All the Pretty Horses*, the actual narrative events seem to undermine John Grady's desire to redeem himself through moral actions. Whatever his intentions, his actions bear almost uniformly catastrophic consequences. However, narrative shifts into John Grady's interior world illustrate his keen and increasingly anguished sense of moral responsibility. If his actions depict him as a failed hero, his internal responses indicate a quite different trajectory: as John Grady's external failures increase, his internal recognition of those failures suggests that he may mature from a callow boy to a morally responsible man. These glimpses into John Grady's intentions are unusual enough in McCarthy's corpus that they seem to demand interpretation. In the end, the novel seems to offer a possible caveat for Ben's relentlessly high standard for redemption. It may be impossible to fully redeem oneself, but the intention to do so—the will and the courage to act morally despite external failures—counts for something.

Thus, revelations of John Grady's internal world are critical to any interpretation of the novel. However, such revelations are rarely revealed through such explicit devices as first-person narration or even thought-tags, such as "he thought." The absence of explicit indications of interior thought does not, of course, mean that such interior thought is actually absent. Arthur Palacas claims that "voice," in literary terms, is a function of "the actual linguistic material observed on the page, the stuff that causes perception of voice" (508). While this definition of parenthetical "voice" seems fairly basic, it is important to clearly identify when a text not only can but *must* be interpreted as "voice." Palacas calls moments of voice "[l]inguistic worlds" (LWs), where LWs are "the interacting product of two worlds—the speaker/author's present time *factive* world and the speaker/author's present time *reflective,* or evaluative, world—two speaker/author real worlds distinguished solely by the opposition between the factive mentality and a reflective mentality" (509, italics his). In general, then, an "interior voice" is the "reflective mentality" of the speaker. In all of McCarthy's work, discussing "interior voice" or "reflective mentality" becomes problematic because the narratives are generally in the third person; so any indications of "reflective mentality" may belong either to a particular character or to the omniscient, unknown narrator. Palacas claims that parentheticals (any information occurring between ellipses, dashes, commas, or parentheses that reflects an evaluative consciousness) always indicate an alternating linguistic world, the intrusion of another "voice." But, again, McCarthy does not use parentheticals. Rarely does he even use such linguistic mental indicators as thought-verbs or speech tags. In *All the Pretty Horses,* however, McCarthy does indicate parenthetical or personal voice revelations. In this novel, the intrusion of a different "voice" is signaled syntactically rather than parenthetically.

The style shift that demonstrates a narrative perspective shift from omniscient narration into the limited third-person perceptions and thoughts of a character typically takes the form of a shift from simple narrative sentences (subject-verb-object sequences linked, if at all, by coordination) into subordination-heavy prose or syntactic fragments. For example, at the end of *All the Pretty Horses,* John Grady prepares to leave Mexico. Pausing to examine himself in a mirror, he begins to reflect on the events of his sojourn in Mexico and, more importantly, on his moral complicity in the many tragedies in which he has participated:

> He studied his face in a clouded glass. [. . .] He remembered things from the night of whose reality he was uncertain. He remembered a man in silhouette at the end of a street who stood much as Rawlins had stood when last he saw him, half turned in farewell, a coat slung loosely over one shoulder. Who'd come to ruin no man's house. No man's daughter. (255)

In this section, John Grady's observations about his bruised and stitched-up face shift to reflection with an explicit verbal tag, "remembered." But the concrete memory—a man in silhouette who reminds him of Rawlins—is transformed from a reflection of observation into an expression of guilt in the two following syntactic fragments. In these fragments, John Grady's description of Rawlins as a man who came to "ruin no man" isolates and intensifies the unmentioned—but implied—comparison person, the one who *did* come to ruin a house and a daughter. These verbal phrases bury the comparison person, but that person is, of course, staring at John Grady from the "clouded glass." In this section, John Grady's intense feelings of guilt are demonstrated through the symbolic self-division of the cloudy mirrored face and through the absence of the self in the recriminating interior reflections. Revelations of John Grady's interior world appear throughout the novel through such syntactic shifts from standard (subject-verb-object) constructions into fragments or run-ons. These revelations also consistently demonstrate his moral awareness. As the boy recognizes his own culpability in the violence of his world, his heroism shifts from external "heroic" behavior to an internal struggle to redeem himself.

Although Billy Parham, the similarly youthful and idealistic protagonist of *The Crossing*, is also a moral character, stylistic shifts in the second novel of the Border Trilogy almost never indicate a shift into Billy's interior perceptions or thoughts. Instead, ornate syntactic structures indicate only the evaluative voice of a removed narrator. In the few instances when the thoughts or attitudes of characters are revealed, the revelations are offered rather diffidently by the distant narrator. *The Crossing*'s paucity of interior revelations makes that novel stylistically more akin to *Blood Meridian* than to *All the Pretty Horses*. For example, in one section of *The Crossing*, Billy comes back from Mexico, and upon his crossing the border, the syntax breaks down into sentence fragments indicating interior perception and then evaluation. These interior revelations, however, are attributed to a crowd of people and are dictated in an omniscient narrator's voice:

> When he walked out into the sun and untied the horse from the parking meter people passing in the street turned to look at him. Something in off the wild mesa, something out of the past. Ragged, dirty, hungry in eye and belly. Totally unspoken for. In that outlandish figure they beheld what they envied most and what they most

reviled. If their hearts went out to him it was yet true that for a very small cause they might also have killed him. (170)

In this example, three syntactic fragments (beginning with "Something in off the wild mesa") indicate a shift into the perspective of an observing crowd, but in contrast to the use of syntax shifts in *All the Pretty Horses*, the crowd remains faceless and unnamed, and the following evaluative voice can be attributed only to an omniscient narrator, someone capable of judging the thoughts and intentions of a crowd.

The archaic and elegant transformations of the two evaluative sentences (beginning "In that outlandish figure") reflect the ornate diction of the narrator's voice in *Blood Meridian* more than they do the interior passages of *All the Pretty Horses*. For example, in *Blood Meridian*, Judge Holden is also observed and interpreted by a watching crowd, but the interpretation is filtered, as in the example from *The Crossing*, through the elevated diction of the narrator:

> The judge looked about him. He was sat before the fire naked save for his breeches and his hands rested palm down upon his knees. [. . .] None among the company harbored any notion as to what this attitude implied, yet so like an icon was he in his sitting that they grew cautious and spoke with circumspection among themselves as if they would not waken something that had better been left sleeping. (147)

In this passage, the convolutions of the narrative voice, fronting the simile at the expense of reversing the subject and verb ("was he" rather than "he was"), reflect the judge's opacity and the audience's "circumspection" around such a cipher. This remarkably self-aware diction reflects the poetic reversal in the previous passage from *The Crossing*, where Billy appears as what the crowd "envied most" and "most reviled" (170). Both of these examples of syntactic panache, however, are focused *on* the central characters, Billy and Judge Holden, rather than from *within* their minds, in contrast to similar passages in *All the Pretty Horses*. In that novel, "poetic" diction consistently reveals the interior workings of John Grady's mind—his self-recrimination, for example, as he reflects that, unlike his cousin, he is a "ruiner of men." *The Crossing* thus stylistically resembles *Blood Meridian* rather than the first novel of the Border Trilogy. However, an exploration of revelations of interior and narrative styles in *Cities of the Plain,* the concluding novel of the trilogy, offers an intriguing explanation for the disparity between the first two novels. An extended examination of *The Crossing* will be left for another study, since that novel does not offer as remarkable a stylistic departure from McCarthy's corpus as does *All the Pretty Horses.* Furthermore, the major themes and character from *The Crossing* are present in and extended by the narrative in *Cities of the Plain,* which melds the contrasting patterns of interiority in the first two novels of the trilogy.

In *Cities of the Plain,* John Grady is granted moments of interiority similar to those in *All the Pretty Horses,* while Billy, just as in *The Crossing,* is given almost no such moments of interiority. Syntactic shifts from the pared-down simple narrative style to complex, lyrical sentences and sentence fragments in Billy's narrative do not necessarily reflect his internal awareness but are instead typically the interpretations of an outside observer. For example, when Billy sees that John Grady has died, his reaction is described with an evaluative adjective, one that interprets the expression in terms of the man's interior world: "He was crying and the tears ran on his *angry* face" (261, italics mine). But that evaluative adjective must be attributed to a narrative voice rather than to Billy himself. Billy may feel angry, but he would not normally be aware that his *face* looked angry. In this scene, the narrative voice remains outside of Billy, observing him, although, of course, Billy *is* a moral character, and in mourning John Grady, Billy distinguishes himself from the uncaring, nonempathetic members of McCarthy's corpus, such as the kid in *Blood Meridian* and Culla Holme in *Outer Dark.* Studying the syntax of key moments in the Border Trilogy novels thus reveals a fascinating pattern of revelations and restrictions of interior thought that describe the third level of consciousness, in particular the revelations of John Grady's interior journey as his conscience is awakened and he begins to reflect on the implications of his actions and, in contrast, the lack of revelations of Billy's thoughts and perceptions even at times when he demonstrates moral awareness and active compassion.

The significance of the narrative perspective differences in the three novels becomes clear when the perspective shifts are examined in conjunction with the novels' thematic explorations of internal morality. The Border Trilogy's first novel, *All the Pretty Horses,* is an intriguing one because it introduces an unusually sympathetic hero, John Grady Cole, whose naive optimism and heroic instincts make him relatively unusual in McCarthy's corpus. The external journey John Grady takes is marred by failure, but his internal journey, while dark, is also heroic in the sense that his appreciation of his own culpability deepens and matures. So for instance, at the commencement of *All the Pretty Horses*, John Grady sets out for Mexico with his cousin Lacey Rawlins. They meet another runaway, Jimmy Blevins, and the prose during this meeting is clear and fluid narrative. Often, independent clauses are linked together with coordinate conjunctions, but these simple sentences have no subordination. In addition, there is a great deal of dialogue. At the end of this passage, the boys camp out the first night and they are "like young thieves in a glowing orchard, loosely jacketed against the cold and ten thousand worlds for the choosing" (30). The "ten thousand worlds" suggests thematically John Grady's initial hope; he sees Mexico as a sort of paradise where his dreams of living with horses and vast expanses of land will come true. Eventually, the boys' relationships become strained and broken. John Grady's affair with Alejandra, the daughter of the ranchero for whom they work, lands Rawlins and John Grady in jail and so alienates them. And Blevins is shot on suspicion of horse theft. In the novel's concluding paragraph, John Grady heads out into the sunset, "the world to come" (334). The transformation from "ten thousand worlds for the choosing" to "the world to come" reflects the sobering journey John Grady has taken.

The novel's first sentence indicates why an examination of the novel's revelations of John Grady's interior life is so fascinating. That sentence is a vivid example of paratactic prose, that is, prose distinguished by its use of subordination rather than coordination, the prose style that characterizes the impersonal omniscient narrative of *Blood Meridian* (Donoghue, "Teaching *Blood Meridian*," 258): "The candleflame and the image of the candleflame caught in the pierglass twisted and righted when he entered the hall and again when he shut the door" (3). The paucity of punctuation draws immediate attention to the sentence's ambivalent placement of the subject. After the deleted subordination marker, "that was," in the second of the two subjects ("the candleflame and the image of the candleflame"), the sentence contains two paired subordinate clauses, "when he entered" and "when he shut the door" (3). Only at the end of the second subordinate clause is the novel's subject introduced. And not only is the novel's protagonist buried in a subordinate clause, but he is introduced only by the anaphoric pronoun "he" without a specific reference. Ordinarily, subordination implies a hierarchical structure of a sentence, with the important information appearing in the main clause and background information in the subordinated clause. But this opening line violates any presuppositions of relative importance within the world of the text. In this novel, the syntax implies, the "hero" may be no more than an afterthought to a reflection. Not until the end of the novel's third scene are readers finally told, "The boy's name was Cole. John Grady Cole" (7). The relegation of the "hero" to a nonreferenced anaphor in a relative subordinate clause casts a shadow over his role as hero and his agency, and this linguistic method creates an empathetic distance; the reader's relationship with the story is fragile, existing only in this tenuous relationship with a "he."

The novel subjugates the character to the external world in more ways than just unreferenced pronouns. Another example of such subjugation is the narrative's reversion to conversational Spanish again and again, such as in the passage in which John Grady returns from the church (where the body is) to his house, where the Mexican housekeeper serves him dinner:

> I appreciate you lightin the candle, he said.
> Cómo?
> La candela. La vela.
> No fui yo, she said. (4)

The dialogue continues in Spanish without translation (untranslated Spanish appears in most of McCarthy's novels). Also, when John Grady and his companions cross the Mexican border, they dialogue in Spanish with the Mexicans they meet. John Grady and Alejandra, his lover, often converse in Spanish. And when he is thrown into prison, John Grady's interrogator questions him in Spanish. All of these passages, though not necessarily pivotal, are at least centrally located, and none of them are translated. In many of McCarthy's novels, untranslated Spanish suggests that the reader overhears the characters in the novel, the lack of translation thus distancing readers. In *All the Pretty Horses,* however, the narrative perspective is so closely tied to John Grady's interior mental life as to suggest to readers that when translation is omitted it is because John Grady needs no translation. For the reader, then, the existence of the narrative itself is mediated by the character's interiority. The fact that the character is introduced only as "he" and that so much of the dialogue is untranslated highlights the temporal quality of texts and characters. At the end of the novel, John Grady recognizes his own frailty, and the last image in the novel is his shadow paling in the darkening land. Essentially, the "textual self-consciousness" of *All the Pretty Horses* reflects the depths of the reflective and evaluative consciousness of the character (Holloway 21). That is, John Grady is not a "narrator" in any traditional sense, but he is a character through whom the text is mediated. This tenuous relationship between character and text deepens readers' awareness of the importance of the character's moral reflections. In other words, if the character himself associates morality or immorality with certain actions, interpreters of the text must understand those actions through his eyes, because the text is inarticulate outside of him. John Grady, then, holds not just the "narrative" authority in the text but also its "meaning," its moral consciousness.

Four key scenes in the text are narrated from John Grady's perspective; in contrast, the observing narrator relates physical actions, such as the flickering of a candle flame, without interpreting them. However, in none of these four passages is there a single instance in which McCarthy allows dashes, ellipses, or parentheses to indicate parenthetical (personal voice) realizations in the text. Furthermore, commas indicate a shift only when they set off phrases or subordinated clauses; where they set off independent clauses, they typically do not mark the appearance of a parenthetical thought. Despite the absence of punctuation or verbal tags, however, when narrative sentences break down syntactically into fragments and run-ons, a shift into "personal voice"—interior perceptive or evaluative consciousness—occurs.

The first example of this syntactic indication of interiority appears, not surprisingly, in the novel's opening scene, where John Grady views his grandfather's casket:

> He looked down at the guttered candlestub. He pressed his thumbprint in the warm wax pooled on the oak veneer. Lastly he looked at the face so caved and drawn among the folds of the funeral cloth, the yellowed moustache, the eyelids paper thin. That was not sleeping. That was not sleeping. (1)

The action is described in narrative sentences that create the existing fictional world, so that the action itself is perceived by the character. That is, in the fictional world, "he looked" (narrative action). However, "he looked" is followed by a list of perceptions ("the yellowed moustache, the eyelids paper thin"). But the repeated syntactic fragment "That was not sleeping," is an ambiguous construction; it could be a complete sentence (a noun phrase plus a verb phrase), where "That" is a pronoun whose antecedent is "the face." Or "That" could be a relative pronoun, in which case the phrase is a sentence fragment, emphasizing that the face is dead rather than "sleeping." In either case, the repeated phrase suggests that the image, a dead visage, has made a profound impact upon the consciousness narrating the events, and it makes little sense to interpret this impact as an emotion felt by the omniscient narrator. Instead, the repeated clause indicates a different perspective from the narrative surrounding it. Unlike "the yellowed moustache" or "the eyelids paper thin," this clause cannot be understood semantically as a perception. Instead, it indicates the presence of John Grady's consciousness, his thoughts directly revealed through the text. The narrative perspective, in other words, has narrowed to the gaze of the protagonist without any explicit indications of such a narrative shift.

Throughout the novel, marked shifts in syntax—such as the repeated, syntactically ambiguous clause in the previous example—indicate that John Grady's consciousness is now narrating the events of the novel. However, the predominant narrative style, simple narrative sentences (subject, verb, and object) or simple clauses linked by the coordinating conjunction "and," is dictated by an omniscient third-person narrator similar to the narrator of *Blood Meridian*. For example, when John Grady sets out for Mexico, the text is characterized by lightness of syntax and lengthy passages of dialogue that are visually poetic with their short, jagged lines. After John Grady finalizes his plans to leave, he picks up Rawlins and the two of them head south to a land they envision as "ten thousand worlds for the choosing." The beginning of John Grady's relationship with Alejandra demonstrates the novel's first explicit shift in prose style. In this section of the novel, McCarthy's use of subordination and syntactic fragments indicates that the narrative has shifted from the omniscient perspective to John Grady's directly revealed perceptions and thoughts.

This second key passage that reveals John Grady's interior world comes early in the text, when John Grady and Alejandra's relationship moves from distant admiration to that of lovers. The scene begins with typical narrative sentences and dialogue:

> Five nights later asleep in his bunk in the barn there was a tap at the door. He sat up.

LINGUISTIC INTERIORITY AND REDEMPTION IN THE BORDER TRILOGY 89

> [. . .]
> What is it? he whispered.
> It's me. (139)

As they begin talking, however, the sentences become more and more convoluted. Simple structures become cluttered with coordinated and subordinated clauses:

> She looked up at him and her face was pale and austere in the uplight and her eyes lost in their darkly shadowed hollows save only for the glint of them and he could see her throat move in the light and he saw in her face and in her figure something he'd not seen before and the name of that thing was sorrow. (140)

"She looked up at him" is paralleled by "her face was pale," "her eyes [were] lost," "he could see," and "he saw." All of these independent clauses are linked by the conjunction "and," repeated four times. However, the sixth "and" sets off a sentence that is not a simple narrative: "and he saw in her face and in her figure something he'd not seen before." There is a significant deletion in this sentence. The underlying structure would read: "[he saw] in her figure something [*that*] he had not seen before," revealing a subordinate clause set off by the relative pronoun "that." The next coordinate clause, "the name of that thing was sorrow," seems to represent John Grady's thoughts.

The scene's climax, when the young couple swim together, is narrated almost exclusively in fragments or subordinated sentences and must be interpreted as John Grady's perspective:

> She paused midway to look back. [. . .] Do not speak to her. Do not call. When she reached him he held out his hand and she took it. She was so pale in the lake she seemed to be burning. Like foxfire in a darkened wood. That burned cold. (141)

"Do not speak to her. Do not call" are in the imperative mode and are obviously not attributed to the novel's omniscient narrator, but rather to John Grady thinking to himself that he must not speak or call to Alejandra. The following sentence returns briefly to external narrative, "he held out his hand and she took it." However, the last complete sentence has a deletion of the subordinating "that" ("She was so pale in the lake [that] she seemed to be burning"), reminiscent of both the initial "That was not sleeping" evaluative moment and the moment just preceding this one which signals the shift into John Grady's interior thoughts ("that he'd not seen before"). And, with a relative pronoun (here deleted) readers are nevertheless once more plunged into John Grady's mental life. The concluding phrase of that sentence, "she seemed to be burning," and the final two fragments of the passage, "Like foxfire," and "That burned cold" are completely "interior"—they reflect an evaluative mental life. These last few phrases contain the highest concentration of verbals, as well, with "burning," "darkened," and "burned." The intensity of John Grady's emotions, then, is reflected in verbal and syntactic intensity.

The interplay of these two different narrative perspectives, omniscient third person and close third person directly revealing John Grady's thoughts and perceptions, creates the emotional vitality of the scene. Convoluted coordinated and subordinated sentences shatter into breathless fragments. The sentences and fragments are also strongly verbal. In this one brief section, ten semantically active verbs appear: "paused," "look," "do not speak," "do not call," "reached," "held," "took," "seemed to be burning," "darkened," and "burned." This verbal concentration, however, is effective only in its connection with syntactic fragmentation and vivid imagery. The shift between dialogic and descriptive sentences, sentences as intimate as self-referential imperatives like "Do not call" and vivid descriptions like "foxfire in a darkened wood," give the scene an intimacy and a tenderness that are quite rare in McCarthy's corpus.

The interiority in the love scene contrasts with the flatly rendered third critical event in John Grady's story, the knife fight in which he kills a man. In this scene, the brutality of the prison in which John Grady and Rawlins have been incarcerated without formal accusation, certainly without trial, has worn both of them down. Rawlins has been stabbed and is missing and John Grady does not yet know if his cousin is alive. John Grady barters a knife from an "insider." During a meal, the dining hall suddenly empties and John Grady finds himself faced with a young man wielding a knife. He realizes that the *cuchillero* has been chosen to do away with the *Americano*. The knife fight is related primarily in brief, standard narrative sentences. Fragments in this section are semantically descriptive and emotionally sterile. In contrast to the passion of the previous passage, these fragments are noun phrases rather than verb phrases.

> The boy came opposite him. He passed. John Grady watched him with a lowered gaze. When the boy reached the end of the table he suddenly turned and sliced the tray at his head. John Grady saw it all unfold slowly before him. The tray coming edgewise toward his eyes. The tin cup slightly tilted with the spoon [. . .]. (199)

The effect is intense, but not dramatic. And by the time the climax arrives, the scene seems to have emotionally flatlined:

> The cuchillero lowered the tray. He set it quietly on the table. [. . .] As he did so John Grady brought his knife up from the floor and sank it into the cuchillero's heart. (201)

This scene is most shocking not in the fact of its violence but in its *lack* of drama or human emotion related to the violence. The technical straightforwardness and the concentrated brevity of the sentences, unalleviated throughout the passage, are instrumental in creating a breathless rhythm that, in contrast to the breathlessness of the love scene, is deprived of sensory or mood indicators. The resulting text feels disjointed and detached.

The contrast between the love scene and the knife fight demonstrates a conspicuous difference in the narrative presence of interior mental activity. In the love scene, fragments and sentences with subordinate clauses occur thirteen times. Nine appear in the last paragraph, the climax of the scene. That paragraph is almost exclusively parenthetical; that is, most of the passage is not a description of events or actions but is rather a revelation of John Grady's own mental activity, demonstrated by phrases such as "Standing there trembling in the water and not from the cold for there was none" (141). With the sudden intrusion of the imperative mood, "Do not speak to her," readers understand that John Grady is so mentally "alive" that his interior voice has taken hold of the text. He is essentially talking to himself. The knife-fight scene, by contrast, has only three fragments, but all three do indicate that the perspective of the narrative is John Grady's. The tray is "coming," a directional word that implies that the camera angle of the text is firmly anchored behind John Grady's gaze. But in this knife-fight scene, the perspective reveals John Grady's *perception* of events rather than his interpretation of what he sees, in contrast to his active mental life in the love scene. Additionally, the emotional index of the love scene is significantly higher than the emotional index of this scene. The two syntactic fragments cited previously, "The tray coming edgewise," and "The tin cup slightly tilted," are noun phrases. Although the phrases possess two verbals, "coming" and "tilted," those verbals seem rather dull when compared to the verbals of the earlier scene ("burning, darkened, burned"). More significantly, "coming" and "tilted" are verbals that represent perception rather than evaluation. That is, John Grady thinks that Alejandra is "burning" like foxfire, an evaluation. But seeing a "tilted" tray is merely a perception. The knife scene is thus clearly positioned in John Grady's consciousness (he *perceives* it all, as evinced by the two fragments), but evaluative interior life is notably absent. Linguistically, then, John Grady's humanity—the personal voice that appears in a parenthetical—is silenced during this moment of violence. It is in this respect that John Grady's mental life reflects his moral consciousness. When he later expresses a haunting guilt and even shame over the knife fight, readers understand that the divorce between perception and evaluation during the scene was an instinctive decision on the character's part, but a decision that he nevertheless later regrets. Within the text itself, the struggle between moral responsibility, failure, and shame plays out syntactically, the literary level reflecting what is happening at the syntactic level.

The "ten thousand worlds for the choosing" that John Grady looks to hopefully in the beginning find a stark parallel scene in the fourth and final key moment, the end of the novel. This moment is, importantly, very interior. The final two sentences are a sentence with a subordinate clause and a fragment, respectively:

> He rode with the sun coppering his face and the red wind blowing out of the west across the evening land and the small desert birds flew chittering among the dry bracken and horse and rider and horse passed on and their long shadows passed in tandem like the shadow of a single being. Passed and paled into the darkening land, the world to come. (302)

The first sentence in this quotation does not reflect evaluative interior monologue as much as perception; it employs coordinate clauses. The second is subordinate, and it is semantically ambiguous. The image of the paling rider and the two horses seems to be observed by distant eyes, the epic pan readers expect at the end of McCarthy's saga-inflected literary universes. However, this final scene commences with an indication that even the distant epic-shot angle may be a reflection of John Grady's growing self-awareness.

Just before this final scene, John Grady passes a group of Indians who "st[and] and watch[. . .] him pass" (301). The camera angle remains inside John Grady's perspective, the unusual epic shot explained by an explicit modal that indicates the character's mental evaluation:

> The indians stood watching him. He could see [1] that none of them spoke among themselves or commented on his riding there nor did they raise a hand in greeting or call out to him. They had no curiosity about him at all. As if [2] they knew all that they needed to know. They stood and watched him pass and watched him vanish upon that landscape solely because he was passing. Solely because he would vanish. (301)

The modal "could" [1] reflects John Grady's capability to perform the following verb: the boy is able to see the Indians, and his sight (his perception) precipitates an evaluative "as if" phrase [2]. In other words, although the novel concludes with the silent Indians watching John Grady pass and pale, the text has not really shifted into their perspective. Instead, John Grady's mind is still controlling the text, *imagining* himself through their eyes. Of course, this final scene evokes John Grady's first dream of the Indians in the novel, "a dream of the past" in which the Indians are "pledged in blood and redeemable in blood only" (5). In that dream, John Grady imagines that he lives in a world where a former race, the Native people of the land, have evaporated, mystically bequeathing the land to him. Early in the novel, the narrator indicates that John Grady interprets the "passing" of the Native people as a cosmic judgment upon their history, a history steeped in violence. Thus, this Native group's moral iniquity has required blood sacrifice and, having paid their debt, they vanish from the earth, leaving it to the idealistic youth eager to claim his inheritance. However, the last scene shows a radical readjustment of this early philosophy. In the final scene, John Grady acknowledges that the Indians remain, watching him. These descriptions of the Indians, one a vision he sees in "canted light" and another stimulated by a perception (seeing Indians watching him), are semantically parenthetical. But the two different images reflect very different conclusions about whose existence is transient and ephemeral and who remains alive, who is guilty of bloodshed and who is justified in passing judgment. John

Grady imaginatively cedes the right of perception—and, by extrapolation, the right of evaluation—to the Indians, suggesting that he has concluded that his own bloodguilt outweighs that of the Native inhabitants. However, because the narrative's perspective remains tied to John Grady, the novel implicitly suggests that the boy's conclusions about the magnitude of his guilt and the value of sacred violence are in fact moral conclusions. He has learned to shoulder responsibility for his own actions and to question the efficacy of redemption from bloodshed through further bloodshed, and the narrative thus demonstrates John Grady's maturity through his recognition of the irreducible other-ness of the Indians: they have not vanished and they are neither guiltier nor more innocent than he or, perhaps, any other human being.

All the Pretty Horses thus foregrounds the critical importance of personal responsibility by tying the text's perspective to that of the main character. At the same time, however, the novel refuses to mitigate the complex and ambiguous nature of morality. At the semantic level, the stripping of sense-making mechanics through the use of anaphoric pronoun references without antecedents and sentences lacking punctuation reflects the impossible dichotomy of the moral universe in the novel. At one point, the boys are discussing judgment day, and Rawlins asks John Grady if he "believe[s] in all that." John Grady replies, "I dont know. Yeah, I reckon" (61). He also believes in moral responsibility (291). He does not, however, know where to find God or where to find absolution. The world of the boys is a stark and harsh reality, where man is temporal yet cannot escape a belief in the eternal; man is sinful yet cannot escape the shame of morality.

However, the novel rejects nihilism through its recognition of some inherent value to moral choices. Even if the significance of morality or the efficacy of moral actions remains ambiguous, the main character's agonized internal struggle forms the heart of the narrative. The novel seems to suggest that although immorality is the inescapable corollary of morality, the character—and perhaps all of humanity—cannot escape the mystical obligation to reach for "what is right." When John Grady testifies before the judge at the end of the novel, the judge, after hearing his story, says, "I've heard a lot of things that give me grave doubts about the human race but this aint one of em" (289). The fading and disappearing horse and rider at the end of the novel are somber but not nihilistic.

Cities of the Plain echoes and intensifies the corollaries of the first Border

Trilogy novel's if-then proposition. However, this concluding novel tentatively proffers an answer to John Grady's agonized attempts—and failures—at achieving morality. In *Cities of the Plain*, Billy's quest is to valorize John Grady's life and death, but the novel suggests that narrative itself is the means through which Billy's quest may be valorized. In this book, meaning resides in relationship.

In order to argue that meaning resides in the interaction between people and consciousnesses, it is necessary first to explore the development of consciousness in the novel. It begins in a distant narrative following the character Billy. The first sentence reads: "They stood in the doorway and stomped the rain from their boots and swung their hats and wiped the water from their faces" (3). As in the first sentence of *All the Pretty Horses*, a series of narrative clauses are joined together by the conjunction "and." Similarly, the subject of the sentence is a nonreferenced pronoun. Readers do not, at first, know who "they" are. Directly following "their" entrance into the bar, Billy speaks: "Damned if I aint half drowned, Billy said. He swung his dripping hat. Where's the all-american cowboy at?" (3). From his comment, it is clear, first, that the narrative is following Billy and, second, that the narrative action is Billy searching for John Grady (the "all-american cowboy"). Later in this first scene, readers are told that Billy "c[an] hear the rain rattling on the metal roof," suggesting that perception (hearing) is tied to Billy's perspective (5). The next section begins, "It was still dark when John Grady woke him" (7). The use of the nonreferenced "him," in contrast to the introduction of John Grady by name, indicates that the narrative camera angles remain close to Billy's head. But the camera never reveals his mind, beyond brief sensory verbs such as "hear." Billy's section is comprised of narrative sentences, and the dialogue is also without speech tags or any indirect speech at all. Billy is the focal character, but he is a character without the capacity to control the evaluative voice of the text.

However, when the narrative shifts from following Billy to following John Grady, the syntax becomes strikingly different. In the first section that follows John Grady, there is an instance of indirectly reported speech, "He said that he was waiting for someone" (37). The next section follows John Grady as he rides up into the Jarillas:

Atop a raw rock bluff he sat the horse and studied the country. The flooded saltflats shining in the evening sun seventy miles to the east. The peaks of El Capitan beyond. All the high mountains of New

Mexico paling away to the north beyond the red plains, the ancient creosote. (38)

John Grady's perception (he "studied the country") is followed by a series of noun phrases. These sentence fragments list what John Grady perceives, but they also indicate that the perception is happening through his eyes. That is, while Billy's sections follow Billy's actions and may relate *what* Billy hears, in John Grady's section the fragments indicate that readers are seeing the salt flats and mountains *through* his eyes. John Grady is a subjective character, even in this novel where he is not the only moral protagonist.

The novel's contrasting use of interiority for its two protagonists is explained through its use of imagery, particularly Christian symbolism. In *Cities of the Plain*, the presupposition of Christian ethics is that "goodness" means something because it is required by, observed by, and judged by an omniscient and presumably moral "God." If there is no God, the morality of his adherents is ambiguously valuable at best. In other words, the Christian imagery and, ultimately, the Christological image of John Grady's dead body emphasize the importance of an outside "judge"—an outside consciousness, like God watching Sodom and Gomorrah, to turn unmitigated tragedy into a story of (possibly ambiguous) redemption. This imagery helps interpret the contrasting use of interiority because it highlights the importance of relationship, particularly the relationship of an observer and narrator imposing meaning on another's life through narrative and through love.

In *Cities of the Plain*, the relationship between the two boys and the interweaving, conjoining narrative impose meaning in a profoundly communal way. For example, John Grady's analog, the lonely kid of *Blood Meridian*, is a tragic character. The kid is completely amoral. He refuses to acknowledge "right" or "wrong," and in the end he is strangled in an outhouse, his dead body hidden from the reader's view. It is important that the kid's excuse for his failure to face the judge and condemn him is that "he [the judge] aint nothing" (*BM* 234). John Grady, who seems to step in as the kid's dialectical opposite in many ways, reverses the kid's decision to opt out of moral commitment. In *Cities of the Plain*, Tiburcio, John Grady's nemesis and the Satanic figure of evil, repeats the kid's phrase to Magdalena shortly before he kills her. "What are you?" he asks her, and answers his own question, "You are nothing" (183). And it is for this woman, this "nothing," that John Grady dies.

The most telling difference between the kid's death and John Grady's death is the difference between mental intentionality. The kid goes into an outhouse and is presumably strangled; his death is completely unintentional on his part and almost an afterthought to the historical events of the narrative. John Grady's death, however, is not only clearly inevitable from the perspective of narrative events (he deliberately gets drunk and goes in search of Eduardo with a knife in his hand), but through the use of interiority, his actions are made to seem consciously intentional as well. When he first faces Eduardo, the narrative explicitly indicates his interior mental life: "Perhaps he'd palmed it in his hand the while" (247). The word "perhaps" is an evaluative adverb implying implicit mental attitude (a judgment of some sort). Shortly after this expression of evaluative interiority, two sentence fragments appear, indicating perception. John Grady sees light winking off the blade of Eduardo's knife: "And then the wink again. As if he were turning it in his hand" (247). The first fragment semantically indicates visual perception (light on metal). The second indicates a mental judgment, a comparison and then an assumption (explaining the wink of light by the action of hiding the knife).

During the knife fight, Eduardo taunts John Grady, telling him that his love for Magdalena is meaningless. Most of the fight is related in direct narrative sentences. Toward the beginning, John Grady's mental life flickers awake through some syntactic fragments indicating evaluation ("As if he were turning it [. . .]"). However, as the fight progresses, Eduardo's taunts grow in intensity and the interior fragments diminish. In the middle of the fight, Eduardo evokes the image of Christ's sacrifice, telling John Grady that he is crazy and that he must believe his craziness is sacred, "[a] partaking of the Godhead." But, Eduardo says, "what does this say of God?" (251). At this point, references to John Grady shift abruptly. Where he was "John Grady" up to this point in the fight, he suddenly becomes "the boy." This distancing common noun, replacing the more intimate proper noun, also reflects a mental distancing. For the next few minutes of the fight, there are no fragments indicating mental life, and the distant term "boy" is used to refer to John Grady fourteen times. And then Eduardo's taunts take a more specific turn. Eduardo begins to remind John Grady why John Grady came to fight in the first place. "For a whore," Eduardo reminds him. "For a whore" (253). The next sentence begins, "John Grady stood holding himself," and the more intimate use of the proper name reflects a sudden rejuvenation of John Grady's interior evaluative mental life. Reminded of his purpose, his single-minded love for Magdalena, John Grady's interiority returns. After that telling shift in reference, the description of the duel is scattered with interior moments, such as "He swung the knife. [. . .] Like a man hacking randomly at weeds" and "He was suddenly very low before John Grady. Almost kneeling. Almost like a supplicant" (249). Both of these fragments are similes and indicate an evaluative consciousness; someone is making the comparison.

In an interesting contrast to the knife fight in *All the Pretty Horses*, where John Grady's interior voice is in abeyance until the fight is over, his interior voice in *Cities of the Plain* syntactically diminishes as soon as the knife fight is over. The last sentence fragment appears when he looks down at the dying Eduardo, who gazes back at John Grady "[t]he way a man might look getting on a train." Shortly after that, John Grady looks at the now dead Eduardo and cuts his shirt away "from his dead enemy" (254). From that point until John Grady's death, there are no sentence fragments and no indications of interior mental life. On a literary level, John Grady has named his enemy and has lost his life revenging a dead prostitute. The narrative action, his revenge of the girl and the syntactic revelation of his active mental life during that defense, indicates that John Grady consciously confronted evil and, also consciously, chose to die for a woman he loved.

John Grady, then, unlike the kid of *Blood Meridian*, faces evil, names it, condemns it, and offers himself as a gesture of expiation. The kid's death is insignificant in comparison with the grief caused by John Grady's death. Meaning is imposed through relationship and through naming, and the syntactic level of the narrative demonstrates that morality (John Grady's love for Magdalena and hatred of Eduardo) is expressed through revelations of interior mental life. The kid, who lacks an interior mental life, also lacks morality. Refusing to enter into the world of either love or hatred, the kid dies in an outhouse, or rather, fades from existence into a nonbeing while the judge lives on. John Grady, by offering himself up, imposes meaning on Magdalena, imbues her "nothingness" with his own life and essence; she is "something" to him.

This shift from nihilism to significance, from "nothing" to "something," reflects the role of archetypal Christian images in *Cities of the Plain*. These images do not necessarily indicate that the worldview of the novel is "Christian," any more than the Gnosticism or nihilism of previous works indicate that the whole of the work or of McCarthy's corpus should be read as

Gnostic or nihilistic. That is, *Cities of the Plain* offers a possibility of meaning through the incarnation of mystical religious imagery in human, "this-world" forms, but the extant substance of those forms is left ambiguous. After all, as the stranger tells Billy at the end of *Cities of the Plain*, "[w]here all is known, no narrative is possible" (277). In the final analysis, the Christian imagery of this novel does not make it "Christian," but it does indicate a method of interpreting or understanding the novel's force. Leo Daugherty argues that *Blood Meridian* is a Gnostic text, where Gnosticism is the belief that the world is inherently evil and the "quest" of humankind is to escape the physical and real world and the "evil" incarnate in it (160). Therefore, the kid, by abdicating his moral essence, nullifies the meaning of the physical world. This reading explains why the only "real" person, in the end, is the judge, and he is "real" only because he chooses to impose his own meaning and morality upon the world. If *Blood Meridian* emphasizes a Gnostic corruption of the physical realm, *Cities of the Plain* employs Christian archetypal images in order to emphasize the mystical power of human communion. Some of the central images are sacramental indications of such radical unity, from the image of John Grady as a pietà to the image of the Eucharist in the cracker-sharing between the stranger and Billy at the end of the novel. These sacramental images indicate that if any meaning is to be found, it is to be found in relationship.

In *All the Pretty Horses*, interior revelations depict John Grady's sense of morality and suggest a means for interpreting the novel. In *Cities of the Plain,* the relationship between interiority and morality is slightly more complex, for Billy also is a "moral" character, but he is not given an interior voice. Unlike John Grady but like almost all other McCarthy protagonists (with the possible exception of Suttree), Billy is observed by outside consciousnesses. In fact, there are outside observing consciousnesses in all scenes except John Grady's. Even more significantly, many characters—even minor and unnamed ones—are permitted moments of interior thought, while Billy is not. Only once in the novel does the narrative shift into Billy's mind, and that shift is, perhaps, ambiguous. At one point, a Mexican tries to grab Billy's arm, and readers are told: "Mistake. [. . .] He was so light" (237). The evaluation ("Mistake") and perception (that the Mexican was "so light") seem to take place inside Billy's mind, although they could be attributed to the omniscient narrator. In any case, even if these comments reflect a narrator interpreting the Mexican's actions as a "mistake" because he was "light" compared to Billy's superior strength, it is an oddly intimate gesture for the ordinarily removed narrator. This instance of interior life on Billy's part is matched and superseded by the interior life of characters appearing in only one or two scenes.

Like *The Orchard Keeper*, *Cities of the Plain* often shifts into the perspective and evaluative consciousness of different characters, seemingly at random. For example, early in the novel there is a section that takes place inside the mentality of Mac, the cowboy who runs the ranch where John Grady works. Certain sentences in this scene semantically indicate interiority, such as when readers are told, "He [Mac] was about out of the cattle business anyway" and then "His wife would be dead three years in February" (116). These instances are clearly Mac's ruminations. In the epilogue, Socorro is observed with an ash-mark on her forehead "to remind her of her mortality. As if she had any other thought" (264). This last sentence fragment syntactically indicates an interior moment, and indeed it seems evaluative, but it is unclear whether this evaluation is Billy's or Mac's, as they stand at the graveside with her, or whether it is that of an omniscient narrator. Finally, when the woman in the concluding scene of the novel pats Billy's hand, readers are given a nominal phrase of adjectives, "Gnarled, ropescarred, speckled from the sun," unlikely to be Billy's thoughts, but not necessarily the woman's either (291). Each of these moments emphasizes moments of connection or the weight of separation, in Billy's violent confrontation with the Mexican, in Mac's and Socorro's loss, and in the woman's tender hand on Billy's. In other words, *all* moments of interiority underscore the significance of human connection and interaction, even moments when the interiority belongs to random or even unnamed and unidentified observers.

Perhaps the most significant manifestations of observations by outside consciousnesses, plot-wise, appear during scenes with Magdalena. In the pivotal scene describing her epileptic fit, a distinct evaluative voice narrates, one similar to the distant, omniscient, and evaluative narrator in *Blood Meridian*. For example, in a scene where Tiburcio, the "pimp" (as Billy calls him) who oversees the prostitutes, takes care of Magdalena during her fit, the narrator observes that he is "[a] morbid voyeur, a mortician. An incubus of uncertain proclivity" (183). Later, as Magdalena, deceived, goes to her death rather than to John Grady, she is "observed" several times; a woman looks at her "as if to remember her. Perhaps to read [. . .]. What was lost or what was ruined. Whom bereft" (211). Then Magdalena walks into a restaurant and two men watch her: "Pale and dirty waif drifted by mischance [. . .]" (213). Unnamed observers remark on Magdalena. Readers, however, are never shown Magdalena's interior world, and, interestingly, readers are also not shown her death, which occurs "off stage." She sees Tiburcio (225), and the next time readers see her it is through John Grady's eyes as he views her corpse (228–29). The distance of narration surrounding the girl lends her the same ambiguity that haunts the kid in *Blood Meridian*. She is an object of ambiguous pathos; she is objectified both by observers in the novel and by the main characters. Both Eduardo and John Grady love her, but, like Billy, readers are given no reasons for their love. This distance is a peculiar antithesis to the close narrative that follows John Grady and slips so easily inside his mind.

In most of McCarthy's novels, the omniscient narrative voice of an outside observer tends to create a feeling of distance, a cold, unemotional consciousness that neither knows nor cares about the character(s) being observed. The narrative voice that follows Magdalena has much in common with this typical McCarthian narrator. Elsewhere in *Cities of the Plain*, however, a narrative voice appears in moments of broken syntax (run-ons or fragments) that seems both intimate and morally concerned. At times these unusual narrative voice-overs can be attributed to minor characters or a watching world, but at other times this mental consciousness is not attributable to any character in the text. The evaluative voice is "outside" either John Grady or Billy and all other characters in the novel, creating an effect that is weirdly evocative of the stranger's surreal dream at the end, a dream in which a man dreams that he is a man in a dream. This intimate observer always watches Billy, drawing readers' attention to Billy, to his struggles, and to his suffering.

In *Cities of the Plain,* John Grady's scenes are redolent with such indications of consciousness, while scenes devoted to Billy, or with Billy in them, typically lack any sort of indication of interior voice or consciousness. However, in Billy's last scene, there are suddenly two subjective adjectives of perception/evaluation ("angry" and "broken") in an instance of reported speech, "[H]e called out to God to see what was before his eyes," and a speech tag with a reference ("cried" to "broken day" and to "God"): "He was crying and the tears ran on his angry face and he called out to the broken day against them all and he called out to God to see what was before his eyes. Look at this, he called. Do you see? Do you see?" (261). Because there is no clearly identified source for the reported speech, the "reporting" being done (the voice telling us that Billy "called out") must be attributable to an omniscient third-person narrator. In *Unspeakable Sentences*, linguist Ann Banfield claims that literary subjectivity emerges most clearly in dialogue; speech tags or instances of reported speech are indications of a consciousness that Banfield claims must be attributed to the narrator (49). So, for instance, if a character says something "loudly," this is an evaluative remark. Likewise, reported speech is by its very nature "reported" by someone, indicating a conscious mentality. If there is no "speaker" to whom the reader may attribute these evaluative remarks, the reader must assume the evaluative voice is a "narrator." Although Banfield does not discuss the significance of deictic terms and modifiers in depth, her argument regarding speech tags or instances of reported speech can be claimed about evaluative deictic words and modifiers as well. That is, if a text includes terms such as "today," or "here," the time frame and place reference must be understood to be the speaker's (or the narrator's). Likewise, modifiers (adjectives or adverbs) describing a scene or a character are evaluative, and the evaluation must be attributed to a specific speaker. If there is no identifiable "speaker," the modifiers are ordinarily attributed to a third-person omniscient narrator. Since most instances of interior voices attributable only to omniscient third-person narrators in McCarthy's work are sterile and devoid of feeling, even when they express deep emotion, such as the pathos expressed in scenes where Magdalena is observed, that emotion distances even as it pities. In the last scene of the novel proper, however, the third-person interior voice is almost shockingly vulnerable.

But the scene in which John Grady views the dead body of Magdalena contrasts with this scene and highlights the difference in attribution of interiority. When John Grady views the body of the girl, he sees "[t]he girl to whom he'd sworn his love" lying with "[h]er hair damp and matted. So black" (229). The emotion here is rich, pitiful, clearly an expression of John Grady's interior agony as he views her, a perception wracked with grief. All of John Grady's actions in this scene (crushing his hat, holding his head) are followed by wrenchingly descriptive fragments and reported speech. The fragments and reported speech do give a sort of distance, but a distance infused with John Grady's sense of fragmentation and loss, which, of course, is really rather intimate. In Billy's scene with John Grady's body, readers are presented with that same echoing sense of loss through adjectives and reported speech, but it is Billy, not John Grady's body, being described, whereas in Magdalena's death scene, it is her body being described from the perception of the mourner's (John Grady's) eyes. Thus, Billy himself is described with the same intimately grieving voice that John Grady uses when looking at Magdalena.

In that climactic scene, when Billy takes up the dead body of John Grady, the narrative shifts to the perception of a passing group of people:

> They could not take their eyes from him. The dead boy in his arms hung with his head back and those partly opened eyes beheld nothing at all out of all that passing landscape of street or wall or paling sky or the figures of the children who stood blessing themselves in the gray light. (261)

In the world of the novel, all the characters recognize the weight of the religious symbol, the pietá, in the dead boy carried in Billy's arms; even the children are alert to the Christological imagery, blessing themselves in his shadow. The archetypal imagery is reinforced, toward the end of the novel, through two characters' verbal evocations of Christian ethics.

The stranger and Betty, the woman at the end of the novel, both draw on Christianity, the woman rather ambiguously, but the stranger in a weirdly direct way. The woman soothes Billy with a simplistic belief both in an afterlife and in the possibility of moral redemption (she "knows" Billy, yet finds him worth caring for, even though in his own estimation he "aint nothing"). The stranger, one of the most two-dimensional characters in the entire book, is a seer/prophet who floods Billy with a seemingly endless and deeply philosophical "dream." The import of the dream seems to be nothing more than an ambiguous and rambling reposing of the questions of blood, guilt, mortality, and worlds to come, until he ends and suddenly addresses Billy directly. They exchange a few farewell platitudes ("I got to get on" and "I wish you well"), and then the stranger speaks again, once more in oddly archaic and archetypal images:

> Every man's death is a standing in for every other. And since death comes to all there is no way to abate the fear of it except to love the man who stands for us. We are not waiting for his history to be written. He passed here long ago. That man who is all men and who stands in the dock for us until our time come and we must stand for him. Do you love him, that man? (288)

This speech is so directly Christian that the stranger seems to be a contemporary version of Evangelist in *Pilgrim's Progress*. But he is also evoking the final image of John Grady through John Grady's shadow image, Christ. That is, Christ is the ultimate image of the "man who is all men and who stands in the dock for us until our time come and we must stand for him" (288), but John Grady also "stood in" for someone, the prostitute Magdalena. As the stranger indicates, symbols are given their weight in the context of narrative, and human behavior is given its own merit by association with symbols and with narrative. Observing, then, becomes inextricably linked to the act of narration, an act that becomes both ethical and sacred.

The identity of the outside observer watching Billy's reaction to finding John Grady's dead body is important because Billy is crying out to God "Do you see?" even as the "broken" day and Billy's "angry" face are, in fact, being "seen." While it is by no means clear that the outside observer is "God"—and, in fact, later observations of Billy are clearly *not* any sort of divine "other"—it is nevertheless important that Billy's explicit cry for a divine presence to give meaning to John Grady's death is met by an implicit, exterior presence. Recognizing one's responsibility to others, naming the "other," is what gives meaning to morality in McCarthy's literary universe. Relationship, in the sense of a responsibility to the other, is that which mitigates death and offers a sense of hope.

The final instance of evaluative consciousness in the novel is, like many moments of evaluative consciousness, ambiguous in attribution. After telling Billy that he will see his dead brother Boyd again, the woman with whom Billy is staying, Betty, pats Billy's hand. As she pats it, his hand is observed in its world-creating symbolism, possessing "God's plenty of signs and wonders [. . .]. To make a world" (291). While this evaluation is not, in and of itself, very intimate, the phrase "to make a world" suddenly resurrects the dread of mortality that has haunted Billy, the dark "worlds to come" that unravel for him in *The Crossing*. This final evaluative voice is as shockingly intimate as the one that observes Billy's anger and grief over John Grady's body, for it understands the fear that haunts Billy, and it grants Billy the role of hero. This evaluative voice finds in the record of Billy's suffering, his scarred hands, an expiatory love able to "make a world."

By the end of *Cities of the Plain*, then, the fundamental questions of both earlier Border novels, morality and mortality, have been explicitly addressed by the stranger and Betty. The stranger tells Billy, "This life of yours is not a picture of the world. It is the world itself and it is composed not of bone or dream or time but of worship" (287). Ultimately, the stranger answers both questions, the problem of morality and its inescapable corollary, immorality, and the haunting devastation of mortality, a demolisher both of narrative and of meaning. The answer to bloodguilt cannot be redemption by bloodshed; instead, redemption seems to reside in empathetic connection, in an individual's recognition of her or his need for others, a recognition that offers the possibility of this-world redemption and that is hallowed by narrative descriptions that suggest such connection is in fact sacramental. As Billy and the stranger talk, they share a packet of crackers in a Eucharistic gesture, an evocation made more intense by the sacramental image of the drinking cup a few scenes later (267, 272). The evocation of the Eucharist in their bread-sharing is also reaffirmed when the stranger makes his final proclamation: "And since death comes to all there is no way to abate the fear of it except to love that man who stands for us" (288). Here, the evaluative voice "takes on" the enigmatic voices of the stranger and Betty. It also appears elsewhere throughout *Cities of the Plain*, but it is always identified by its function; it is the voice that imposes meaning on Billy, watching him throughout his wanderings. Essentially, the omniscient narrator's function in *Cities of the Plain* is to "tell" Billy's story. Ultimately, both John Grady and Billy are savior figures, but neither one is unambiguously redemptive; neither one is certain, at the end, that he has achieved anything meaningful. In other words, while John Grady must be the controlling mentality, he cannot grant himself meaning after he dies. Billy gives John Grady's death, and therefore his life, meaning. But Billy also needs someone to stand in for him, someone to "narrate" meaning into his life, someone to "see him." And in fact Billy is consistently observed, from the moment of John Grady's death through the end of the novel.

Why is it important that John Grady possesses an interior world but Billy is subjected to objectification, to evaluation by an unknown "outside" voice? The importance lies in the fact that meaning, in McCarthy's novels, resides in relationship. In *Cities of the Plain*, Billy mourns John Grady's death, but ultimately Billy also is "mourned." Billy also is "known." Even as John Grady is a savior figure, Billy also is a savior. In *The Crossing*, Billy hears an old man talking about how he (the old man) looked for a reason for destruction, maybe that God was angry (evoking Daugherty's suggestion of Gnostic devaluation of the subspiritual world). But, the old man concludes, "[t]hings separate from their stories have no meaning" (142). All things, then, are meaningful only if there is a narrator, someone to weave them into the cosmos and give them meaning. Billy is also a savior, but, like John Grady, the efficacy of his salvation is extremely dubious. His first salvation attempt, in *The Crossing*, is an attempt to save a she-wolf, but the she-wolf dies. Then he saves his younger brother Boyd, but Boyd also dies. And in *Cities of the Plain*, Billy tries to save John Grady, but John Grady dies. In *The Crossing*, as Boyd is dying, Boyd tells Billy that he is all right, but Billy says, "I know you are, but I aint" (330). Billy's suffering, his "expiatory" act of violence, is his self-nullification. In losing the objects of his salvation, he loses his own identity. At the end of *The Crossing*, in the passage cited earlier, a crowd of people on the street watch him emerge from the mesas and they observe him to be "[h]ungry in eye and belly" and "[t]otally unspoken for" (170). This ambiguous savior identity haunts Billy; he has emptied himself out for his brother (becoming "hungry in eye"), but for all his heroism, he is "totally unspoken for," and his very meaning hovers over the void. He needs someone to see him and impose meaning on his sacrifice, someone to tell his story, or he is "nothing," nullified as the kid is nullified by the judge, as Magdalena is nullified by Tiburcio.

At the end of his journey in *Cities of the Plain*, Billy meets a stranger, "another such as he [. . .] solitary and alone" (266). This stranger resurrects the echo of John Grady's dilemma in *All the Pretty Horses*. His dream-man commits a blood crime in which he "w[ill] become an accomplice in a blood ceremony that was then and is now an affront to God" (280). Then, when Billy requests an interpretation of the dream, the stranger asks him to hold out his hand. Billy wants to know if this is a pledge, and the man replies: "You are pledged already," invoking John Grady's dream in *All the Pretty Horses*, which indicates that John Grady believes those "pledged in blood" are "redeemable in blood only" (*COTP* 287; *ATPH* 5). In other words, the stranger reiterates John Grady's quest, to expiate himself from the guilt inherent in a world "pledged in blood." But what way is there to lift off that burden, to pay off that pledge? The stranger does not say that there is a "redeemer," but says instead, "The thing that is sought is altogether other" (*COTP* 287). The stranger ends his weird interlude of philosophy by claiming that morality is found in an act of relationship. The image he uses evokes Christ, the "man who stands in the dock" for all men (289). The stranger's philosophy assumes an inherent holiness in alterity, and in this respect his philosophy reflects Jacques Derrida's explanation of the "other" in poetic language.

In *Writing and Difference*, Derrida claims that his own description of the "anxiety" between the written word, the word's original intent, and the word's interpretive meaning reflects a similar anxiety in post-Holocaust ethical philosophy. "In the work of Emmanuel Levinas," he says, "can be found the same hesitation, the same anxious movement within the difference between the Socratic and the Hebraic, the poverty and wealth of the letter, the pneumatic and the grammatic" (73). Derrida likens the written word to the broken tablets, the Ten Commandments that Moses shatters on the mountainside. The fragmentary nature of the letter resides in its distance from what it intends, an irreducible alienation. Even more profound is the separation between the living force of a word and its limited "actual" meaning, the anxiety between the "pneumatic and the grammatic," as he calls it. However, that distance between the force of meaning and the physical letter creates poetic language (74). For Derrida, this mysterious relationship can be likened to the metaphor of the human relationship with an extant God, the "Being" that is entirely separate from human "being" but who is sought and recognized as the source of "being." Essentially, the capacity of poetic language to mean anything is inextricably linked to its potential to mean *different* things; the gestational potential of poetic language is linked by analogy to the creative energy of the human-divine relationship. The disposition and purpose of poetic writing always reflects an "other," to the extent, Derrida says, that "[i]f writing is not a tearing of the self toward the other within a confession of infinite separation, [. . .] then it destroys itself" (75–76). Derrida articulates a post-Holocaust ethical philosophy deeply influenced by Martin Buber's *I and Thou,* through his assumption that poetic language is ethical *because* it demands a separation of sign and signified, suggesting that meaning is language's irreducible "other." The "other" becomes the birthplace of ethics, be it a religious ethics demanding the worshipper to see God as other or a linguistic ethics demanding the speaker to see the addressee as other. *Cities of the Plain* draws attention to both the spiritual and the linguistic uses of "otherness." The Christian substitution narrative (Christ for the sins of the world) underpins the novel's symbolic trajectory, and the contrasting uses of subjective and objective narration illuminate the ethical possibilities of novelistic discourse. In this novel, once characters recognize and value the sacredness of the "other," a narrative voice draws attention to those characters' sacred otherness.

There is an omniscient "evaluative voice" in almost all of McCarthy's novels, but the speaker rarely deviates from the role of distant narrator. In

Cities of the Plain, by contrast, the omniscient narrator sometimes actively interprets characters or offers them sympathy. In this novel, John Grady clearly "doubles" psychologically for Billy as Boyd, his little brother, but John Grady is more than just a double for a younger brother. John Grady is a man fanatically devoted to a sort of redemptive goodness—saving contrary horses, saving epileptic whores, seeking justice. When Billy devotes himself to looking after John Grady, therefore, he is "protecting" a voice of morality in an immoral world. Billy implicitly recognizes what the stranger claims explicitly—that the greatest Christian symbol of morality is expiatory suffering. If symbols can impose meaning on reality, then John Grady's death for the prostitute may be an act of great heroism rather than the drunk and stupid violence of an infatuated teenager. Billy's attempts to translate meaning onto John Grady's death become, in the end, his own act of substitution, replacing one brother with another, one loss with another. But in the world of the novel, Billy's own sacrifices may also be hallowed.

While the novel self-consciously extricates itself from any sense of finalized or concrete "meaning" of John Grady's sacrifice and Billy's attempts at salvation, it nevertheless achieves a vague impression of finality. The solution to the questions haunting the earlier two novels is proposed in the ambiguous nature of the unseen narrative voice that haunts Billy and, through Billy, John Grady. The nature of this omniscient narrator is expressed in the novel through archetypal Christian images, evoking the strange dichotomy of a God watching Sodom and Gomorrah burn—where death and annihilation do not necessarily indicate a universe bereft of morality or justice. Whether Billy believes he has been seen, known, and loved, readers do not know. Whether Billy *has,* in fact, been seen, known, and loved, readers likewise do not know. But as the stranger explains, the twin quests of these two heroes, John Grady and Billy, are not unambiguous failures, because they are not wholly devoid of meaning; they are incarnations of a strong sense of hope. According to the stranger, after all, the only way to struggle through this dream where all humanity has been "pledged in blood" is to acknowledge the one who "stands in" for humankind, a recognition that suggests that all such standings-in are inherently meaningful. Readers therefore are meant to hear the stranger's words and understand that the haunting beauty of John Grady's passionate last sacrifice and the suffering, nurturing love of Billy Parham are, ultimately, "acts of worship." Their acts are "worship" in the sense that they bear the agonizing potential to redeem the sin of violence, subsuming fragmented and isolated lives in a sacramental sense of community. Furthermore, *Cities of the Plain* indicates that narrative—the power to weave meaning and significance out of the unknown, the evil, and the ordinary—is in itself a sacred and ethical rite. If humankind is the cause of its own hurt, the Border Trilogy suggests, then it can also author its own redemption.

4
"HE'S A PSYCHOPATHIC KILLER BUT SO WHAT?"
MORAL STORYTELLING IN *NO COUNTRY FOR OLD MEN*

The bible is full of cautionary tales. All of literature, for that matter.
—CORMAC MCCARTHY, *The Sunset Limited*

Characters in narrative folklore and literature are completely different. In literature they are unique individuals; they typify a period or social milieu, generalize the features of many people and reflect a great number of prototypes, but they remain individuals. They have their own names and possess their own personalities. In the wondertale, the hero does not normally have a name.
—VLADIMIR PROPP, *Theory and History of Folklore*

No *Country for Old Men* (2005) tells the story of a sheriff struggling along in the bloody wake of a psychopathic murderer. This novel is narrated primarily in the omniscient third-person style that typifies McCarthy's darkest novels, such as *Blood Meridian* (1985); but unlike *Blood Meridian*'s narrator, the third-person narrative voice in *No Country for Old Men* is stripped of McCarthy's characteristic convoluted and archaic diction. As many of the novel's earliest reviewers pointed out, its characters resemble iconic caricatures of evil portrayed in earlier novels, such as Lester Ballard and Judge Holden. But *No Country for Old Men*'s syntactic landscape is shorn of the rich, Faulkneresque language typical of these earlier works, leaving the characters flat and two-dimensional, so much so that James Wood calls the novel's villain, Anton Chigurh, a "hollowed" representation in a "morally empty book" (92). At one point, a character describes Chigurh as "a psychopathic killer," but the speaker shrugs at the description, adding, "but so what? There's plenty of them around" (*NCFOM* 141). Because the stripped narrative permits very few revelations of interior thought, the novel does not necessarily privilege the worldview of either Chigurh, the psychopathic killer, or Bell, the lawman who hunts him, and the violence is indeed so ubiquitous that upon first reading, the novel's audience may very well also shrug at the seemingly crazed killers rampaging around. The story itself is narrated by a distant, omniscient narrator who offers few interpretive comments, much like the opaque narrator of *Blood Meridian,* although the two moral men, Moss and Bell, are granted some narrative authority through passages that reveal their thoughts and intentions. However, the unusual aspects of this novel that drew critical acclaim and horror in almost equal measure illustrate the novel's larger argument about the nature and purpose of storytelling. In particular, this novel explores the relationship between storytelling and morality by evoking archaic tropes and modes of narration more typically associated with the folktale.

Released in July of 2005, *No Country for Old Men* was McCarthy's first novel since *Cities of the Plain* came out in 1998. Perhaps because of the author's growing fame, the novel met with polarized responses. For example, William J. Cobb's review gushes praise, claiming that McCarthy "is nothing less than our greatest living writer, and [*No Country for Old Men*] is a novel that must be read and remembered." Wood's review in the *New Yorker,* in contrast, describes the novel as "an unimportant, stripped-down thriller" that aggravates McCarthy's already tenuous literary status (88). Similarly, Edward St. John's review for the *Library Journal* lacerates the novel, claiming that in it "McCarthy stumbles headlong into self-parody," while Walter Kirn, at the end of a rather positive review, concludes that "[a]t times, the whole novel borders on caricature." *No Country for Old Men* is certainly an unusual addition to McCarthy's corpus, since it reads like a pulp thriller. The seeming superficiality of *No Country for Old Men,* in comparison to *Blood Meridian,* for instance, derives from the novel's iconographic landscape described through minimalist syntax, vis-à-vis the complicated and archaic syntactic style used in *Blood Meridian. No Country for Old Men*'s style is unique among McCarthy's novels, but the metatextual attention to narrative is not unique in his larger corpus. In a conversation with the Coen brothers regarding the process of translating the novel into film, McCarthy cites a comment David Mamet once made regarding script-writing. Mamet, McCarthy claims, "says that the ideal venue for a playwright is to write radio plays, because then you have nothing, just—this is what somebody said. That's it. You have nothing to fall back on" (Grossman 63). Like Mamet, McCarthy seems to admire the challenge of minimalist writing, writing that strips away trappings to reveal the naked skeleton of the art form. If an ideal play is one that relies solely on the sounds of voices, then *No Country for Old Men* may be close to McCarthy's ideal of a novel—one that reduces narrative to the bare depiction of events, coupled with ambiguously related snippets of prophetic interpretation.

In general, McCarthy's nonnovelistic texts, his screenplays and stage plays, tend to be more explicitly concerned with questions of epistemology and ontology and more didactic in form than his novels. *The Sunset Limited*, for instance, reduces its few digressions into literary language to the commonplace by offering self-conscious commentary on those turns of phrase. When Black happens to use a poetic expression, "the lingerin scent of divinity," White repeats the phrase. Black questions him, "You like that?" and White responds, "It's not bad" (14). The play's metatextual attention to artifice in language strips artifice of its shamanistic creative power. White denies the capacity of language to evoke a sense of commonality or brotherhood, and by drawing attention to its very artificiality, White questions the capacity of language to mean anything at all. *No Country for Old Men* poses questions similar to those in *The Sunset Limited*, but by subsuming the questions into a high-octane crime thriller, the novel avoids didacticism. McCarthy demonstrates a rather consistent awareness of and interest in the fine line between a narrative voice that suggests interpretations and a narrative voice that instructs readers to produce certain interpretations.

McCarthy explicitly addresses this crucial distinction in the opening stage direction for *The Stonemason* (1994). In that play, he divides the stage in a manner reminiscent of Irish playwright Brian Friel's divided stage in *Philadelphia, Here I Come* and *Dancing at Lughnasa*, both plays that rely on a character not part of the main action of the scene to interpret a deeper layer of meaning. As Friel does in his plays, McCarthy uses a narrator separated from the main action as a device to reveal deeper layers of meaning, though he does not permit the narrator to interpret the play as a whole. Thus in *The Stonemason* Ben stands behind a podium to the side while the action—his memories—plays out on the center stage. The stage direction notes: "*Above all we must resist the temptation to see the drama as something being presented by the speaker at his lectern, for to do so is to defraud the drama of its right autonomy*" (6). The screenplays and stage plays push the boundaries of narrator-as-interpreter to the point where McCarthy finds it necessary to warn against stepping across to the other side, where the narrator *teaches* the play's lessons. As the stage directions point out, Ben ought to be seen instead as a narrator who can impose his own interpretation on the play's actions while leaving the audience to come to their own conclusions about the play as a whole, the narrative that spans both Ben's monologues and the drama playing out on center stage. In the same way, *No Country for Old Men* presents a side-staged character, Bell, whose interpretive voice cannot be understood as "presenting" the text in any way. Rather, Bell's voice offers a metaphysical counterpoint to the nihilistically inclined narrative events of the novel. The two literary forms, story and thinly veiled philosophy, counter each other, undermining facile attempts at interpretation and so, perhaps, assuring the novel of its "right autonomy" (*TS* 6).

Bell's italicized monologues may elucidate themes that drift like cordite through the explosive narrative events of the novel, but they do not interpret those events. Jay Ellis, in his chapter on the novel, claims that "for the first time since *Suttree*, and fundamentally in a different way, McCarthy has characters thinking all over the place in *No Country for Old Men*" (251). This statement is perhaps misleading, since the only examples of "thinking" that Ellis cites occur in Bell's italicized monologues. In the novel, the "thinking" that takes place differs in interpretive weight depending on the literary form in which the thinking appears. *No Country for Old Men* is structurally more fragmented than many of McCarthy's novels, with the text broken up into eight "chapters" and each "chapter" broken into smaller sections, each one following one of the main characters, Bell, Moss, or Chigurh. Most strikingly, each "chapter" begins with an italicized section in the first person from Bell's point of view. The first-person italicized sections are narrated in Bell's south-Texan dialect (e.g., "*I dont know what them eyes was the windows to*") (2), rendering them closest in style to the sections of italicized first-person memory in *The Orchard Keeper* and in *Child of God*. Since these sections are narrated in the first person, it comes as no surprise that Bell "thinks" out loud, as when he says, "*I dont know*" (2). Moreover, as in *The Orchard Keeper* and *Child of God*, the first-person narration in *No Country for Old Men* exists on a separate plane from the rest of the novel. The contents of the italicized sections may relate thematically to the novel, but they differ in style and tone, as if they are fragments of another type of text altogether. Because of their stylistic differences, their symbolic content, and their heavy emphasis on philosophical musings about ontology and epistemology, these italicized sections should be read as examples of novelistic *heteroglossia*—the coexistence of many narrative voices blending together, counterbalancing each other, and decentralizing narrative authority. In other words, there may be "thinking" in these italicized sections, but revelations of thought in monologues function as Ben's narrative frames in *The Stonemason* do: they reflect the side-staged narrator's worldview without necessarily reflecting the worldview of the main text. And although revelations of interior life *within* the main narrative do not reveal the mentality of the omniscient narrator, they do draw systematic attention to the moral struggles of the particular character.

The distinction between interior thoughts revealed in monologues and interior thoughts revealed in third-person narrative is an important distinction, since there *are* third-person passages in *No Country for Old Men* that depict interior thought. The main narrative, as mentioned previously, variously follows the three main characters, Chigurh, Bell, and Moss. Chigurh is *No Country for Old Men*'s Judge Holden—evil, erudite, and seemingly immortal. Like Judge Holden, Chigurh holds forth in long, rambling speeches that depict an archaic and nihilistic cosmos, ruled by fate and characterized by senseless savagery. In his speeches, Chigurh occasionally provides glimpses into the machinery of his mind, if not his soul. When he explains to Carla Jean why he must kill her, for example, Chigurh says that if he were to demonstrate mercy, he would "make [him]self vulnerable and that [he could] never do" (259). For Chigurh, the fickle fates are the only deities worth serving. If, as Denis Donoghue claims in "Teaching *Blood Meridian*," "Nietzsche is Judge Holden's philosopher," then he is surely Chigurh's philosopher as well (277). Chigurh is also like Judge Holden in that, beyond what he reveals in his speeches, his interior world remains entirely mysterious. Bell, in contrast, is a moral character. Aside from his italicized monologues, however, Bell's interior world remains for the most part as shrouded from view as does Chigurh's. Throughout the unitalicized text, Bell provides indications of his philosophy through dialogue, but beyond that, the machinations of his mind and the motivations of his heart are not generally revealed. The notable exception is the last third-person section of text in the novel, which takes place primarily inside Bell's head. But since this section is framed by lengthy italicized monologues, and since its two other central characters either are dead (Moss) or have disappeared (Chigurh), it seems that the novel itself has narrowed to Bell's perspective.

Moss, by contrast to the strongly moral and philosophical Bell, is an ambiguously moral character: he is beset by greed but is at least free of the homicidal sociopathology that seems to afflict the truly evil characters. Moss's interior world is revealed several times. These revelations are sometimes indicated by explicit thought tags such as "he thought," but even more commonly, shifts into Moss's thoughts are heralded by changes in syntactic patterns, in the same way that John Grady Cole's interior world is revealed in *All the Pretty Horses* and *Cities of the Plain*. Furthermore, Moss's mental life blossoms whenever he is conscious of a moral dilemma, underscoring his capacity to think and behave morally, even if that capacity is underutilized. Moss's internal struggles with morality are depicted from a point of view inside his mind rather than inferred by an outside observing narrator, and in general all of the portions of text that follow Moss remain close to his perception, as opposed to the portions of text that follow Chigurh and Bell. For example, in the first narrative section of the novel, Chigurh kills a police officer. The point of view remains distant, observing both men from a distance: "He [the police officer] was slightly bent over when Chigurh squatted and scooted his manacled hands beneath him to the back of his knees [. . .]. If it looked like a thing he had practiced many times it was" (5). In this scene, the actions of both men are observed, the police officer in front, Chigurh behind, placing the "camera" controlling the text's perspective in front of the police officer. The final sentence in this example indicates the presence of an evaluative voice, a voice that explains Chigurh's action by providing a bit of backstory—that Chigurh has practiced this maneuver and is therefore to be understood by the reader to be an old hand at escaping police custody. Because the voice is capable of providing backstory but at the same time is clearly observing Chigurh rather than relating events through his perspective, the voice must be attributed to an omniscient and removed narrator.

The next section in the novel follows Moss and is strikingly different in terms of the distance between the narrator and the character: "He [Moss] lowered the binoculars and sat studying the land. Far to the south the raw mountains of Mexico. The breaks of the river" (8). In this passage, the viewpoint of the text remains close to Moss's head. Moss looks out at the landscape and the following observations are unmediated by a narrative voice. That is, the syntactic fragments represent Moss's perceptions without the added interpretive weight of an observing and interpreting narrator. Later, Moss faces his first moral dilemma after he steals a bag of money and leaves a dying drug smuggler in the desert. That night, Moss wakes up, haunted not by the money but rather by the dying man's thirst. As Moss approaches the truck where he left the dying man, the text remains close to his mind and at times shifts into his perception:

> He approached with the .45 in his hand. Dead quiet. Could be because of the moon. His own shadow was more company than he would have liked. Ugly feeling out here. A trespasser. Among the dead. [. . .] He felt like something in a jar. (27).

The narrative events in this passage are related in standard narrative form (subject-verb-object), but the first syntactic change, a sentence fragment ("Dead quiet"), indicates a shift from external narrative to revelations of Moss's interior world. The first fragment indicates perception—the "quiet" of the nightscape—but the second syntactic fragment ("Could be because of the moon") introduces an evaluative voice, a voice interpreting the physical landscape. Unlike the interpretive voice in the section following Chigurh, however, this voice cannot be attributed to an outside narrator. The modal verb "could" possesses a level of uncertainty that would not plague an omniscient narrator. Instead, the "could" represents Moss's internal attempts to explain his presentiments. Syntactic fragments in this passage consistently represent Moss's perceptions and thoughts, and this example ends with an explicit indication of Moss's interiority: he "felt." Although his thoughts are not depicted in the first person, Moss is truly a "thinking" character, just as he is a character who possesses the ability to experience empathy and to act on compassionate urges. In these two respects, he has much in common with John Grady Cole. These commonalities suggest that in terms of the connection between morality and interiority, *No Country for Old Men* does not differ significantly from the Border Trilogy or any other novel in McCarthy's corpus: transparently thinking men are moral, but evil men, even if they are thinkers, remain shrouded by a narrative opacity that denies readers access to any of their mental processes.

Despite thematic similarities to other novels in the corpus, what differentiates *No Country for Old Men* from earlier works is its explicit attention to literary forms. From Bell's monologues to narrative tropes, the novel plays with literary forms and, through the paucity of descriptive passages, draws readers' attention to those forms. Ellis notes this novel's patterned forms and provides an extended analysis in which he claims that the novel is actually made up of two different "books," a "Young Man" book whose central character is Moss and an "Old Man" book whose central character is Bell. The first "book," Ellis claims, fits the crime-novel genre with its prototypical noir characters and the "salient characteristic" of the genre, a weapons fetish (228). The second "book" takes over when Moss dies and readers are compelled to recognize the "true protagonist," Bell (236). This second book, Ellis claims, collapses into prophetic lamentation, and he characterizes the new narrative type as a form of contemporary jeremiad (243). This reading of the novel's twin literary forms is deeply compelling, but Ellis's recognition of the competing styles ultimately does little to reveal the novel's unity. While both the noir crime novel and the jeremiad clearly infuse the narrative style of *No Country for Old Men*, other literary forms are also at play.

The striking difference between McCarthy's typically dense prose style and the prose style in *No Country for Old Men* cannot be fully explained by citing the noir tradition. There are, after all, stylistically "dense" noir thrillers, such as Irish noir-writer Ken Bruen's Jack Taylor series or Pat McCabe's *The Butcher Boy*. Even William Faulkner's foray into the genre, *Sanctuary*, for the most part bears all the characteristics of his typically opaque prose. As Steven Frye notes in his extended analysis of the influence of the W. B. Yeats poem "Sailing to Byzantium" (from which the novel derives its title) on the novel, *No Country for Old Men* demonstrates a "deliberate shift in style" from McCarthy's other works (33). This "shift" away from syntactic artistry in the main narrative contrasts a world that is "external and objective, [. . .] of artless violence, disorder, and bloodshed," with the more artistic interior monologue passages, passages that reveal "human love, spiritual transcendence, and a mild and mitigated acceptance" (40). But perhaps the stylistic departure draws attention to more than just the atavistic nature of the external world. The novel's stripped prose seems to draw attention to the *act* of narrative rather than the substance of narrative. The novel foregrounds the artifice of storytelling in particular, through rigid narrative structures and through archaic and folkloric tropes, symbols, repetitions, and character depictions. *No Country for Old Men* can be read as a glorified pulp thriller, but the pared-down prose and narrative frames draw attention to another literary ancestor: the archetypal, folktale-type parable.

Of course, McCarthy has explicitly distanced himself from literary traditions that deviate from strict realism. In his dialogue with the Coen brothers, he claims that he is "not a fan of some of the Latin American writers, [i.e.,] magical realism." His problem with magical realism, he explains, is that "it's hard enough to get people to believe what you're telling them without making it impossible. It has to be vaguely plausible" (Grossman 63). But McCarthy's professed attachment to realism can be a bit of a red herring. While his novels generally ground the characters and actions in real-world settings, certain characters stretch the category of realism almost to breaking point. One of the most obvious examples, of course, is Anton Chigurh, the devil figure who flits through the landscape of *No Country for Old Men*. As Vladimir Propp points out in *Theory and History of Folklore*, characters in folklore differ from characters in literature primarily because in folklore, characters are "types," not individuals. Chigurh, however, is not much of an individual. Instead, he seems to be a blue-eyed, vaguely ethnic version of *Blood Meridian*'s Judge Holden, who himself is more caricature of evil than complex individual. Not only is Chigurh a typed character, but he is also depicted with strongly supernatural overtones. At one point in *No Country for Old Men,* Sheriff Bell assures himself and another deputy that Chigurh is, in the final analysis, not a ghost. The other man replies, "*I guess if he was a ghost you wouldnt have to worry about him*" (299). However, Bell's final "encounter" with Chigurh is overshadowed by Chigurh's weird (in the archaic sense of the word) escape. Chigurh gets into his truck and watches Sheriff Bell pull up to the motel (243). Bell goes into the motel room, realizes that Chigurh is still on the premises, goes outside, and calls for backup. He and the other cruisers then search all the trucks in the lot, but Chigurh is gone, having "outgeneraled" the police once again (245). While it is conceivable that Chigurh drove away, the text does not indicate how he accomplished that deed without alerting the otherwise vigilant Sheriff Bell. In the Coen brothers' film *No Country for Old Men*, this final encounter is depicted with a heightened sense of "weirdness." Bell approaches the motel room door, sees the shot-out lock, and stands watching a shifting reflection on the convex metal of the lock cylinder. The next shot depicts Chigurh's face in shadow with only a cylindrical light shining on it. The film's montage connects the two scenes using the single image of a shot-out lock, indicating that the men stand on either side of the door. Yet when Bell finally pushes the door in, Chigurh is gone. The apparently inexplicable vaporization of Chigurh in the film is thematically consistent with his depiction in the book. Chigurh, repeatedly associated with "devils" and "ghosts," has a strong lingering scent of magical realism, much like the ageless and undying Judge Holden.

Chigurh is not the only example of "magical" or folkloric imagery in *No Country for Old Men*. The novel exhibits folktale elements at many levels. It possesses a folktale narrative structure and a frame citing a folktale purpose: to explain a phenomenon. In other words, the novel presents an "and this is how it came to be" tale, exploring how the contemporary violence of the Texas-Mexico border in particular and the modern world in general came to be. The novel presents a "fairy-tale"-type initial landscape that gives way to a dark and foreboding "cursed" landscape by the end of the novel. Additionally, the story is framed by italicized sections narrated by Bell that attempt to interpret the *"signs and wonders,"* the folkloric portents, of the narrative (298). At the end of the novel, Bell articulates the "moral" of the story when he answers a reporter's questions about what happened. He says that his narrative demonstrates *"where we're headed"* (303). Shortly after this, he reflects that the old people around him are, like Rip Van Winkle, characters who *"woke up and they dont know how they got where they're at"* (304). Thus, in addition to mythic, folkloric qualities of the novel's central characters, the framed tale structure compounds the folkloric feel of the novel.

In her article "Folk Narrative," Linda Degh claims that folktales can be categorized by three basic qualities: first, a framed, narrated structure (a voice framing events with cues such as "once upon a time" to indicate the beginning of the story); second, figured or formulaic speech patterns and description patterns; and third, formulaic narrative arcs and character types (60–61). In addition to its cautionary-tale theme, *No Country for Old Men* demonstrates all of these formulaic qualities. Perhaps most obviously, the novel utilizes an eye-catching framed narrative device, the italicized sections at the beginning of every chapter. Although Bell's italicized sections initially indicate that he plays the role of the narrator, he does not actually narrate events or control or dictate them, suggesting that the narrative sections in this novel are playing a different role than would be played by first-person narration in a typical novel. There seem to be two Bells, in other words, the narrator Bell of the philosophy texts and the character Bell, who plays a Rip Van Winkle–type sheriff in the main text. Bell's evocation of "Rip Van Winkle" suggests the function of the italicized sections of the novel—a function typical to folktales, namely, the framing device.

Framing devices typically signal the commencement of a tale rather than a novel, and an example of such a framing structure is, of course, Washington Irving's *The Sketchbook of Geoffrey Crayon, Gent.*, in which "Rip Van Winkle" originally appeared. *The Sketchbook* is ostensibly a compilation of sketches presented by an authorial alter ego, Geoffrey Crayon. Within the *Sketchbook*, Crayon claims that he culled two tales, "Rip Van Winkle" and "The Legend of Sleepy Hollow," from the folk wisdom of the historian Dietrich Knickerbocker, who is Irving's other authorial persona, erstwhile known to readers as the narrator of the wildly outrageous and heavily ironic *A History of New York*. Irving's different narrative personae are critical figures in balancing the sly skepticism and slapstick humor of the stories. The narrators also distance the story from the actual author, primarily so that Knickerbocker, who is at least a bit susceptible to the superstitions Ichabod Crane swallows whole, can express a naive credulity that the audience is not expected to share. *No Country for Old Men* loses, for the most part, the humorous aspect of the authorial stand-in. However, the novel's authorial narrative frames, like Knickerbocker, intensify the supernatural elements in the story by suggesting that the "narrator" possesses a level of belief in the supernatural aspects of the story. For example, Bell describes Chigurh as a devil and a ghost. Although he professes to believe in rational explanations for the man, he nevertheless suggests at one point that he is *"startin to lean"* in the direction of believing in an incarnate Satan. *"He [Satan] explains a lot of things that otherwise dont have no explanation,"* Bell claims (218). Bell is a rational man and a modern skeptic, but in his mind there is at least a niggling fear that Chigurh just might be a walking, breathing personification of the Prince of Darkness. More than in most of McCarthy's novels, this narrative does not settle for mere symbolism. Chigurh is not "like" Satan; at some level of the story, he just might *be* Satan. The story elements themselves thus demonstrate a folkloric quality, melding the supernatural with the natural in order to explain a real-world phenomenon.

In addition to framing devices that heighten the mystical or magical quality of the tale, Degh points out that fairy tales' narrative structure follows a "ruling action of tri-episodic action-repetition" (61). *No Country for Old Men*'s narrative traces the physical transgressions of the Texas-Mexico border in a complex style of triplicate patterning. In the opening section of the novel, Bell describes sending a boy to death row. Bell claims that he *"visited with him two or three times. Three times"* (1). Events happen three times throughout the novel. In addition, *No Country for Old Men* follows three central characters, Llewellen Moss, who steals a suitcase full of drug money; Anton Chigurh, who chases Moss to retrieve the money; and Sheriff Ed Tom Bell, who chases Chigurh. The chase is segmented by major plot events that occur in triplet. For example, Moss encounters Chigurh three times. He escapes from Chigurh twice but is killed during the third encounter. First, Moss runs to Del Rio and cleverly outwits Chigurh, barely escaping him (99–103); next, Moss goes to Eagle Pass and gets in a shoot-out with Chigurh but manages to escape (161); and last, Moss takes his wife to El Paso, puts her on a bus, and flees north to Van Horn, but when he stops at a hotel there, he is caught and killed in a shoot-out (201, 224, 236–39). Likewise, Chigurh narrowly escapes death three times. He is first caught with a distinctive murder instrument that could be linked to his past crimes and earn him the death penalty, but he escapes by killing the deputy (6–7); next, he gets shot in Eagle Pass but lives (161); and finally, he goes to El Paso to shoot Carla Jean and gets hit by a car but lives (261). Bell almost encounters—but just misses—Chigurh three times as well, completing the tri-episodic narrative patterns for the three characters. First, arriving at Moss's Desert Aire trailer after Chigurh has left, Bell "just misse[s] him" (93); second, Bell surveys the wreckage after the shoot-out in Eagle Pass at "nine-fifteen in the morning," having missed Chigurh, who quit the town when "the new day [was] paling" (134, 122); and last, Bell arrives at the Van Horn motel while Chigurh is (presumably) still in the parking lot, but Chigurh manages to escape (243–45). The Coen brothers' film again emphasizes the intensity of Bell's near misses. When Bell arrives at the Desert Aire trailer in the film, Chigurh has left so recently that the glass of milk he was drinking still sweats on the coffee table. Given the collaborative relationship between the Coen brothers and McCarthy during the filmmaking process, the film's amplification of the novel's events is a cinematic change rather than a thematic one. Chigurh eludes Bell's grasp in the film with more cinematic panache, but in the novel he occasionally behaves in more erratic and inhuman ways than he does in the film; in his feral attack on the deputy in the novel, he leaps on the man, as compared to his savage but relatively silent and motionless attack in the film, where he strangles him while prone on the floor (*NCFOM* 6; *No Country* [film]).

Degh next talks about "patterned figures of speech," which she calls cues-descriptions, such as "handsome" princes and "beautiful" princesses. The descriptions also codify the settings, placing the story within a framework meant to inform readers how to understand each narrative event's significance. For example, Degh says, "sparkling, metallic radiance represents fairyland [. . .] and riches, whereas dark and bleak hues signify [. . .] the site of evil" (61). In the novel, Moss sees the world originally, before the opening of the money bag, as a world covered with a "low haze of shimmering dust and pollen," dawn shining down on an earth made of glittery volcanic gravel (8–9). After he finds the treasure, evening falls, and he is in a "blue world. Visible shadows of clouds crossing the floodplain" (26). The novel ends with Bell imagining himself as a lone survivor riding out "*in all that dark and all that cold*" (309). The color hues of the novel, then, darken symbolically in keeping with the growing darkness of the threat.

Finally, the novel's characters are described with certain traits common to folktales. The formulaic central characters, Moss, Bell, and Chigurh, seem initially more at home in a medieval morality play than a Texas-Mexico border thriller. Moss, an ordinary "everyman," stumbles upon a temptation (the cash) and, upon succumbing to the temptation, is pursued by a vice character, Chigurh, who is also an archetypal "Devil," and a virtue character, Bell, who tries and fails to get Moss to do the right thing, turn in the money to the police. The classic story line of the everyman's temptation and subsequent fall from grace is more consistent in some ways with the Judeo-Christian folktale tradition, since the existence of a fundamentally evil character has little in common with most Texas-Mexico American Indian traditions, in which devil characters cannot be described as purely "evil" in the Western sense of the term. But upon further analysis, it can be seen that *No Country for Old Men*'s depiction of Chigurh as a "devil" character uses tropes more consistent with border folklore, specifically with the shape-shifter character in border folklore. For example, Chigurh is a terrifying character primarily because he does not seem to kill out of malice. Rather, as Wells, a hit man, points out, Chigurh "has principles" (153). These "principles" involve his absolute adherence to seemingly arbitrary promises, such as making a victim's life depend on a "promise" that precedes a coin toss. Thus, Chigurh's allegiance is to a world of rules that does not mesh with that of most civilized human societies. Because Chigurh is so inexplicable, he seems less intentionally malicious than the Judeo-Christian devil, who is often depicted solely in terms of his desire to thwart human beings. Chigurh is rather an instrument of an archaic type of Anglo-Saxon "fate" or an arbitrary wreaker of havoc like many American Indian tricksters.

Chigurh's otherworldliness is consistently emphasized throughout the novel. In introducing the narrative, Bell calls Chigurh a "*true and living prophet of destruction*" and, later, a "ghost" (218). Chigurh also refers to himself as "the devil" (60, 256). And, in the mode of villains in fairy tales, he ritualistically dialogues with his victims before killing them. Like the wolf "huffing and puffing," Chigurh forces his victims into a prescribed conversation before destroying them. He asks them if they understand the role he plays, and he corrects their answers by telling them that he is God-like and devil-like (57, 260). In addition, Chigurh's survival from three near-death experiences reinforces his tricksterlike ability to escape death. But it is his essential character that differs from traditional trickster types and that so profoundly affects Bell. Bell begins the narrative by saying that he will tell the story of this strange and terrible creature because he wants to provide a reason for his decision to give up his job as sheriff. He says that Chigurh made him realize that a job requiring a man to decide other men's fates (as a sheriff, like himself, or as a hit man, like Chigurh) does not depend solely on what you do, but also on "*what you are willin to become. And I think a man would have to put his soul at hazard* [to make those choices]" (4). In other words, the novel's central conflict is not the actual chase—Moss with the money, Chigurh after Moss, Bell after Chigurh—but rather Bell's encounter with the soulless "prophet of destruction." These two characters, then, are juxtaposed like the twin faces of Janus, each envisioning a different possible world. Chigurh, the "prophet of destruction," follows an archaic code of destruction and annihilation, while Bell, haunted by prophetic visions of hope, looks into the future and the past in order to construct a sense, however elusive, of transcendence.

The novel's archetypal figures and its focalization on moral choice are thematically consistent with fairy-ale structure, but however much the novel suggests patterns and tropes similar to those in fairy tales, it is nevertheless a plot-driven, naturalistic novel. The significance of such structures, in the end, is that they are aesthetic devices that encourage the audience's moral engagement with the events of the novel. That is, such structures, like the fairy tale, tell a deceptively simple story. In the same way that Red Riding Hood meets a wolf in the woods, *No Country for Old Men* describes a war veteran meeting drug dealers in the desert. But, as all children know, Red Riding Hood's narrative is not simply the fabulistic story of a child meeting a talking wolf. Instead, it is a story meant to encourage children to draw the conclusion that strangers ought not to be trusted. In a similar manner, *No Country for Old Men* encourages readers to recognize the dangers of human greed, that small actions like picking up a bag of money or neglecting to say "ma'am" and "sir" are perhaps minor lapses into uncivilized, vatic behavior, but however minor, those actions may reap an unimaginably violent retaliation: a world in which brute instincts crush the rule of law and destroy human love and hope.

Perhaps the best way to illustrate the novel's stimulation of response from its audience is to examine the predominating narrative style. As many reviewers of the novel noted, *No Country for Old Men* employs a markedly simplistic narrative style, void of the dense, polyphonic language that sends readers running for a dictionary, the language so typical of McCarthy's heavier tomes, such as *Blood Meridian*. But such simplistic syntax may mask a complex narrative aesthetic in which the text encourages readers to construct a counternarrative to the deceptively straightforward story printed on the page. In *Analyzing Prose*, Richard A. Lanham describes two primary prose styles, parataxis and hypotaxis. Parataxis refers to prose comprising primarily compound sentences (clauses joined by coordinating conjunctions), and hypotaxis refers to prose characterized by hierarchical syntax, prose that encourages readers to "know how things rank, what derives from what," usually through the use of subordination (29). Yet novels whose prose relies heavily on parataxis may in fact encourage readers to infer a hierarchical meaning in the same way that allegory sets up a transparent, simple narrative while requiring readers to understand that there is a much more complex shadow narrative behind the visible story line. For example, Lanham examines Ernest Hemingway's famous parataxis-heavy opening to *A Farewell to Arms*, which begins, "Now in the fall the trees were all bare and the roads were muddy" (Hemingway qtd. in Lanham 29–30). While Hemingway's narrative links descriptions using the coordinating conjunction "and," Lanham points out, the intuitive reader will understand that the point of the passage is not, in fact, the realization that trees in the Italian countryside are bare in the fall. Instead, the reader understands that the novel's narrator is capable only of observing his world. He is incapable of translating or understanding meaning behind the physical landscape because of some psychological disability numbing him to the world outside himself (30).

Lanham's description of Hemingway's allegorical use of parataxis—setting up a deceptively simple narrative that requires readers to recognize a shadow narrative behind the events described—provides insight into McCarthy's prose style in *No Country for Old Men*. For example, when readers are first introduced to Chigurh, the distant, omniscient third-person narrator describes the scene using a combination of both parataxis and hypotaxis. Unlike Hemingway's almost exclusive reliance of *asyndetic* parataxis—compound sentences without explanatory connectors—McCarthy's hypotactic prose demonstrates *polysyndeton*, that is, a variety of compound and complex connecting words, in addition to straightforward paratactic sentences employing the ubiquitous "and" (Lanham 33). So, for instance, the scene in which Chigurh attacks and kills a deputy who has arrested him is described with seemingly straightforward prose filled with enough explicit hierarchical subordinators that readers feel as if they have been given sufficient information to understand the scene:

> When he [the deputy] stood up out of the chair he swung the keys off his belt and opened the locked desk drawer to get the keys to the jail. He was slightly bent over when Chigurh squatted and scooted his manacled hands beneath him to the back of his knees. In the same motion he sat and rocked backward and passed the chain under his feet and then stood instantly and effortlessly. If it looked like a thing he'd practiced many times it was. (5)

In this section, the primary connector between clauses is "and," but there are subordinating, causal connectors as well: "to" ("in order to"), "when," and "and then." These hypotactic connectors ostensibly emphasize the reasoning behind the actions, but they function as in the example from Hemingway's *A Farewell to Arms* to which Lanham refers, in which the very "asyndetic world" (a syntactic world typified by its connector "and") that Hemingway creates ironically insists that such a world is one in which "connections cannot be made" (Lanham 33). In the same way, this section from *No Country for Old Men* invites readers to join in the act of deducing reasons for the actions—that the deputy opened a drawer with the intention of fetching keys, for instance, or that Chigurh was prompted to attack the deputy by the deputy's bending over—but such a basic level of causal revelations in fact only underscores the *lack* of logical reasons behind the actions. The deputy, after all, cannot be thinking too carefully if he turns his back on such a weird and dangerous captive; and Chigurh is prompted to kill the deputy not, readers come to realize, because of any recognizable motivation but rather because of his inexplicably barbaric instinct to destroy all that he comes across.

In another example, when Chigurh confronts Carla Jean at the end of the novel, the prose style employs almost exclusively *asyndetic* parataxis, independent clauses linked only by the conjunction "and," with one significant exception:

> He [Chigurh] straightened out his leg and reached into his pocket and drew out a few coins and took one and held it up. He turned it.

> For her to see the justice of it. He held it between his thumb and forefinger and weighed it and then flipped it spinning in the air and caught it and slapped it down on his wrist. Call it, he said. (258)

The primary syntactic mode, of course, is relentless parataxis, the conjunction "and" being repeated eight times. However, in a sudden nominative-phrase sentence fragment commenced by the conjunction "for" ("For her to see the justice of it"), readers are given an explanation for the otherwise unjustified actions related in the passage. Chigurh engages in a coin toss "for" Carla Jean to recognize that her death is not arbitrary but will be instead a just death. After Carla Jean mis-calls the coin, Chigurh launches into a detailed explanation of justice, fate, and the workings of the universe. He repeatedly asks for her acknowledgment that she understands the justice of her doom, repeating, "Do you understand?" and "Do you see?" until at last Carla Jean sobs, "I do. I truly do" (260). Following Carla Jean's admission, the narrator relates Chigurh's response: "Good, he said. That's good. Then he sh[oots] her" (260). Like the ostensibly explanatory conjunction "for," the adverb "Then" explains the relationship of the event—his shooting her—to his words. Because Carla Jean has finally understood that her death is just, Chigurh kills her. Yet readers, witnessing this explanation, will likely come to precisely the opposite conclusion. Chigurh shows Carla Jean a coin "[f]or her to see the justice" of her death, but readers recognize that Chigurh's definition of justice has little to do with merit; Carla Jean, after all, is entirely innocent in the story. Likewise, Carla Jean's weeping admission of defeat, "I do. I truly do," likely does not indicate that she accepts the justice of her own impending death. Rather, she seems to accept that Chigurh will kill her, that she is helpless to stop it, and that the only choice remaining in her power is to claim admission of defeat and so end his deranged, drawn-out monologue. Readers, in other words, must engage in a rather complicated reinterpretation of the narrative, unprompted by linguistic cues, in order to accurately read the emotional content of this scene. The plain narrative style of the scene insists, like Chigurh, that the girl's murder is straightforward and makes sense. The style produces a heart-wrenching pathos as readers reject the narrator's conclusions and at the same time reject Chigurh's explanations, instead mourning an innocent young woman's murder and thereby recognizing the pointlessness of an event that both the central character and the narrator insist makes sense.

No Country for Old Men's deceptively simple prose style thus works in conjunction with the deceptively simple narrative events to construct a fairy-tale-like parable, a story whose straightforward constructions in fact encourage readers to actively participate in constructing a deeper, more meaningful shadow interpretation. In other words, through its unusual narrative patterns, No Country for Old Men requires readers to participate in constructing an ethical interpretation of the novel if the narrative is to have any meaning beyond the blandishing amorality embodied by Chigurh. Folklorist and novelist Americo Paredes, in his article "The United States, Mexico, and Machismo," explains that folklore tropes play a unique role in constructing an ethical component to the literary canon. Because folklore requires readers' interpretation to find the larger moral behind the simple narrative, Paredes claims that readers of folklore have a moral obligation to interpret such tales in an ethically responsible manner. For example, Paredes explains that the European-American assumption that "machismo" is a particularly Mexican characteristic is based on an unethical interpretation of folklore images. He claims that, while tropes depicting male courage are common in older Mexican lore, the characteristic traits of machismo—the phallic symbolism, the identification of the man with the male animal, and the man's ambivalence or brutality toward women—were associated only with buffoons and weaklings. However, naturalistic writers like Frank Norris and Jack London adopted the "machismo" trait and associated it with heroism and "true" masculinity, reinventing the term and its use (27). The point, Paredes says, is that machismo is an attitude that does not describe the Mexican so much as it describes the urge of "[u]pward-moving groups" to shake off feelings of oppression and inferiority and to exult in images and lore of grandiose heroism (37). "Machismo," in this analysis, says more about the European culture's latent prejudices and misogyny than about Mexican culture. Paredes argues that the naturalistic writers' appropriation of "machismo" folklore reflects negatively on the American culture of the time but that, even more, it epitomizes the danger of mis-using folklore. Folklore should not be used as a means of measuring or describing the psychology of the culture from which it comes. Rather, Paredes says, folklore should be used—and reshaped if necessary—to create commonalities between groups and to motivate groups toward what is humane and noble.

Despite McCarthy's general commitment to realism, No Country for Old Men actually uses folklore in a manner consistent with Paredes's vision. Throughout the novel, repetitious imagery of loss and destruction is pitted against imagery of renewal and re-creation, culminating in the novel's final image, a dream of fire being built in darkness. The novel's archetypal figures and narrative tropes therefore gesture beyond the violence of the border region to recognize universals of human communion and hope. Furthermore, by associating magical or folkloric qualities with its characters and story line, the novel is able to transcend the ethical limitations of the "thriller" genre and the naturalist movement of which it is ostensibly part. While the naturalistic novel may warn against a form of human corruption, the folktale typically calls for a response or poses a clear moral to the audience. Of course, *No Country for Old Men* is hardly the first of McCarthy's novels to foreground narrative tropes and types so prominently. *Outer Dark*, as Russell Hillier points out, is stylistically evocative of John Bunyan's *Pilgrim's Progress*, to the extent that Hillier calls the novel a "subversive parody" of the older text (58). Likewise, *No Country for Old Men*'s tropes and archetypal figures reflect older Judeo-Christian forms such as the medieval morality play. But its strong folkloric flavor and its attention to questions of identity place the novel inside the tradition of Texas-Mexico border literature. The novel seems to comment on larger epistemological questions, but in a way specific to the border region. Critics like Linda Woodson and Robert Jarrett reflect the extent to which the novel is rooted in border sensibility by explaining the novel in terms of its historical and physical context. Woodson begins her article "'You are the battleground': Materiality, Moral Responsibility, and Determinism in *No Country for Old Men*" by citing a series of news stories from the *San Antonio Express-News* that depict real-world mindless bloodbaths similar to those in the novel (5–6). Jarrett likewise contends that Chigurh's "senseless" violence is only senseless if the novel is removed from its context; placed in context, "for the last decade Nuevo Laredo on the southwestern border has been the center of a series of drug wars and drug-related violence—a violence that makes a great deal of 'sense'" ("Genre, Voice and Ethos" 79). Certainly the violence in *No Country for Old Men* is contextually relevant. But even more importantly, the patterned narrative is contextually relevant, examining universal human crises in the location and in the lore of a specific and deeply troubled region.

In *No Country for Old Men*, McCarthy makes explicit reference to the universality of violence through the use of varying region-specific examples. The novel's core event—a particular drug sale gone wrong—creates a kernel from which discussions of regional, national, and universal penchants for violence are discussed. If Chigurh's math is correct, *No Country for Old Men* takes place in 1980 (56). The infection of violence in the novel therefore reflects the historical peak in violence along the border in the early 1980s. This spike in border crime reflected the concurrent catastrophes of, first, a shift in heavy drug trafficking from Florida to the Mexico-U.S. border and, second, the subsequent crackdown on border immigration along the border (Martinez 142). An example of the mostly unilateral crackdown on immigration, the "Tortilla Curtains" constructed in El Paso, Texas, and San Ysidro, California, in 1979 prompted sprees of racial crimes along the border and served as graphic depictions of the severance of communities and communications (134).

Although the "Tortilla Curtain" may symbolize division and violence along the border, such a symbol hardly touches on the roots of the problem. Oscar J. Martinez, in his analysis of the U.S.-Mexico crisis, claims that the "War on Drugs" has focused attention on Mexican causes for the drug-trade expansion, but this emphasis on Mexico overlooks "the voracious consumption of drugs in U.S. society" (146). In *No Country for Old Men*, Bell chastises a young female reporter who blames him (and by association U.S. law enforcement) for the rise in drug crime. "*I told her that you cant have a dope business without dopers,*" Bell says, suggesting the futility of attributing blame exclusively to one side of the crime equation (304). The novel consistently suggests that violence is born in a single human choice, but once born it spreads like a disease and its infection spreads beyond national and temporal boundaries. At one point, Bell visits his uncle, Ellis, who reflects, "How come people dont feel like this country has a lot to answer for?" (271). Ellis believes that the United States has a particularly vicious history. During this interaction, Ellis and Bell exchange recollections of war, and their reminisces sketch a history of twentieth-century America that is a veritable slag heap of violence, from abandoned mothers in World War I to psychologically devastated soldiers in Vietnam (268–71). Yet the novel is predicated on Bell's philosophical musings on the existence of human souls, indicating that if the United States is infected with an incomprehensible violence, the country is only a specific example of a larger human brokenness (2).

According to Bell, a fundamental absence—the absence of a "soul"—marks the boy he sent to death row, who murdered his girlfriend for no reason, and also marks Chigurh, who murders at a coin toss (2). Although Bell does not define what a "soul" is, the juxtaposed characters of Bell and Chigurh provide sufficient evidence to suggest that, in McCarthy's universe, characters who recognize their ethical responsibility to nature and to humankind possess a "soul," while those who do not are empty shells of flesh. Bell epitomizes this recognition of the crucial necessity of human interconnection. Toward the end of the novel, he describes how he has created an imaginary relationship with his dead daughter, attributing to her all the good qualities he wishes he possessed. He says that he has *"give[n] her the heart [he] always wanted for [him]self"* (285). In this relationship with a dead girl, Bell evokes McCarthy's first published short story, "Wake for Susan," where the young man Wes imagines a love affair with a name on a headstone. Both texts suggest that the central characters are haunted by their need for an "other"—even if that "other" is dead. Bell later describes his ethical recognition of his need for an "other" when he claims that his core identity lives in the love of his wife. Without her, he says, *"I dont know what I would have. Well, yes I do. You wouldnt need a box to put it in neither"* (305). Bell defines himself as a composite self, a self whose core identity exists in constant relation to other people. Love and goodness, for Bell, occur only in relationship, and outside of such relationships, all that a human possesses would not need a box.

Chigurh, of course, recognizes no such ethical or metaphysical obligations and therefore epitomizes the disease whose symptom is catastrophic violence. And at first glance, Chigurh's disturbing ethics seem to be supported by the novel's patterned imagery. Chigurh uses a coin toss to explain fate and to determine the fate of one of his victims in the beginning of the novel (56–57) and then with Carla Jean at the end of the novel (259). The two events counter each other. The first time, Chigurh's would-be victim calls heads, the coin falls to heads, and the man survives. Carla Jean also calls heads, but the coin falls to tails. Chirgurh uses the image of a coin toss to explain fate to his victims. He claims that history works like a series of coin tosses, probabilities becoming singularities. The coin, he says, had "been traveling twenty-two years to get here. And now it's here," as though all of history has unfolded to the precise moment of the coin toss (56). Later in the novel, when Bell visits Ellis, the older man briefly takes an oracular role. Ellis apparently subscribes to Chirgurh's view of the world as an unfolding of sequences, a heads-or-tails division of possibility, which he calls "good times and bad times" (265). But Ellis's worldview is more nuanced than Chigurh's. Caught inside the juggernaut of history, Ellis claims, people are only able to choose between happiness and despair (265). These characters' tunneled and prescriptive view of history explains the internal logic of the novel's narrative structure. Events are heralded by symbols, unfold in sequence, and arrive at conclusions foretold from the beginning. The narrative, in other words, is as immutable and predictable as a folktale. The only possibility for change lies in the reader's interpretation: faced with the predictable and immutable events of the novel, the reader is only able to choose hope or despair.

By flattening the narrative into a series of prescribed events, McCarthy restricts the possibilities to those ontological questions at the heart of the novel, questions about identity formation and the critical possibility of hope in an increasingly chaotic world. In "Sailing to Byzantium," Yeats describes the transcendence found in art as the "artifice of eternity" (line 24). *No Country for Old Men* applies the poem's argument to narrative and describes transcendence as the "promise" of a single act of creation in the face of pervasive destruction (305). Thus, Bell ends his narrative by telling of a dream in which he stood outside in the dark and cold world and saw his father in the distance building a fire (309). In condemnation of the soulless Chigurh's worldview, Bell instead evokes memories of his father, a man who believed in "a promise" of essential, irreducible human goodness. Retelling stories about his father provides Bell with the means to revivify hope in humanity's capacity to create, even in a world filled with evidence of humanity's capacity to destroy. In other words, although the narrative style in *No Country for Old Men* does not demonstrate the same virtuosic syntactic technique of other McCarthy novels, the "stripped-down" prose style does draw attention to literary artifice and the creative potential of that artifice (Wood 88). When Wells laconically describes Chigurh's evil, then dismisses it—"He's a psychopathic killer, but so what?"—he suggests that evil is, like Chigurh, inexplicable, and because inexplicable, impossible to defeat. But Bell's final dream-vision poses an implicit answer to Wells's assertion. Despite the pervasive violence of the border region, and of humanity itself, there are also aspects of human nature capable of achieving great beauty and ethical meaningfulness. Through folktale-like narrative structures, *No Country for Old Men* draws attention to the power of storytelling to create alternate identities and realities and to pose a transcendent meaning that helps to heal the wounds of human violence with images of hope.

5
"THERE IS NO GOD AND WE ARE HIS PROPHETS"
HEROISM AND PROPHETIC NARRATIVE IN *THE ROAD*

He tried to talk to God but the best thing was to talk to his father and he did talk to him and didnt forget. The woman said that was all right. She said that the breath of God was his breath yet though it pass from man to man through all of time.
—CORMAC MCCARTHY, *The Road*

The battlefield is symbolic of the field of life, where every creature lives on in the death of another. A realization of the inevitable guilt of life may so sicken the heart that, like Hamlet or like Arjuna, one may refuse to go on with it. [. . .] The goal of the myth is to dispel the need for such life ignorance by effecting a reconciliation of the individual consciousness with the universal will. And this is effected through a realization of the true relationship of the passing phenomena of time to the imperishable life that lives and dies in all.
—JOSEPH CAMPBELL, *The Hero with a Thousand Faces*

IN *The Road* (2006), two nameless characters, a father and a son, travel through a postapocalyptic world from the ruins of the father's ancestral home in eastern Tennessee down to what is likely an abandoned, darkly futuristic Galveston, Texas. *The Road* symbolically bridges the geographical divide between McCarthy's earlier Appalachian novels (*The Orchard Keeper, Outer Dark, Child of God,* and *Suttree*) and his Texan novels (*Blood Meridian,* the Border Trilogy, and *No Country for Old Men*), but *The Road* also spans a thematic rift cutting through McCarthy's corpus. The darkest novels, such as *Blood Meridian,* depict a world beyond the pale of civilization and beyond the reach of redemption, while novels such as *The Orchard Keeper* and *All the Pretty Horses* alleviate an overwhelming pessimism by depicting a few individuals who recognize their ethical obligations toward animals, nature, and other humans. *The Road* depicts a world even bleaker (if possible) than the world of *Blood Meridian,* but the novel nevertheless privileges the haunting obligation of ethical behavior, indicating that the darkest possible world may not be entirely bereft of people able to believe in human goodness. In *The Road,* the father believes that he has a mystical duty to keep his son alive, but, even more important, he believes that his task is to shore up all that remains of goodness in humanity by telling the boy "[o]ld stories of courage and justice" (35). Through hero stories, the father attempts to rekindle a prophetic vision of goodness and beauty in a devastated world. However, the father's quest is of dubious consequence. At one point, the father and the son stumble upon a wandering prophet figure with a nihilistic bent. "There is no god," the wanderer tells the father, "and we are his prophets" (143). Like the despairing prophet, the father is caught in an agnostic crisis. He doubts that his stories have any capacity to "mean" in such a morally bankrupt universe, and so his attempts to describe goodness to his son may, in the final analysis, make him nothing more than the prophet of a nonexistent god. However, the father's doubts are revealed almost exclusively through narrative revelations of his internal anguish: his external actions demonstrate a stubborn refusal to give up hope. The novel's revelations of the father's internal despair, juxtaposed with his external endurance, depict the conflicted morality of a postapocalyptic hero. In this bleak new world, the act of storytelling becomes an act of heroism, and stories themselves become the sacraments and rites of a new religious order haunted by despair but hallowed by hope.

The Road is a remarkable addition to McCarthy's corpus, primarily because of its landscape that resembles the moral abyss of *Blood Meridian* coupled with its atypically moral heroes. While early critical discussion of the novel is consistent in noting the surprisingly humane and tender relationship between the two protagonists, the novel is not as much of a departure from McCarthy's more typical themes as it may initially appear to be. Instead, the novel combines the two worlds—moral heroism and bleak nihilism—that contend for center stage throughout his literary universe. The few insights into this novel's conception that McCarthy has provided illustrate how the novel follows a dismal trajectory consistent with his corpus's generally pessimistic outlook on human depravity while nevertheless focusing readers' attention on those few glimmers of humanity that cannot be quenched in the darkest tide of calamity. In his July 2007 interview with Oprah Winfrey, McCarthy describes the inspiration for *The Road* as an idea that occurred to him one night when he and his youngest son, John Francis McCarthy, were staying in a hotel in El Paso. Standing at the hotel window, McCarthy says, he imagined "El Paso in a hundred years" (McCarthy, interview). Later, when he was in Ireland, he spent about six weeks developing the idea into the novel. In the novel, El Paso seems to have been translated into the port city of Galveston, since the father and the son finish their journey at a coastal city with a dock and a shipyard. The most interesting translation from idea to novel, however, is that the "hundred years" into the future, for McCarthy, is a grim apocalypse. Some early reviewers, such as Phil Christman, assume that the shearing light that heralded the end of *The Road*'s human age was a nuclear holocaust, although the novel remains intentionally vague about the cause of the catastrophe that stopped the clocks at 1:17 A.M. (40). In his interview with David Kushner, McCarthy "suggests that the ashcovered world in the novel is the result of a meteor hit," although, Kushner says, McCarthy admitted that "his money [was] on humans destroying each other before an environmental catastrophe sets in" (par. 43). In any event, like Robert Frost's ambivalence toward ice and fire, *The Road*'s uncertainty about the primary cause of the world's end ultimately emphasizes the inevitability of that end, along with the transience and relative unimportance of the human race. Whether it arrives through avarice and corruption or through the arbitrary violence of nature, McCarthy seems to suggest that the end is both inescapable and imminent.

The play *The Sunset Limited*, written at roughly the same time as *The Road*, demonstrates McCarthy's characteristically pessimistic view on the trajectory of human history (Luce, "Beyond" 3). In the play, the suicidal academic White claims, "The darker picture is always the correct one. When you read the history of the world you are reading a saga of bloodshed and greed and folly the import of which is impossible to ignore" (112). At first glance, White's prognostication seems to speak for the eschatological world of *The Road*. In this vision of a future world, the flora and fauna of (at least) the central and southern United States are ash, and, not content with the destruction of nature itself, the few human inhabitants now devour each other. But this grim picture is the story's backdrop rather than its main action. Through this hellish world a father and a son trek south, their telos not a precise location but only an instinctive determination to survive the coming winter by reaching a warmer climate.

Despite their journey's vague physical telos, however, the father's spiritual goal is clear, if potentially untenable: he must preserve human goodness by turning his son into a messianic moral compass. William Kennedy, in his review of *The Road,* claims that the "oracular presences" of evil in novels such as *Blood Meridian* speak with more clarity and interpretive force than do the father and the son, who are, comparatively, "tongue-tied." The father in particular, he says, "is as inarticulate on his Promethean son as he is on his own obsession with their forced march" (par. 14). In McCarthy's novels, if human goodness appears at all, it appears as ephemeral and mysterious, an affinity for animals, perhaps, or an inarticulate pity for the afflicted. In *The Road,* however, "goodness" may have all the concrete substance of gossamer, but its role in this, the postapocalyptic universe, is foregrounded in a way that is perhaps unique in McCarthy's corpus. The father cannot define goodness, and when he attempts to define it, he consistently fails to live up to his own definitions, causing his son to question the veracity or the practicality of those definitions. Nevertheless, the father sees his role of storyteller as an almost sacramental vocation. The father's hero stories lack the syntactic elegance of Judge Holden's nihilistic philosophizing, but they burn instead with a religious fervency and an aching exigency. In the end, even the father does not—perhaps cannot—fully believe in the worth of stories or in his own efficacy as a storyteller. However, the novel consistently draws attention to the father's courage as he acts out belief in the face of his own agnosticism. The father evokes archaic, classical, and Judeo-Christian religious symbols throughout the novel, transforming storytelling into a ritual of redemption by his association of meaning with the broken signs of the physical world. While he internally questions his own task, the novel closes with the boy, a herald of morality, finding a new human community—a scene that is a full realization of the father's quest to recreate a moral civilization. Despite its darkness, then, *The Road* ultimately undermines White's assertion that "the darker picture is always the correct one" (*TS* 112). In this novel, the darkest possible future has become reality, but that picture is not, in the end, wholly correct: despite his own agnosticism, the father effectively demonstrates the prophetic, reality-creating potential of storytelling.

McCarthy's postapocalyptic novel is in many ways itself a classical hero story. The world of *The Road* is constructed out of symbols, and the quest narrative structure evokes all the parameters of the mythological hero's journey. Joseph Campbell's *The Hero with a Thousand Faces* divides the mythological journey into three sections, the departure, the initiation, and the return, a narrative pattern that underpins *The Road*. The novel commences at the father's ancestral home. From there, spurred by a desire to survive the coming winter, the father and the son journey south, where the father will struggle against incipient death in order to ensure his son's survival. In McCarthy's novel, the boy seems to possess the primary qualifications of the hero. He is the son, the source of his world's salvation, and the character who achieves "*apotheosis*," the breath of his father passing on to him (Campbell 149; *TR* 241). Campbell claims that a hero is "the champion of things becoming" and that in this respect the boy most clearly plays the role of the novel's focal character, practicing hope in a hopeless world, haloed by the novel's concluding image of fish whose scale patterns are "maps of the world in its becoming" (Campbell 243; *TR* 241). However, Campbell also points out that the process of a hero's journey is sparked by "the awakening of the self," a call that "rings up the curtain, always, on a mystery of transfiguration—a rite, or moment, of spiritual passage, which, when complete, amounts to a dying and a birth" (51). If there is any "awakening of the self" in this novel, it can only be on the part of the father, since he is the only character with a "self." And the father's narrative does seem to be precipitated by an "awakening" moment. The novel commences with the father's realization that his quest may be, as his wife claimed, a self-serving mission, that "the boy was all that stood between him and death" (25). Questioning whether his salvation of the boy is an act of cowardice, the father begins a journey that will end in his sacrificial death, his journey becoming an anguished quest to prove to himself that his son is his world's messiah and that his life and the life of his child matter. Thus, while the boy in *The Road* plays the role of the hero, the narrative itself spotlights the father's journey. In the traditional hero story, the mentor character is ancillary to the central character's journey. In this novel, by contrast, the father's internal journey is focalized, transforming the father into the true hero of this tale, elevating the role of the oracle or prophet figure to that of the narrative's true heroic protagonist.

The son therefore plays the "messiah" figure, but narrative revelations of the father's mental life shift the focus of the hero journey from the son to the father. The narrative of *The Road* is closely linked to the father's interior world, so closely that at times the narrative's perspective moves inside his mind, shifting from third-person narration to the first person. For example, in the novel's opening descriptive passages, a first-person sentence fragment indicates a shift into the father's head without any explicit verbal cues: "He [the father] lay listening to the water drip in the woods. Bedrock, this. The cold and the silence. The ashes of the late world carried on the bleak and temporal winds to and fro in the void. [. . .] If only my heart were stone" (9–10). This passage begins with a third-person pronoun ("he"), but by the end of the passage, "he" has taken over the narrative point of view. The father's observations of the rocky outcroppings around their camp shift into his agonized desire to be, like nature, destroyed beyond any further capacity to feel pain. In revealing the father's interior world rather than the son's, *The Road* suggests that heroism is inextricably linked to storytelling and that thus the storyteller becomes the quest's actual hero.

Throughout the novel, the narrative remains close to the father's perspective and frequently moves inside his mind. This narrative style is noticeably different from McCarthy's typical style of removed narration. Only one novel published before *The Road* uses this narrative style, and that novel is McCarthy's most autobiographical work, *Suttree*. Both Suttree and the father are given instances of unmediated first-person narrative control. The unnamed father thus possesses a mental vulnerability and a focal subjectivity paralleled only by McCarthy's Joycean proto-author character. As an important distinction, the first-person sections of both *Suttree* and *The Road* are stylistically and semantically different from first-person narration in other McCarthy novels. *The Orchard Keeper* (1965), *Child of God* (1973), and *No Country for Old Men* (2005) all have passages of first-person narration. However, the first-person sections of these novels are all "spoken" in the characters' regional dialects. The passages' dialectical structures keep them distinct from the actual narrative. In contrast, both *Suttree* and *The Road* are narrated in a close third-person voice that sounds linguistically identical to the dialects of the protagonists. Most distinctively, the narrative in these two novels remains so close to the protagonists' minds that the novels' narrative perspective at times shifts to the first person.

For example, the following passage from *The Orchard Keeper* illustrates the omnisciently narrated text's shift into first-person narration. The shift here is obvious, and the philosophical content of the first-person thought is unambiguously attributed to the thinker, Arthur Ownby:

> He [Ownby] eased himself slightly in the chair and shifted his weight. Most ever man loves peace, he said, and none better than a old man. *Or even knows they need attendin to. But I never done it to benefit myself. Shot that thing.* (229)

The first-person internal monologue "*I never done it*" is in the same dialect as Ownby's speaking voice, "Most ever man loves peace." This dialect-infused voice remains clearly distinct from the narrator's voice, "He eased himself slightly in the chair." Such distinctions between interior first-person narration and omniscient third-person text are not present in *Suttree* and *The Road*.

In *The Road*, revelations of the protagonist's interior world are tightly interwoven with the narrator's, to the extent that the two viewpoints merge and are frequently indistinguishable. For example, at one point the father and the son hide from other travelers who might or might not be members of the cannibalistic blood cults. The father realizes that his revolver has only one bullet, and he decides that he must use the bullet to kill his son and so spare the boy the fate of being kept alive as food by the blood cult:

> They lay listening. Can you do it? When the time comes? [. . .] Could you crush that beloved skull with a rock? Is there such a being within you of which you know nothing? Can there be? Hold him in your arms. Just so. The soul is quick. Pull him towards you. Kiss him. Quickly. (96)

In this section, as they lie listening for the travelers, the father is haunted by the idea that he might have inside himself the capacity to kill his own son. The father counters this idea by kissing his child. However, the paralleled actions in this section, listening and kissing, are recounted using different narrative perspectives. The listening is related in the third person, while the kissing is in the implied first person—an imperative command that is not voiced out loud and therefore must take place inside the character's mind. There can be no clear delineation between narrators, since, in this case, even the narrative action is related as much by the first-person narrator as it is by the third-person narrator.

A comparison of these two passages, however, raises the problematic question of what such a narrative means about the morality of the character controlling the text. In general, McCarthy's novels grant readers insight into the minds of moral characters, such as John Grady Cole or Llewellen Moss, but not into the minds of immoral or amoral characters, such as Culla Holme or the kid in *Blood Meridian;* and at the very least, a transition into the perspective of a single character highlights that character's moral choice. But the passage from *The Road* cited above reveals instead a relatively ordinary and moral man's recognition of a hidden and monstrous potential within himself, suggesting that this time, a revelation of interiority reveals moral degradation.

Ultimately, though, *The Road* follows a man actively pursuing fatherhood, creating the loving relationship almost ex nihilo, out of the atavistic chaos around him. While revelations of the father's interior world often reveal his anguish over his own corruption, or his suicidal despair, such revelations also expose the raw courage the man exhibits as he attempts a journey fraught with horrific danger in order to forge the possibility for a future out of an apocalyptic waste. His journey, in other words, is a moral quest to become a father, but the fathering of a human child is merged with a metaphoric journey toward authorship. *The Road* in particular emphasizes the creative force of language as a prophetic "fathering" of humanity. And the most significant aspect of this author-quest novel is that it is a primarily interior journey. The narrative reveals its protagonist's inner struggles with moral failure and so emphasizes the redemptive role of storytelling, the means by which the man attempts to foster in his son a reality he himself cannot quite grasp. Unmediated first-person revelations of the father's mind in *The Road* may thus reveal his recognition of his moral failures, but that recognition proposes to the reader that he possesses the capacity, however damaged, to become a better human being. For example, when the father kills a man who he believes threatens his son's safety, he contemplates his own moral complicity in the devastation of the world around him, and those contemplations are revealed through a shift from third- to first-person narrative.

> The wet wood hissed in the flames, the snow continued to fall. [. . .] This was the first human being other than the boy that he'd spoken to in more than a year. My brother at last. [. . .] The gray and rotting teeth. Claggy with human flesh. Who has made of the world a lie every word. (64)

The shift into first-person, "My brother," illuminates the father's recognition of the humanity of his victim. His victim, a cannibal whose teeth were "claggy with human flesh," may have deserved death, but the act of killing has pushed the father closer to the precipice of all that he dreads, the loss of what it means to be human.

Despite the father's moral ambiguities, the novel draws explicit attention to his interior angst, his attempts to grapple with, and understand, his own ethical obligations and what ethical failure means about his own humanity. And while the first-person revelations illuminate the father's struggles with morality, there are also third-person indirect revelations of his thoughts. These indirect revelations of the father's fears draw attention to his heroic commitment to survival and to stories of courage in the face of his overwhelming doubts. In other words, the most significant aspect of the multiple narrative modes in *The Road* is that the father's revealed consciousness, whatever the mode of revelation, draws attention to his role as a narrator, a storyteller. His ultimate success as a storyteller is significant, however, because it is expressed in his *son's* embodiment of his ideals rather than in his own redemption. The father dies without overcoming his moral agnosticism, but he leaves behind a son who seems to possess a relatively intact belief in humanity's capacity to be good. His journey describes the transference of morality through the act of storytelling, suggesting that storytelling possesses a world-creating power greater than the flaws of the human orator. Because of this mystical ability to *mean*, storytelling seems to be imbued with a particularly Roman Catholic sacramental quality. In the Roman Catholic tradition, for example, the human errors of the priest cannot negate the divinely inspired transubstantiation of the Eucharist. In the same way, the father's moral failures do not empty from the sacred rite of storytelling its numinous power to bring healing and hope to humankind.

Storytelling is consistently described as a rite, a ritually practiced act with sacramental significance, in *The Road*. For example, near the end of the novel, the father attempts to convince his son that their story is a good story because they have survived so far. His unimpressed son questions that definition of "good," but the father objects that the mere fact of their survival "counts for something" (227). And indeed, the ritualistic practice of survival—the acting out of hope—is all that matters in this morally devastated world.

The novel develops this argument through systematic patterns of indirectly and directly revealed interiority. Specifically, indirectly revealed interiority tends to illustrate the father's fear and despair at moments when he physically behaves in direct contradiction to that despair. Directly revealed interiority likewise reveals a man catastrophically crippled by despair, but these revelations also describe the depths of the father's love for his son, moments that create brief respites of tenderness in the otherwise tragic narrative. Finally, certain direct revelations of the father's interior world are phrased in the imperative mood. These depict the father silently urging himself on, and as he manages to carry on despite horrific physical calamities, they indicate the reality-creating power of language. The father's imperatives create an incantatory refrain throughout the novel. Even though the father remains in doubt over the efficacy of language, these interior revelations illustrate the power of language to inspire, to give strength, and to conjure possibilities for hope out of existential despair.

Throughout the novel, indirect revelations of the father's thoughts tend to illustrate his worry, fear, or anger in contrast to his efforts to appear confident in front of his son. At one point, the father looks at his son's cadaverous face as the boy sleeps, and "[h]e f[ights] back the rage. Useless" (81). The adjective "useless" intensifies the narrative description of the father's internal struggle, a struggle apparent to no one but the father himself. Shortly after this, he dreams about his son dying, and when he wakes up, the narrator explains that "[w]hat he could bear in the waking world he could not by night" (109–10). These examples illustrate the function of indirect revelations of the father's thoughts in the novel. The revelations paint a picture of a man losing an internal battle to hold onto hope. Even more dramatically, third-person revelations of the father's thoughts sometimes counter his actions, depicting a battle that McCarthy's more typical distant and objective-sounding third-person omniscient narrators would not illustrate. So, for example, when his son questions what will happen to them, the father answers the boy, "You'll be all right," but the following narrative sentence undercuts that verbal assurance: "He [the father] was terrified" (208). Twice, indirect descriptions of the father's interiority suggest the possibility of hope, but it is at best an agonized and despairing hope. At one point, looking at the wasted and bleached northern lights, the father feels something; he "had this feeling before, beyond the numbness and the dull despair" (75). But that feeling is one of savage desperation, since the father believes that he is losing memories of color or of warm and human things now lost in the barren apocalyptic world. Finally, the father, knowing he is dying, sends his son away. He tries to convince the boy that his task is to leave and to "carry the fire." Imagining his son's future, the narrator informs readers, "[h]e wanted to be able to see" (233). The semantic implication of the verb "want" is that the father is doomed to tragedy; desire, after all, is defined by what it lacks. Although these moments of revealed interiority are brief and scattered throughout an arid and depopulated literary landscape, when they are culled together, they describe a fragile heroism. In spite of an overwhelming despair, the father still tries to pass on hope to his child.

The father's actions are tainted with suspicion, terror, and dread, but his very commitment to survival marks every decision he makes. He fails to live up to his own definitions of "goodness," but he nevertheless transmits those definitions to the boy and to the world of the novel. His efforts at regeneration seem to face defeat around every twist in the road, but he struggles on. One time, the father cajoles his son into an abandoned house in search of canned food and blankets. The son, born after the end of civilization, is terrified by houses and does not want to enter, but the father prevails and, later, builds a fire in the dining room, cooks canned goods, and serves the food in "bone china bowls" on the dining room table. They eat with utensils, seated at a table with a candle between them, the father's re-creation of a familial tableau from an era vanished before the boy's birth (176). The formal meal mimics the decorum and gestures of a world irrevocably lost, and this mimicry of a preapocalyptic world stands in stark contrast to the horror of the novel's previous dinner scene, the campfire with the charred remnants of a human child—the dining style of the new, postapocalyptic world (167). The father acknowledges that ultimately his playacting of old charades of civilization may be just more evidence of his "placing hopes where he'd no reason to hope" (180). However, as the two eat their dinner, the "warming house creak[s] and groan[s]. Like a thing being called out of long hibernation" (176–77). The cannibalized infant may be the sign of the new order, but the father resists surrendering to the collapse of human society.

Instead of relenting to despair, the father resurrects and recreates symbols of the past, attempting to construct a symbolic "road" stretching from the past, where signs had meaning, to the future, where the boy may represent a new generation with a meaningful mythology of its own. In *The Road*, human survival depends on knowing symbols and being able to interpret them in a meaningful way. However, the novel underscores the connection between symbol and reality: symbol interpretation is meaningless if it is not matched with action. The father fails to fully live up to his claims that there is such a thing as human "goodness," but at least he tries. And his efforts seem to empower the son to embody a more generalized and deeper ethics, a self-sacrificial and universal compassion for humanity. *The Road*, in other words, suggests that symbols may be shorn of their referents, but the attempt to reunite the symbol with ethical action is of paramount importance. Even if it ends in failure, the attempt to construct meaning is what matters. As the man tells his son, "[t]his is what the good guys do. They keep trying" (116).

The juxtaposition of revelations of the father's internal lack of belief with his external actions expressing belief represents the monumental weight of the argument at the heart of the novel. The father, poised between two disparate possible realities, chooses to *act* as though the more hopeful possibility is the true reality. At one point, the boy looks at his father and sees his face in the firelight "like some old world thespian" (9). While the boy is consistently pictured in terms of a religious vessel, the father is pictured as an actor. Unlike the boy, he does not really believe in the reality behind religious forms that grants terms like "goodness" and "beauty" meaning; he is, at heart, a skeptic. But his refusal to quit "acting" as though forms still carry religious significance is the source of his heroism. The father's memory of his final argument with his wife captures this tarnished yet crucial definition of heroism. In their conversation, his wife claims that suicide is her only option left in a world that has become meaningless. She criticizes his decision not to commit suicide by saying, "You cant even see." The man responds, "I dont have to" (49). Although he cannot "see" hope, he chooses to keep living and to protect and nurture his son, offering him a heritage of hero stories with which he might be able to recreate a humane world. Indirect revelations of the father's thoughts and emotions, in other words, depict his internal heroism—a technique that is rare and, because rare, significant in McCarthy's corpus.

Shifts into direct revelations of the father's thought process, indicated by the narrative's perspective changing from third- to first-person narration, similarly draw readers' attention to the father's blind sight, his despairing hope. But first-person passages humanize that heroism by illuminating the father's fragile internal moral compass. For example, when the father shoots the cannibal who threatens his son, a shift into the first person indicates that the father recognizes the man as "[m]y brother at last" (64). The father's voice seizes the narrative from the third person long enough to acknowledge his absolute culpability in the stranger's death. Even in self-defense, that killing was a violation of humanity. The savage violence in this passage is typical of McCarthy's literary world, but it is unusual to have these moments trigger a first-person point of view. The first-person reflections make the violence all the more terrible because they demonstrate a moral human being violated by the brutality he has committed. The father's feelings of moral culpability in this case are even more piercing because there is no mediator between the sufferer and the reader.

First-person narrative is also used to highlight the father's musings on what it means to be human in a posthuman universe. At one point, the boy thinks he has seen the reflection of another boy in a window, and wanting to find and keep the boy, he starts crying. The father tries to distract his son from his grief by pointing to a map. The father identifies written signs that locate them, symbolically counteracting their loss and isolation. The boy, however, "w[on't] look" and instead begs that they find the boy and "the dog" (73). The next section of text is narrated in the first person. This passage explains the boy's reference to a dog: "The dog that he remembers followed us for two days. I tried to coax it to come but it would not. [. . .] I promised I would not hurt the dog. [. . .] That is the dog he remembers. He doesnt remember any little boys" (74). This passage demonstrates two significant aspects of the function of first-person narration in the novel. Thematically, the father's interpretation of the episode indicates that he believes the boy practices a radical connection between sight and empathy. The boy's desire for the dog—his primal yearning for something to hold and to "keep"—is, when thwarted, transformed into a visual hallucination of an "other," a potential playmate and friend. The father's interpretations of the son's motivations may or may not be true. Because this section is in the first person, the interpretation indicates only the father's perspective, so that the reader is compelled to interpret this passage as revealing the *father's* instinctive connection between sight and empathy, thus demonstrating the second significant function of first-person narration. The father wants to "see" in the prophetic sense—he wants to foresee a better future, a world where hope is possible—but all of these prophetic visions are bound up in the primary role of sight, which is to connect the seer with the "other."

The last moment of interior voice in the novel comes after the father has woken up from a restless sleep. He leaves the campsite and walks out to the road, where he reflects that he will soon be dead. The scene ends with a sudden shift into the first person: "He is coming to steal my eyes. To seal my mouth with dirt" (220). At this point, the father's greatest fear is his own death, which he sees as abandoning his child. He imagines this fear in terms of a personified death who first blinds and then silences him. The horror of death, for the father, is blindness, the absolute conclusion to a life lived in spiritual darkness. Although the man "cant see" hope, he nevertheless attempts to give figurative sight to his son. The first-person point of view forces the reader to perceive the literary world through the eyes of the main character, the person directly experiencing that literary world, rather than through the eyes of a distant observer. In this case, the literary world is almost unbearably cruel, and shifting to a first-person narrator who is spiritually blind yet linguistically prophetic makes for a brutal yet oddly transcendent literary experience. In this way, the first-person sections of text depict a character who is morally aware, who recognizes that his world is teetering over an abyss of hopelessness, and who acts out hope anyway.

One of the most important functions of the stylistic use of the first person is that these passages profoundly deepen the reader's comprehension of and connection to the father's tenuous morality and anguished humanity. In *Language in Literature,* Michael Toolan describes the interpretive potential in studying the narrative modes a text uses to depict characters' thoughts. Toolan claims that there is a marked difference between a reader's experience of a text that uses free direct thought ("What's going on?") and the experience of "framed direct thought" (She thought, "What's going on?") (109). The difference, he says, is that direct thought creates a "vivid experience of real people" (117). In fact, Toolan claims:

> [a] text rich in these modes [i.e., direct thought] is one in which we sense that real people are speaking out, in their own words, and disclosing their thoughts in their own words. Instead of a detached and summarized telling of what happened, we witness an involved and elaborate showing of what happened—and in fact that phrase "what happened" ceases to be entirely fitting as a result: when the showing is sufficiently direct and displayed, through the pages of a text, we feel we are witnessing "what is happening" rather than merely "what happened." (117–18)

The temporal immediacy of directly revealed thought heightens readers' experiences of the text, shortening or erasing altogether the gap between narrator and event and, consequently, between reader and event. The distance imposed by removed narration, as in *Blood Meridian,* isolates the events on the page. The narrator remains floating above and out of reach of the action, and the reader remains with the narrator, coldly observing without any emotional attachment to the actions. So, for example, in *Blood Meridian* when the narrator observes "[b]lacks in the fields, lank and stooped, their fingers spiderlike among the balls of cotton. A shadowed agony in the garden," the reader understands that the slaves are objects of some pathos, being explicitly linked to the suffering of Christ, but the text nevertheless retains a rather emotionally sterile feel (4). Compared to this removed narration, the pathos involved in a scene with direct first-person narration burns with intensity. When the father realizes that he has only one bullet left in his gun, for instance, the text is narrated in free direct thought: "What if it doesnt fire? It has to fire. What if it doesnt fire? Could you crush that beloved skull with a rock? [. . .] The soul is quick. Pull him toward you. Kiss him. Quickly" (96). The stream-of-consciousness repetition of "What if it doesnt fire?" mimics the frenzied worry the father feels, and since the text is related directly through the eyes of the father, readers are compelled to empathetically enter into that frantic horror. The emotional index of the second style of narration is, quite clearly, far greater than that of the first.

The most significant aspect of first-person narration in *The Road*, however, is that most instances of this directly revealed thought are syntactically phrased in the imperative mood. Compared to the five instances of first-person narration that use the first-person pronoun "I" (10, 27, 64, 74, 200), there are eleven sections where the text is technically narrated in the first person but there is no "I" narrator (24, 27, 58, 63, 64, 96, 98, 111, 164, 210, 220). Instead, these passages are in the imperative mood, indicating that the reader is being allowed to overhear the father talking to himself. These imperative commands are almost always associated with ritualized behavior. For example, the first time the imperative mood breaks into the text, the father is musing on the ephemeral traces of civilization in his barren world. He recalls the survivors during the first years after the catastrophe who demonstrated "the frailty of everything revealed at last" (24). This "frailty" prompts him to make a philosophical observation about the tenuous nature of existence and the subsequent role of the observer: "The last instance of a thing takes the class with it. Turns out the light and is gone. Look around you" (24). As in this example, the imperative mood almost always depicts the father commanding himself to codify the remains of a vanishing world, to recite a litany of things past, or to otherwise construct a ritualized means of preserving and revivifying civilization. Because of their semantic content and because of their syntactic mode, these passages accentuate the father's prophetic role. And these incantatory refrains weave a shamanistic creative energy through the blasted and ash-darkened wasteland of a postapocalyptic narrative.

The imperative-mood moments, while also depicting the courage of a ravaged soul, more importantly illustrate the capacity of language to support human life. For example, the man recalls a good memory of his wife (the only good memory of her related in the novel). At the end of that memory, the syntax switches to the imperative mood: "Freeze this frame. Now call down your dark and your cold and be damned" (16). The father's existence is one in which all feelings are abhorrent and memories are dangerous sirens. Yet he chooses to "freeze" one good memory—a memory tainted by his wife's subsequent suicide—and he dares the darkness of his world to swallow the frail beauty of that memory. The father's happiest thoughts are not exactly cheery, but they do demonstrate his commitment to resurrecting images, symbols, and stories of human community and warmth in a world where he cannot see, is lost in darkness, and feels utterly "damned."

After another harrowingly pleasant memory, the father is tempted to close himself to all memories but then refuses to do so. The imperative mood once again breaks into the narrative and commands: "Make a list. Recite a litany. Remember" (27). This command is echoed shortly after, in the passage where he sees his son as a prophetic figure and tells himself, "So be it. Evoke the forms" (63). In this second case, he recognizes that he may have "nothing else," but he chooses nevertheless to resurrect old images that once brought beauty and grace to the world. In other words, he chooses to act as though he possessed precisely what he fears he has irrevocably lost. This conscious decision to act over against the darkness inside of him is again revealed through the imperative mood when he realizes that they have only one bullet left in their revolver. Knowing that if they are threatened, he will use that bullet to kill his son to spare his child from marauding cannibals (the "bloodcults"), he says, "You will not face the truth. You will not" (58). And, later in the novel, the father realizes he is dying and, in his fear, "[h]is mind [i]s betraying him." The imperative mood breaks in again: "Correct for that" (98). The imperative mood consistently reflects the father's choice to keep moving, to keep surviving, a choice based on his blind hope that surviving will "count for something" (227).

Revelations of the father's thought processes in the imperative mood also suggest that he sees the world in terms of narrative and, despite his agonized agnosticism, assumes some sort of "narrator." For example, the father at one point strokes the hair of his sleeping son and imagines the boy as a "[g]olden chalice." The narrative then shifts to the imperative mood: "Please dont tell me how the story ends" (64). The father's plea reveals his fear that his son will die, but even more significantly, it demonstrates the way the father perceives their journey—as a story. Later, when he imagines death coming "to seal his eyes with dirt," the father's fanciful personification of death is prompted by his perception of stones at a crossroads like "the spoken bones of oracles." The oracular bones prompt a self-addressed question: "What will you say?" (220). The father imagines death as a moment of reckoning in which speech will defend both his life and the value of his quest. He interprets his life in terms of story and verbal reckoning, and the text's revelation of his imperative-mood thought underscores the importance of reality-creating language. The father imagines his role as an oracle for the boy, and faced with the oracular bones of a long-dead world, he does not know what he will say. But as he commands himself to hold onto memories of color and love and to keep going, those memories increase, and he goes on until the boy is able to go on without him. In the end, the father becomes his own oracle.

    The prophetic and oracular role of storytelling is depicted through revelations of the father's interior world, but this idea is also developed thematically in the novel through recurring imagery that associates the transmission of meaning and morality with fire. For instance, prophetic storytelling is consistently pictured as "carrying the fire" (182). Like revelations of interior life in the novel, moments of light and color are rare yet significant. The postapocalyptic world is described as gray and dark, but the father dreams in color (18). Near the beginning of the novel, the father fears that even his dreams of color are bleeding away to darkness. Colors, like memories of birds and plants, are fragile and fading, "[t]he sacred idiom shorn of its referents and so of its reality" (75). Yet, as the novel progresses, fragments of vivid color, such as the salt wood burning "orange and blue" and flares of lightning, kindle in the darkness (200, 197). And rather than dimming, the father's dreams "brighten" until he starts to wake on a regular basis "out of softly colored worlds of human love, the songs of birds, the sun" (157, 229). Near the end, the father explores an abandoned ship and finds an ancient sextant nestled in its box on "blue baize." The sextant—an archaic device meant to measure the sun and locate people otherwise lost on a featureless sea—"stirs" the father in a way he has not experienced in a long time (192). Finally, after the father dies, the boy joins a small band of people (apparently people of the noncannibal sort), and the final scene conjures up a memory of ancient fish in mountain streams, primordial life forms of a former world whose scale patterns represented the evolutionary progress of a world yet to come, a process that even this nearly demolished planet may yet recommence (241). The father, after all, tells his son that "[g]oodness will find the little boy. It always has. It will again" (236). That statement initially seems as falsely idealistic as many of his assurances to the boy, yet when the father dies, the boy ventures out on the road and sees a man in a "gray and yellow" parka. The deus ex machina appearance of this man, like his yellow jacket and like the child in his traveling community, suggests a resurgence of color and hope and the possibility of some version of the former world's finding a toehold on this new and barren planet (237). The slow flush of color spreading through the grim darkness of the novel likewise seems to counter the father's increasingly despairing interior world, suggesting that the son may possibly succeed in bringing the "fire" of sacred meaning back to the emptied vessels of his universe.

In the novel, then, meaningfulness, hope, and beauty are always pictured in terms of color, fire, and sight. If it is true that the father "cant see," then his choosing to behave as though he could becomes all the more remarkable. In loving his son and teaching him to "see" stories of goodness and heroism in the world around himself, he becomes a consummate thespian. The novel thus suggests that love, morality, and meaning are indivisible and that hope is acting out those qualities even without sight. Without at least the pretence of hope, there can be no life or continuance of humanity, physical or otherwise. So the central conflict in the novel is the father's desperate attempt to bring the "fire" of hope into the bleak and dying postapocalyptic world. His struggle is depicted primarily through revelations of interiority, both explicitly depicted revealed thoughts and emotions and moments in which the narrative actually *becomes* his thoughts or emotions. McCarthy's linguistic device in shifting the narrative into the father's head holds the emotional power and poignancy of the father's struggle. The father's struggle is depicted as heroic rather than merely futile or pointless through those passages that reveal his interiority and thereby hallow his courage.

The father plays an authorial role by taking up the prophetic mantle of a storyteller to give his son the capacity to "see" color in a gray and despairing world. The father comes to realize that "to the boy he [i]s himself an alien. A being from a planet that no longer existed. The tales of which were suspect" (129). In this moment, the father acknowledges the impossibility of his task. In spite of his crushing moral culpability, his despair, and his recognition of the profundity of his loss, however, this troubled author acts out hope like a Greek thespian with a smiling mask, the hypocritical yet heroic relict of a past era. At one point, the man and the boy meet a fellow traveler who tells them that his name is "Ely." This prophet, however, turns out to be the nihilistically inclined oracle who tells them that "there is no god"; when the father intimates that it may be possible to bring "god" back, Ely counters, "Where men cant live gods fare no better" (145). Demonstrating a rather perverse sense of humor, Ely concludes their brief encounter with a story in which a personified death, defeated by his own overefficiency, stands around wondering, "Where did everyone go?" (146). The nihilistic prophet insists on the futility of the father's dreams of continuity and survival: in his tragic world, there is little difference between the blood cults and the boy, leading him to conclude that "[t]hings will be better when everybody's gone" (145). The father feebly protests Ely's worldview.

However, before this conversation, when the father and son first see Ely on the road, the father internally debates the merit of stopping to help the old man, in a monologue that is both consistent with and diametrically opposed to Ely's worldview. The father is initially reluctant to befriend the old man, but his son encourages him to "touch him [Ely]," to offer a gesture of human connection (137). The father then fancifully imagines the traveler turning out to be a hidden god who will turn them into trees (137). In the myth to which the father alludes, an old couple, Philemon and Baucis, shelter Jupiter and Mercury without knowing they are offering succor to gods. In thanks for their kindness, the gods turn the couple into trees. The father, it seems, also imagines a world in which the cessation of humanity is a god-given boon. But in the father's imagination, even in stripping them of their humanity, the god would recognize their desire to remain together. The father values relationship to the extent that he cannot imagine a "good" without it. His valuation of life suggests that even his most artificial acting may nevertheless represent a very real belief in the value of life and love, even if that value is mysterious and indefinable.

Ely's dim prognostication, in other words, is not necessarily the full picture. Early in the novel, the father claims that if his son is not the "word of God," then "God never spoke." All that humankind knows of the divine rests in the capacity to imbue the symbols of this world with divine meaning. At one point, the father catches a snowflake that melts on his hand "like the last host of christendom" (13). And indeed, there may be no place for sacraments of divine communion with humanity in this forsaken place. But, on the other hand, rites of community may survive as long as humans survive. The boy, the vessel of images, is described as both "the word of

God" and the "breath of God," so that he becomes a symbol defining God in terms of orality, just as symbolic meaning is described in terms of sight, as fire and color (4, 241). *The Road* travels through a bitter and dark land, but it describes in many ways a journey through despair toward a tenuous and fragile hope, defined by the prophetic vision and oracular power of a despairing storyteller. In fact, the devastation of the physical world of the novel accentuates the transcendence of its fragile victories of human connection. At one point, the father realizes that their road is more passable than he had feared. In this brief respite from despair, he watches his gaunt son sleeping and thinks that his son's face bears a "strange beauty" (87). This description recalls W. B. Yeats's "Easter, 1916," in which a "terrible beauty" is born from a world that has been "changed, changed utterly" by violence (lines 16, 15, 80, 79). In the same way, the novel is, perhaps, a description of the terrible and inexplicable beauty of a hope born out of ruinous despair.

Given its thematic exploration of the crucial role of storytelling in the transmission of a moral sensibility, it is no surprise that *The Road*, in contrast to the novel just previous to it in publication, *No Country for Old Men* (also a Yeats reference), stylistically returns to the "complexity, lyricism, and beauty we often associate with McCarthy's prose" (Frye 27). Richly symbolic, *The Road* begins with a description of the father's recurring dream in which he descends into a classical underworld and sees a mythological creature guarding the dark cavernous place across a "black and ancient lake" (3). Throughout the novel, the characters, especially the father, unfold the world and interpret it through classical and biblical symbols, a feature common to McCarthy's multivalent and densely symbolic texts. In particular, this novel's narrative trajectory is framed with caves, the first scene evoking a classical Hades and the "road" ending with the father's death in a physical cave (3, 236). Both of these caves, unlike Plato's allegorical cave, seem to have no exit to the higher world of forms. Instead, they dead-end in death. However, the unalleviated darkness of the first cave image is counterbalanced by the glimmer of hope in the final cave. In the first scene, the father's dream ends with the hideous Cerberus-type monster "lop[ing] soundlessly into the dark" (4). In the final cave, the father recognizes that there may (still) be no metaphysical "way out," that "[i]n that cold corridor they h[ave] reached the point of no return," but that "point" is "measured [. . .] solely by the light they carr[y] with them" (236). In the literal sense, the father and son cannot see the entrance to the cave because the frail light of the boy's candle does not extend that far. However, although the father cannot see the outside world and, finally, will die without seeing it again, the boy does find his way out of the cave, both physically and metaphorically. The framing symbol of the cave, then, suggests that the novel's metaphorical road may not dead-end in darkness and the absolute cessation of human history.

Just as the caves create a mirroring effect, balancing despair and hope, death and resurrection, the novel draws explicit attention to the importance of symbols and, consequently, the critical role of the interpreter of symbols. At one point while bathing and drying his son, the father imagines that his actions, bent over the blanketed child, are "like some ancient anointing" (63). The father seems to notice, and then consciously accept, the weight of that Judeo-Christian symbol of the prophetic mantling. The text shifts into the second-person form, a syntactic shift that indicates the father mentally addressing himself. "So be it," he tells himself. "Evoke the forms. When you've nothing else construct ceremonies out of the air and breathe upon them" (63). The "forms," ancient and sacred imagery, carry the burden of meaning in the novel, and stories are the vessels that carry those images.

Of course, the great danger posed to the author, a prophet figure who guards the sacred vessels of images, is the question that haunts this novel as it haunts almost every text McCarthy has written. That question is whether or not those symbols can mean anything in such a bleak and morally devastated world. And it is precisely because the father plays an authorial role that his answer to that question becomes of primary importance in any interpretation of McCarthy's corpus. At one point in the novel, the father remembers his final conversation with his wife, who committed suicide sometime after the "apocalypse" that ruined their world and after the birth of their son. In his memory, the wife tells her husband that she no longer cares enough to keep living because "[i]t's meaningless" (48). This conversation evokes a dialogue in *The Sunset Limited* in which Black attempts to dissuade White from committing suicide. White wants to die not because he is in despair, but because he cannot live in a world that is devoid of meaning. He tells Black, "The truth is that the forms I see have been slowly emptied out. They no longer have any content" (139). The play's final scene depicts White, a character who has abandoned (or been abandoned by) meaningful symbols, departing with the intent to kill himself. He leaves Black "*weeping rocking back and forth*" and offering up questions of existence to a stage world whose only answer is to turn off the lights and lower the curtain (142). The father plays Black's role, but he questions from the beginning the value of any of his "forms." Yet after the father dies, his son "talks" to him, imagining the "breath of God" passing from generation to generation, a mystical human connection across the ravages of history. The father's ultimate gift to his son is a tenuous hope that meaning has not fully abandoned the "forms" (4). Unlike Black's God, the universe of this novel has, apparently, given the father the words sufficient to keep hope alive.

The debate at the heart of McCarthy's moral universe is fairly simple: either there is some transcendent "spiritual truth" that is apprehended through religious symbols, or there is none, in which case all symbols and forms are "emptied" and all color is leached from the universe. Many of the novels pose the debate and the first, more hopeful vision, as in *The Sunset Limited,* loses out against the darker vision. But that is not always the case. *The Road* presents an authorial figure who straddles both sides of the debate yet finally chooses to commit himself to the more hopeful vision. In this way, the father defines authorship as identifying religious imagery and "translating" that imagery, and so he becomes a transmitter of stories whose moral obligation is to define the world in terms of sacred images (35).

For the father, the act of transmission is his (and the world's) only defense of humanity, a bulwark against death, and the boy represents the vessel into which he pours these stories. This vessel will become the next prophet-author who will carry the "word of God" into the void of the postapocalyptic future (4). The father pictures the boy as a "chalice, good to house a god" and as a "tiny paradise," and later he sees the boy ahead of him on the road "glowing in that waste like a tabernacle" (64, 126, 230). All of these images are of religious vessels that "house" God—a chalice (such as the Holy Grail with the healing blood of Christ) and a paradise (where God walked on earth) and a tabernacle (a construction meant to house God himself). The boy, then, is imagined in terms of religious "forms" that bring God's presence and healing to humankind, but those forms are meaningless if there is, in fact, no God to be housed in them. The father lies awake one night watching the boy in the light of their campfire and begins to "sob uncontrollably but it wasnt about death. He wasnt sure what it was about but he thought it was about beauty or about goodness" (109). The haunting question for the father, then, is whether or not his quest to imbue the boy with stories of goodness and of God is meaningful. At the beginning of the novel, the father claims, "If he [the boy] is not the word of God God never spoke" (4). That, of course, is precisely the question. The boy is either a form drenched in sacramental meaning, or "God never spoke" and the form is meaningless.

The father may therefore be agnostic regarding the efficacy of his storytelling, but his *purpose* in telling stories is always clear: he believes that heroism can be preserved—or created anew—only through the transmission of archaic ideals enshrined in old symbols and narratives. Even in the absence of real-world references, the novel suggests that such symbols and narratives mysteriously possess meaning. The father tells stories that transmit hero identity to the boy, defining goodness and heroism in ways that seem irrelevant and hopelessly outdated in this ash-covered world. But somehow the boy comprehends the world of the stories and behaves as though that fictional world is more real than his external reality. For example, when the father kills the cannibal, his son later questions, "Are we still the good guys?" (56, 65). The boy critiques his father's definition of "good guys," pointing out that "in the stories we're always helping people and we dont help people" (225). The disparity between the idealism of the stories and the brutal reality in which they live troubles the boy. This disparity indicates that the idealistic definition of goodness the father offers his child may be impossible to achieve, but the child's recognition of that disparity offers hope for his future; if the boy can recognize the connection between belief and actions, then he has the capacity to choose to embody goodness in his future. The boy recognizes his role and actively acknowledges it. When the father strips a would-be thief and leaves him naked, the boy cries. The father tells him to stop crying, but the boy claims that he has to cry, that his role is to "worry" about "everything" (218). The boy, in other words, viscerally comprehends the messianic role he has been raised to play—the role of a savior of human life, but also, even more importantly, of human dignity.

The Road's depiction of heroism and morality is exceptional in the context of the rest of McCarthy's corpus, since his novels in general are peopled with characters who do not even attempt to save others, such as Culla Holme, who watches in silence as a pig herder falls off a cliff (*OD* 218). And in *The Sunset Limited,* White asserts that "people are not worth saving," even if they could be saved, which he doubts (40). Characters such as Billy Parham, by contrast, engage in desperate quests to save she-wolves, brothers, and friends—and yet they fail at their attempts at salvation. Some characters survive, including Suttree in *Suttree* and the child in *The Road,* but they wander into dangerous and nebulous worlds with no guarantee that their fragile belief in the importance of human connection will survive. Ultimately, these bleak literary worlds are unalleviated by any concrete promise of redemption. People die; the world is vanishing. And along with the vanishing world, symbols and stories falter and fade. However, the efficacy of the father's quest is symbolically justified by the symbolism of regeneration at the end of the novel. Humankind, the novel proposes, may yet survive, and with it religious symbols able to bring meaning (a concept synonymous with "God" in the novel) back to the human experience. But survival, if it is possible, will be achieved only through the sacred ritual of storytelling.

This interpretation of the novel's symbols and the significance of storytelling may seem rather naively optimistic, given the general darkness of McCarthy's corpus. However, it may be overly simplistic to focus only on the darkness in McCarthy's novels. Gary Wallace says that, in an unofficial interview with McCarthy in 1992, when the subject of religious experience came up, McCarthy's response surprised him. Discussing the mystery of religious experience, Wallace says, "[h]e [McCarthy] ended with the thought that our inability to see spiritual truth is the greater mystery" (135). Characters in McCarthy's novels display little confidence in mystical experiences, and they are not capable of "seeing" any fundamental truth in their uncertain worlds. But some of these men are drawn to religious symbolism as a means of representing a mystical meaningfulness, their own fumbling apprehension of "spiritual truth." The crucial question, then, becomes whether or not there is some spiritual reality that grants meaning to these religious symbols. For example, John Grady Cole's death scene in *Cities of the Plain* is depicted as a secular pietà. Billy Parham lifts up the dead body of John Grady (who died for a prostitute named Magdalena). He then looks up at the sky and questions, "Do you see this?" (261). Likewise, the father in *The Road* looks at his frail son, then looks up at the sky and cries, "Are you there? Damn you eternally have you no soul?" (10). In both of these novels, God's questioners have sufficient evidence on their side to support their indictments of the divine.

The divine, however, is not entirely undefended. Denis Donoghue, in his study of *Blood Meridian*, claims that McCarthy's literary world is like the Homeric epics, only darker—a world such as Nietzsche described, full of "'luxuriant, triumphant existence, which defies the good and the bad indifferently.' Or a demotic version of such a world" (268). On the one hand,

The Road seems to offer a literary universe similar to the one Donoghue describes. This gray landscape belongs to a blasted planet on which wild animals may be dead, but the humans are utterly feral. In such a world, religious symbols and images of regeneration and hope seem to be nothing more than beautiful delusions. But on the other hand, *The Road*'s narrative valuation of the father suggests that this universe may have more in common with *Suttree*'s. Donoghue argues that that novel is "the strongest of McCarthy's early novels because its sense of life is a sense of life more than the other novels imagine" (263). Like *Suttree, The Road* offers an affirmation of the human project. The very ferocity of this postapocalyptic devastation offers a backdrop against which the staunchness of the father's belief in the possibility of human goodness and his son's ethical instincts glows brightly.

In general, the most grotesque images in the novel are also the sites of its most profound arguments for the value of human life. This premise holds for many of McCarthy's novels. One of the most striking examples of the grotesque image used to affirm the sanctity of life is, of course, cannibalism. In McCarthy's fiction, cannibalism—and especially infant cannibalism—crops up several times. At the end of *Outer Dark*, for example, Culla Holme stumbles on a campsite where three wild men have killed the tinker and are playing with a small child who, readers discover, is the product of Culla's incestuous relationship with his sister. As Culla watches, one of the wild men slits the child's throat and begins to drink his blood. In the next scene, Rinthy Holme, searching for her stolen baby, finds a dead campfire with "the charred billets and chalk bones, the little calcined ribcage" of the devoured child in the ashes (237). In *The Road*, the son stumbles upon the abandoned campfire of one of the roaming blood cults. He finds a fire over which is hung "a charred human infant headless and gutted and blackening on the spit" (167). Both of these images are presented with horrifying simplicity. Like the crawdad-infested dead puppy in McCarthy's short story "A Drowning Incident," these devoured infants bear their own mute testimony to the human race's capacity for cruelty. Their very muteness, however, suggests the importance of language, the testimony of the living. Dead flesh, for McCarthy, symbolizes the dead sign, language stripped of its ability to mean. In these novels, however, the ultimate horror is not the dead corpse but that the dead are left to speak for themselves.

The dead human form consistently represents language in McCarthy's corpus. For example, in *The Sunset Limited*, White claims that he decided to commit suicide because it was his birthday. Birthdays, he says, "are dangerous. Like Christmas. Ornaments hanging from the trees, wreaths from the doors, and bodies from steampipes all over America" (6). He later equates these dangling bodies with language—and all symbols—shorn of meaning. "The truth is," he explains, "[t]hey are shapes only. A train, a wall, or a world. Or a man. A thing dangling in senseless articulation in a howling void" (139). Because the human form is so frequently associated with the linguistic sign, it is no surprise that characters who find no significance in humanity likewise demonstrate no interest in language. And so unethical characters, like Culla Holme, watch the dead in silence. Ethical characters protest the dead human form, as does Billy crying over John Grady's body, or the boy crying over the devoured baby in *The Road*. The word becomes flesh in these novels, but that radical incarnation is offered up with striking narrative reticence, the grotesque image given contradictory interpretations by the stories' characters. According to White, or to Ely in *The Road*, such symbols mean nothing. Even the characters who react in outrage at such visions of violated human flesh seem to recognize that they live in a universe stacked against them. Everyone is dying. Their worlds are decaying before their eyes. At the same time, however, their valuation of flesh and word is granted a mystical significance.

The mystical aspect of language is perhaps its most critical attribute in terms of understanding what language represents in McCarthy's corpus. For instance, the final paragraph of *The Road* describes a memory of fish, living creatures who represent some of the earliest evolutionary forms that gave birth to a world that is now destroyed. The fish, then, are images of "a thing which could not be put back. Not be made right again," but at the same time those fish represent the arc of history that has gone between, and so they are also images of "all things [. . .] older than man and they hum[. . .] of mystery" (241). Kennedy, in his book review, claims that there is a "scarcity of thought" in the novel that makes readers "wish that old humming mystery had a lyric" (par. 15). The point of the mystery, however, is that it is prelingual, existing before the ravages of humanity. The novel's revelations of the father's thoughts demonstrate his awareness of old symbols, such as the fish, and the moral failure of the human race that has destroyed those symbols. But the father also seems to recognize the mysterious force of those symbols of life, a life-affirming energy that burns on after the physical sign has been destroyed. Even in the absence of the physical remnants, like the now-dead fish, the father is able to transmit a primordial recognition of the value and continuity of life to his son. The novel thus implies that lyrics are beside the point as long as there is a voice to hum. At one point, the father recalls a preapocalypse memory in which, as a child about his son's age, he stumbled on a group of half-wild men burning a nest of snakes. In the memory, he claims that the men burned the snakes "having no remedy for evil but only the image of it as they conceived it to be" (159). The men acted out an archaic association of the snake with evil and so indicated, for the father, that humans possess an inherent compulsion to infuse symbols with meaning in order to make sense of the world, to create an illusion of structure, a metanarrative to grant their lives significance (159). The depravity of the human race has reached its culmination in *The Road*, but it has not yet succeeded in defeating humanity's latent and primal instincts for good. The "mysterious humming" at the end of the novel, then, may represent humanity's nascent goodness, a tiny seed holding the promise of regeneration.

In his interview with Winfrey, McCarthy addresses the relationship between the "mysterious" force of language and humankind's instinctive recognition of morality. He explains that he believes there is a Jungian-sounding universal "subconscious" that existed "before language" but which must "understand language" (McCarthy, interview). What McCarthy describes as "pre-linguistic" forces haunt this novel. In general, it is easy to recognize the primal forces of evil surging through McCarthy's writing, but the frailer forces for good are present as well. McCarthy also points out in the same interview a section in *The Road* in which the word "upright" is punned in a way that illustrates the mysterious connection between language and morality. In this section, the father stands in the absolute dark of a night sheltered from all moon and stars, remaining "upright" only because of "the vestibular calculations in his skull" (13). The father realizes that if evolution has given his inner ear the means to keep his body physically upright in all that dark, then he may possess as well the inherent capacity to remain "upright" in the other sense of the word as well. He is morally vertiginous, questioning, "Upright to what?" but he remains physically and spiritually vertical nevertheless (13). McCarthy's connection of moral "uprightness" with evolutionary instincts suggests that an instinctive rectitude is buried as deep in the father's DNA as is his capacity to kill another human being.

After his father dies, the boy in *The Road* meets a traveling group of people. He wants to know if they are "good guys," and so he asks what is, in his mind, the single defining litmus test for goodness: "Do you eat people?" (239). The boy's standards of morality may seem a bit basic, but in the world of this novel, it comes as no surprise that these people, who are not cannibals, are also believers in the mystical value of human life and in the divine capacity of words and stories to create human connections that reach even beyond the boundaries of death (240). White's claim in *The Sunset Limited* that the "darker version" of history is always correct is consistent with the bleak revisionist view of *Blood Meridian*, a novel based on historical sources that portrays history as a juggernaut of senseless violence, a meaning-crushing brutality that shatters images and dreams of spiritual beauty or sense-making (*TSL* 112). But that devastated vision of history is pitted against a corollary vision in *The Road*. A common theme in McCarthy's corpus is sacramental, expiatory acts of violence that create the possibility for redemption. As Tim Parrish points out (citing René Girard), "the sacred becomes the means by which the community controls violence and therefore preserves itself" (36). However, *The Road* modifies McCarthy's traditional use of violence, subjugating the brutal to the beautiful. Violence becomes important only insofar as it is the fire of "pain" out of which grace and beauty are forged. The father verbalizes this contrasting vision of the sacred when he claims, "All things of grace and beauty such that one holds them to one's heart have a common provenance in pain" (46). In this apprehension of reality, the ugliness of the known world becomes a "proving" forge for those ephemeral yet all-important glimpses of goodness that haunt it.

The Road's concept of human depravation and suffering as a "proving" forge for goodness and beauty is an argument that is both compelling and too easily overlooked, since this idea crystallizes for the first time in this novel, out of all of McCarthy's works. Despite its almost overwhelming brutality, then, *The Road* offers an unusual corollary to the majority of McCarthy's dark corpus. The novel consistently draws attention to the father's inner struggles, bearing witness to his heroism. Even more importantly, the father's imperative mood drives the oracular rhythms of the text. Out of his damaged soul, the father manages to construct a fragile future for his son, and out of his own moral culpability, the father reinforces his son's messianic ethics. The novel's systematic narrative shifts indicate the prophetic power of story to weave hope out of chaos. In this universe, even if there "is no god," there are still prophets who live as though a god existed to give their stories meaning. As he lies dying, the father tells his son, "There is no prophet in the earth's long chronicle who's not honored here today" (233). Faced with his own mortality and the fragile hope of a single boy heading out into a barren world, the father suggests that, in the end, all prophecy comes down to this: the ability to find, even in a postapocalyptic world, a "strange beauty" burning in the dark (87).

CONCLUSION
FINDING HEROISM THROUGH EMPATHY IN McCARTHY'S NOVELS

> You tell me that my brother is my salvation? My salvation? Well then damn him. Damn him in every shape and form and guise. Do I see myself in him? Yes. I do. And what I see sickens me.
> —CORMAC MCCARTHY, *The Sunset Limited*

> What I need most is to learn charity. That most of all.
> —CORMAC MCCARTHY, *The Stonemason*

> Readers, which is to say living people, bring empathy to the novel, and they alone have the capacity to convert their emotional fusion with the denizens of make-believe worlds into actions on behalf of real others.
> —SUZANNE KEEN, *Empathy and the Novel*

In the account of his 1992 interview with McCarthy, Richard B. Woodward describes *Blood Meridian* (1985) as "the bloodiest book since *The Iliad*." He points out, though, that in contrast to *The Iliad*, "[t]here are no heroes in this vision of the American frontier" (7). There are no traditional heroes anywhere in McCarthy's corpus. Even "all-american cowboys" such as John Grady Cole betray cousins, defile virgins, and kill people (*COTP* 3). The overwhelming darkness of McCarthy's novels, their often deranged and psychopathic characters, and their typically cold and distant narrators exacerbate the already stunning violence. The novels' most vivid and immediate impression upon readers is of a universe roiling with misfits and bloodshed. Even in the austere and sterile descriptions of place for which McCarthy is known, nature seems to look on uncaring. Jay Ellis claims that in these "photographic" descriptions of nature, "we [. . .] glimpse a world given no distinction, no anthropocentric resonance. And indeed, McCarthy regularly warns us away from anthropocentric consolations." Yet in this dark cosmos, the narrative gaze is shot through with glimpses of human compassion, pity, nobility, and hope. Twin tensions tug at the heart of this literary cosmos: the implacable pull of the natural world away from "anthropocentric consolations" and the opposite draw in the direction of fundamental human kindness (265). Although they are few and far between, characters who affirm the value of life, both human and animal, are granted narrative powers, their perspectives merging with the "camera angle" that controls the text. For this reason, images of affinity and connection in McCarthy's novels should not be underestimated. This study has demonstrated a systematic association of narrative perspective with characters' moral choices, desires for affinity, and expressions of compassion that bear witness to primal urges to "do right" in contrast to the atavistic depravity surrounding them (*ATPH* 331). Furthermore, this stylistic device—associating particular narrative points of view with moral characters—suggests that one of narrative's functions generally is to require readers to practice empathy, making the act of reading and the practice of narration moral acts in themselves.

McCarthy's fiction goes so far as to require readers to recognize an ineluctable bond between thematic explorations of the importance of empathy and the linguistic forms that encourage readers themselves to practice empathy as they identify with moral subjectivities. Examining the bond between aesthetic forms and the practice of empathy is not, of course, anything new. Martha Nussbaum expounds on precisely this link, and in *Poetic Justice: The Literary Imagination and Public Life,* she claims that novels construct meaningful empathy through assuming an established distance or estrangement between the reader and the fictional character. Therefore, the realistic novel, she says, creates characters who demonstrate "general human concerns," permitting the reader to empathetically engage with the characters. These universally recognizable characters are then superimposed against depictions of society or social concepts in such a way that the reader is estranged enough to critique those social structures, questioning their assumptions and functions. Thus, she explains, "the very structure of the interaction between the text and its imagined reader invites the reader to see how the mutable features of society and circumstance bear on the realization of shared hopes and desires" (7). But in McCarthy's novels, characters demonstrating "general human concerns" are rare specimens; most are bizarre, behaviorally inexplicable characters who seem to possess no reflective or evaluative consciousness. McCarthy essentially strips his literary universe of the familiar, but, as Nussbaum predicts, against this uncommonly darkly fantastic landscape, the few glimpses of familiar human drives and desires for connection, respect, love, and home are all the more profound. These brief moments are in many ways reiterations of a very basic assertion that the root of ethics lies in meaningful, moral connections between people. Empathy, then, becomes that simple yet profound expression of the desire for human connectedness that lies at the heart of an individual's ethical engagement with the world.

Yet it is not sufficient to merely recognize that certain characters in McCarthy's corpus demonstrate somewhat primitive impulses toward human connectedness. Such a reading may suggest that McCarthy's novels are more nuanced than some critics have found them, but it does little to explicate or resolve the tension between those few ethically aware characters and the overwhelming amoral or immoral energies of the novelistic worlds. For example, in *Cormac McCarthy and the Myth of American Exceptionalism,* John Cant systematically explores McCarthy's devastating critique of the American—and, more generally, the human—mythology of inherent goodness. Cant points out that *The Road* is an essentially more affecting novel than many of McCarthy's earlier works because of "the loving nature of the relationship between father and son, the complete reversal of the oedipal structure" of his other novels (277). The tenderness of this novel is thematic, but it also plays out in the "inner voice of the main protagonist," which stylistically merges, Cant claims, with "that of the author" (267–68). Despite such narrative and thematic intimacy, however, Cant believes that the novel "expresses the paradox that lies at the heart of all serious pessimistic literature: its literary passion defies the very emptiness that it proclaims. It declares the inevitability of cultural entropy, but is itself an example of cultural vitality" (280).

Cant has identified the undeniably knotty paradox regarding empathy that resides at the heart of McCarthy's fiction. As Ellis points out, narrative attention to the bleakness of the natural world and the atavistic depravity of the human animal undermines any reader's attempts to find "anthropocentric consolations" in the novels (264). But the father's love for his child in *The Road* cannot be reduced to mere animal instinct, especially since the textual revelations of the father's interior life encourage readers to empathize with, sympathize with, and valorize his despairing yet heroic ambitions. This novel's undeniable gesture toward human nobility certainly seems to suggest a level of "consolation," but is that consolation held in irreducible tension with the pessimistic weight of the rest of McCarthy's works? Studying empathy in McCarthy's novels on a purely thematic level may be doomed to end in messy tangles and internal contradictions. Examining the stylistic methodology of the novels in concert with the thematic structures, however, suggests that McCarthy systematically balances an anthropological humility with an equal emphasis on individual moral responsibility. In the course of history, the human race may be less dramatically important than most people like to think, but in the immediate present, human beings are ethically obligated to recognize the value of life by behaving in ways that promote the well-being of others.

The practice of empathy, then, is an undeniably tricky task in McCarthy's universe, but it is, despite its complications and limitations, a profoundly important task. In fact, in this literary cosmos, empathy seems to be the most important task required of humanity. From his first published short stories, all of McCarthy's characters, from the demonic to the heroic, struggle with the question of human connection. Some characters, such as Judge Holden in *Blood Meridian* and White in *The Sunset Limited*, reject their need for others, constructing instead a universe in which humankind is both pointless and heading quickly for extinction. Other characters, such as Billy Parham in the Border Trilogy and the father in *The Road*, recognize such a fundamental need for others that they define themselves by the ones they love and accept no version of the universe in which the lives (and deaths) of their loved ones are not infinitely valuable. In some texts, these competing views are presented in opposition without mediation, for example, the dialogue between White and Black in *The Sunset Limited*. Both men acknowledge the connectedness of the human race, but for White that mystical unity is cause only for despair. He likens the world to a concentration camp, suggesting that depravity encrusts the moral DNA of humankind. Any attempt to rid humanity of its moral baggage is ultimately futile. "The efforts that people undertake to improve the world," White says, "invariably make it worse" (122). Black, in contrast, believes that there exists a "pure ore," a "forever thing," at the core of all humans—a sameness that connects them. According to Black, that sameness is "Jesus understood as that gold [ore]," the sameness, in other words, of a mystical divinity in all human forms (94–95). "And if I said there aint no way for Jesus to be ever man without ever man bein Jesus," he explains, "then I believe that might be a pretty big heresy. But that's all right" (95). McCarthy's universe is so dark that the few feeble gestures toward morality stand out in bold relief. The novels proffer no platitudes and permit no easy consolations about the human condition, but they do suggest that the Blacks of the world who try to save the suffering, who even mourn suicidal misanthropes, are in the final analysis heroic.

The competing worldviews of different characters, such as Black and White, elucidate the competing worldviews held in tension throughout McCarthy's fiction—a tension that is irreducible but not uninterpretable. These characters describe opposing viewpoints on the importance of the human condition and, consequently, the importance of empathy—the primary factor in compassion, justice, and all other attributes of morality. The two viewpoints are contradictory, and in McCarthy's literary world, this contradiction cannot be erased, because it represents the fundamental choice at the core of human existence. Human freedom derives from the capacity of the individual to choose only one of the two viewpoints. At the same time, however, McCarthy's novels do not merely present an unresolved contention. Instead, the novels describe these competing viewpoints while systematically privileging characters who practice empathy.

McCarthy's treatment of empathy is consistent with contemporary linguistic research on the nature and function of empathy in communication. The linguistic field of pragmatics—the study of how language functions in practical, real-world conditions—proposes that effective communication between humans is possible only when speakers recognize and compensate for the inability of other persons to fully express themselves. Basically, pragmatics assumes that there are always missing components in language and that communication can occur only when one speaker infers or reconstructs another speaker's meaning. Pragmatics thus suggests that the ability to empathize—to put oneself in another's place—is at the heart of effective communication. McCarthy seems to be aware of this pragmatic effect, and he articulates an overarching argument through his fiction about the role of empathy in communication and the value of communication in general, through characters who consciously engage or disengage from empathetic encounters with others. If linguists have identified a capacity to infer meaning from implicit information as the root of pragmatic competence, then McCarthy's fiction rests upon an assumption of pragmatically competent readers of literature. Asserting this viewpoint, Wolfgang Iser, in his examination of the reader's participation in and experience of an aesthetic text, argues for a recognition of the pragmatic function of reading, namely, that "the study of literary work should concern not only the actual text but also, and in equal measure, the actions involved in responding to that text"

(20–21). Scholars in the field of pragmatic linguistics often exclude literary language from their study because such language is not, strictly speaking, "practical" language, but Iser nevertheless claims that the "conventions" guiding pragmatic communication are the same as those guiding a reader's interpretation of a text (55).

McCarthy's texts demonstrate an awareness of the compensatory function of pragmatic linguistics, perhaps most identifiably in his characters' dialogues. Some characters empathetically engage with the other speaker in order to ensure effective communication, while other characters reject the notion that effective communication is possible, or even desirable. The characters who are able to effectively communicate—characters who are "pragmatically competent"—are those who value human connection; of course, the reverse is true of the characters who resist effective communication. Linguist Diane Blakemore describes linguistic pragmatics as a study of "how hearers are able to recover the intended propositional content from utterances missing constituents" (19). Blakemore uses the term "pragmatic competence" to refer to the human capacity to infer meaning from missing information. As an example, if two people are standing at a bus stop and Person A says, "It's coming," Person B may have no difficulty understanding A's statement, even though the pronoun has no antecedent and the directional verb "coming" likewise has no referents (Person A did not say what was coming from where to where). Pragmatics understands that human beings constantly make inferences to fill in the gaps left by missing information. In the previous example, Person B would have to infer quite a bit of information, but B may respond without hesitation, automatically compensating for the absent constituent information in A's statement. A pragmatic understanding of how people communicate leads Blakemore to assert that "the fundamental ability in communication is not linguistic encoding and decoding, but the ability to derive inferences which result in assumptions which are entertained as metarepresentations of other people's thoughts, desires, and intentions" (71). McCarthy's texts often play with this linguistic principle, sometimes humorously but often with potentially devastating results. For instance, in *The Sunset Limited,* Black blames on language his failure to convince White of the value of White's own existence. Black asks (presumably of God), "If you wanted me to help him how come you didnt give me the words?" (142). His assumption here is that sufficient words can coerce a propositional understanding in the hearer. But such an assumption, Blakemore says, seems to be pragmatically incorrect; "[I]t is not clear at all," she claims, "that anyone can have a controllable effect on someone's actual thoughts" (68). McCarthy thus often creates dialogues in which a speaker fundamentally fails to control the listener's interpretation of the semantic content of the speaker's propositions.

Blakemore argues that pragmatics is primal—that is, the semantics (the meaning) of a spoken sentence does not encode its actual meaning *unless* the listener engages pragmatically, choosing to infer in the sentence a "metarepresentation," a reconstruction, of the speaker's intent. McCarthy's texts elegantly refuse to permit one character to coerce another into communication, preserving a fictional universe in which the human choice to participate in or to reject communication is primary. At the same time, however, McCarthy describes pragmatic competence and incompetence through subtle yet profound indications of empathetic connection. In his fiction, dialogues are often pared down to fragments of constituent information, leaving the listeners in the text—and the readers of the text—to choose to infer meaning or to fail to participate in the pragmatic re-creation of the speaker's intent. In these literary universes, people are often either pragmatically blind, such as the kid who refuses to understand Judge Holden (or is too stupid to understand him) in *Blood Meridian*, or they intentionally opt out of a pragmatic sense-making dialogue, such as White in *The Sunset Limited*.

An example of pragmatically incompetent communication occurs in *No Country for Old Men* (2005) when Chigurh explains to Carla Jean why he must kill her. Their dialogue demonstrates a fundamental failure on her part to understand the semantic assumptions he makes. When Chigurh says that he gave his word to Moss that he would kill Carla Jean, she says, "He's dead. My husband is dead." Chigurh responds, "Yes. But my word is not dead. Nothing can change that" (257). The two characters demonstrate verbally that they are at cross-purposes. Chigurh believes that human action and even human language are fated and are out of the individual's control. Carla Jean seems to think that free will is the fundamental defining characteristic of humanity. Their dialogue continues and Chigurh finally suggests that he toss a coin to determine her fate. She calls heads, but the coin is tails:

He lifted his hand away. The coin was tails.
I'm sorry.
[. . .]

> She looked away. You make it like it was the coin. But you're the one.
> It could have gone either way.
> The coin didnt have no say. It was just you.
> Perhaps. But look at it my way. I got here the same way the coin did. (258)

The dialogue demonstrates their different sets of pragmatic assumptions. Chigurh sees the coin toss as a cosmic arbiter. Fate, for him, is the final deciding word, and there is no difference between his presence in Carla Jean's home with a loaded gun and a coin falling tails. So when he says, "I'm sorry," he expects the expression to convey a fairly straightforward semantic meaning, namely, that he sincerely wishes the fates had decided otherwise. His subsequent comments reflect his recognition that the woman is innocent and does not deserve death, and by saying "I'm sorry," he believes that he is acknowledging the inherent sadness of the situation and is voicing pity for her death. Carla Jean, however, sees his proclamation of sympathy ("I'm sorry") as an insult. Action, for her, derives from human will, not from some mystical, preordaining fate. Chigurh tells Carla Jean to "look at it my way," but she refuses to join in his pragmatic assumptions.

In fact, all of McCarthy's most flamboyantly evil characters are articulate, erudite men who are nevertheless pragmatically incompetent. Judge Holden, one of the most eloquent men in McCarthy's corpus, is also one of the most spectacularly pragmatically incompetent speakers. At one point in *Blood Meridian*, Holden speaks to some religiously inclined prospectors. He claims that books lie but that God "speaks in stones and trees, the bones of things." The judge continues to use his elevated diction to press his point "until they were right proselytes of the new order whereupon he [Holden] laughed at them for fools" (116). Like Chigurh, Holden practices a manner of speaking in which illocution does not, cannot, and should not result in pragmatically competent communication. In other words, these men demonstrate a *capacity* to use language effectively: they are persuasive, eloquent men whose illocutions are highly functional. But—and herein lies their fatal flaw—they do not attribute any significance to their illocutionary prowess. That is, the linguistic cosmos created by evil characters such as Chigurh (and Judge Holden and the others of their ilk in McCarthy's corpus) is one in which linguistic competence is irrelevant. They speak, but they do not care whether they enable their audiences to join in their pragmatic assumptions, for the sole reason that, in their linguistic universes, language has no relevant meaning. Words, like coins controlled by external forces rather than by the human interlocutor, bear no ethical responsibility, and any possibility for human connection or engagement that words may bring about is meaningless—as, according to these men, human life itself is pointless.

Thus, however elegantly they may phrase their discourse, Chigurh and Holden are not truly pragmatically effective communicators. They may practice pragmatically effective language, but they undermine the fundamental purpose of effective communication: empathetic engagement, the first step toward ethical behavior. Such a failure illuminates the importance of the reader's role in understanding and engaging with a text. Nussbaum points out that ethical behavior is possible in a world devoid of literature, but literature, as it sparks imagination and "summons powerful emotions," has the capacity to engage not just the mind but also the heart of the reader, providing an effective catalyst for the transformation from ethical mental inclinations to actively moral behavior (5). McCarthy's novels demonstrate her assertion as they point to the devastating void at the center of pragmatic language that fails to engage the emotions and that consequently fails to connect two human beings in a meaningful encounter. By contrasting the empty pragmatic competence and egregiously unethical behavior of men such as Chigurh and the judge with the fumbling yet luminous pragmatic competence hallowed by strongly ethical behavior in men such as John Grady Cole and the father in *The Road*, McCarthy's novels underscore the fascinating link between ethical reading and ethical behavior.

McCarthy's novels, in other words, suggest that ethically effective communication requires an emotional authenticity in addition to the ability to construct empathetic engagement. That is, Chigurh provides an example of a man capable of constructing the chimera of a pragmatically competent dialogue—he asks for Carla Jean's empathetic response, to "see things" his way—but his capacity to feel empathy, far less sympathy, in return seems to be nonexistent (*NCFOM* 258). Because his dialogue lacks emotional authenticity, his flamboyant competence as a speaker is effectively nullified. The importance of emotional authenticity in addition to pragmatic competence is exemplified by the contrast between articulate men such as Chigurh and Holden and such pragmatically competent characters as Cornelius Suttree, who is both a magnificently pragmatically competent speaker and an individual capable of authentic emotional feeling. In "Suttree, Linguistic Chameleon," William C. Spencer claims that Suttree demonstrates effective "code switching"—changing his dialect—in order to effectively communicate with his audience. He cites as evidence the passage where Suttree asks the uneducated Willard to "'cast [. . .] off for us.'" Willard blankly asks, "'Do what?'" and Suttree responds, "'How about untying us'" (*Suttree* 321; Spencer 23). In this section, Suttree's rephrased statement indicates that he understands Willard's inability to effectively infer his meaning. He switches his terminology in order to ensure effective communication. But this capacity to communicate effectively is used, typically, with the purpose of reinforcing bonds of communication. Unlike Chigurh, Suttree seeks actual engagement with his illocutionary audience. An even more profound example of the ethical implications of authentic feeling linked to pragmatic communication is found in the father in *The Road*. In many of his dialogues, the father concludes by asking, "Okay?" and pausing until the son responds, "Okay" (e.g., 214, 235). In his world, it is of paramount importance that his son be able to form a "metarepresentation" of his thoughts. The father's role as a story transmitter works only if the son comprehends and can recreate the semantic import of his words. The father thus fuses his love for his son with the exigency of spoken communication. Unlike Chigurh and Judge Holden, the father cares desperately about being understood.

Thus, in McCarthy's texts, there are two types of speakers. One type sees illocution as an action that happens in a void, needing and expecting no successful transmission of semantic content. The other type self-adjusts, repeats information, and uses verbal comprehension checks ("Okay?"), practicing and expecting pragmatic competence. These two types of speakers linguistically demonstrate their opposing views on the significance of human connection. For Judge Holden, the right order of the universe requires a "winner" out of a field of "losers." Human connection is only a fantasy, at best a temporary distraction from grim reality. Suttree seems initially to practice Holden's philosophy. At the beginning of *Suttree*, he has rejected his old society, but he struggles with his isolation. Finally, through his fumbling "fathering" of Harrogate and his brief attempts at connection with others, he learns to grieve death, implicitly recognizing and valuing human connection. A ragpicker with whom he has spoken on occasion dies. When Suttree finds the ragpicker's body, he castigates the dead man for dying alone. "You have no right to represent people this way," he tells the corpse. "A man is all men. You have no right to your wretchedness" (422). The contrast between Suttree's and Holden's worldviews may be reduced to a simple recognition of the relative importance of human connection. When Suttree believes he is dying, he begins to declaim his isolated lifestyle, concluding, "I know all souls are one and all souls lonely" (459). His recognition of the loneliness of the human condition underscores the vast gulf between his world and that of Holden's, a world where, according to the judge, "[t]here is room on the stage for one beast and one alone" (*BM* 331). In Suttree's world, the loneliness of the human condition requires the moral individual to expend effort to combat isolation. Holden, on the other hand, suggests that the most evolved individual recognizes the loneliness of the human condition and exacerbates it. Holden consequently concludes the narrative of *Blood Meridian* by reducing the staged population to one dancing beast—himself. Suttree, in contrast, flees Knoxville at the end of his novel, but his flight is, metaphorically, from the waste of human despair. As he climbs into the truck of a passerby, he imagines himself fleeing the "slaverous" hounds of some mythical huntsman. He is fleeing isolation, epitomized by death, an action precipitated by his recognition of kindness in the blue eyes of a child who offers him water and in a man who stops to pick him up when he has not signaled. The narrative makes a point of the undeserved grace inherent in a single act of kindness: "A car had stopped for Suttree, he'd not lifted a hand" (471). This act of unmerited kindness seems to demand a mystical gratitude on Suttree's part, a ritual recognition of a benevolent "other" in the universe.

The contrasting linguistic competence of Suttree and Holden reflects their corresponding divergence in worldviews, a contrast that is significant because it reflects the link between linguistic competence and morality in McCarthy's novels. The worldviews presented by both men seem to run as crosscurrents throughout McCarthy's corpus, but Suttree's worldview is the one that demonstrates pragmatic competence, suggesting that fiction—which functions based on a similar assumption of pragmatically competent engagement between text and reader—likewise privileges that worldview. The gratitude following a relatively minor act of kindness at the end of *Suttree* epitomizes the worldview practiced by McCarthy's pragmatically competent characters. In fact, for characters who value human life, gratitude seems to be the most natural and necessary emotional response in the face of effective human connection. In his interview with Oprah Winfrey, McCarthy indicates that he practices a worldview similar to Suttree's. McCarthy remarks at one point that he finds it important to be thankful, that life is "pretty good," all things considered, and that people should be grateful for that fact. When Winfrey asks to whom he is thankful, McCarthy humorously eludes giving a direct answer, concluding that gratitude is important even if "you don't know who you're being thankful to" (McCarthy, interview). The mystical gratitude McCarthy describes in the interview does not require the known existence of a benevolent divinity, just as an act of kindness does not lose its merit if the action's recipient fails to be grateful. For McCarthy's moral characters, pragmatic linguistics is an exercise of good faith. They speak in order to communicate and assume that communication is inherently valuable; and when they speak into a void, they assume an illocutionary audience. For example, after he has lost White, Black asks his silent God why that God did not help him save White's life; he concludes, though, "That's all right. If you never speak again you know I'll keep your word" (*TSL* 142). Billy calls the sky to witness when John Grady dies in *Cities of the Plain*, and the son speaks to his father's corpse in *The Road*, telling the dead body, "I'll talk to you every day" (240). These characters practice a radical pragmatics. For them, human connection matters so much that it is possible to pragmatically infer meaning, to construct a conversation, even when there is no other speaker speaking.

McCarthy's unflinching depictions of the universe do not grant any earthly paradise to the few moralists, idealists, and lovers who populate that world. But a consistent and overarching theme of the novels suggests that characters who value kindness are also characters who value pragmatically competent language—language that necessitates empathy and that produces effective communication. And the novels privilege those characters who value kindness by permitting their minds and thoughts to control the point of view and even, at times, the interpretive perspective of the text. The violence in McCarthy's novels is shocking and pervasive, but if this moral darkness shows the extremes to which humans will go to destroy others, the darkness also makes all the more evident the extremes to which other people will go to demonstrate pity, love, and mercy. As the wandering prophet in *Outer Dark* admits, "[t]he grace of God don't rest easy on a man" (226). The pilgrim explains his twisted theology, claiming that his cosmos is one in which Jesus loves "[t]he lame the halt and the blind"—the very ones "scarred with God's mercy. Stricken with his love" (226). But that uneasy grace, that "scarring" mercy, creates an oddly compelling aesthetics of empathy throughout McCarthy's corpus.

McCarthy's theology of empathy is expounded upon by several characters in different works. In all of his fiction, however, characters' descriptions of and responses to this theology remain consistent. Those characters who recognize the ineluctable bond between all living creatures practice empathy and exhibit gratitude whenever effective communication or connection occurs. Characters who reject the value of humanity, of course, criticize the practice of such a theology. White, for example, castigates Black for constructing a theology of "some sort of communal misery wherein one finds salvation by consorting among the loathsome" (*TSL* 128). Community, he says, is repulsive, which is why he has chosen death, a place where there is "[n]o community. My heart warms just thinking about it" (136). Black, of course, resists White's commentary, instead claiming that his only consolation is in this "communal misery." Black's "communal misery" in which lie the seeds of human salvation reflects Suttree's own theology of misery. At the end of *Suttree*, Suttree "lay in his chrysalis of gloom and made no sound, share by share sharing his pain with those who lay in their blood by the highwayside or in the floors of glass strewn taverns or manacled in jail. He said that even the damned in hell have the community of their suffering and he thought that he'd guessed out likewise for the living" (464). For Suttree, as for Black, the suffering of the sinners in hell can be metaphorically inverted into the proving forge of redemption. In community, the meaninglessness of suffering is transformed into something numinous, a quality the father in *The Road* describes as grace and beauty, which "have a common provenance in pain" (46). The characters who subscribe to this theology of suffering seem to believe that human empathy is the sole source of this-world redemption.

The fact that their perspectives at times control the text's point of view in turn creates narrative strategies that encourage readers to practice a similar empathy. In *The Road*, the father's first-person narrative passages require readers to experience an empathetic suffering that is truly hellacious, but it is possible that the postapocalyptic inferno of *The Road* is that place "wherein one finds salvation" (*TSL* 128). If any salvation is possible in *The Road*, of course, it resides in the same place where redemption hides in the Border Trilogy—in the capacity of individuals to recognize their own moral obligation to the world around them. And it is no accident that the characters whose thoughts are textually revealed—such as the father in *The Road* or John Grady Cole in the Border Trilogy—are characters who practice an empathetic engagement with humanity.

McCarthy's novels systematically reveal the internal worlds of characters who practice empathy, requiring readers to empathetically connect with those characters. The justification for examining narrative perspective in McCarthy's novels therefore resides in his formal attention to empathy attributions. That is, the narrative perspective structurally directs a reader's empathy toward moral characters while emotionally distancing readers from the immoral and the amoral. Susumu Kuno claims that "[e]mpathy is the speaker's identification, which may vary in degree, with a person/thing that participates in the event or state that he describes in a sentence" (206). In terms of "camera angles," Kuno describes how readers automatically identify with "given descriptors" (main characters in the subject position in a sentence). McCarthy associates the text's camera angles with characters in a manner that illuminates, humanizes, and makes sympathetic the moral inclinations or impulses of certain characters. This technique, of course, would not be so remarkable, nor would its effect be so profound, if McCarthy did not also systematically restrict the empathetic perspective. His fatalistic universe is scarred by violence, death, and despair. But his fiction both thematically and structurally draws attention to people who struggle against nihilism by affirming their affinity for community and for justice. Even in "Wake for Susan" (1959), the narrative emphasizes the importance of the empathetic perspective. Wes imagines himself kissing the long-dead Susan good night, and as he walks home (alone), he imagines "wind-tortured trees that sp[eak] in behalf of the stars" (4). These trees, on behalf of the stars, say, *"You walk here. Moonwarmed and wind-kissed, you walk here . . . for awhile"* (4). Wes's mental animation of the trees and the stars underscores his fierce belief in the ethical obligation of empathy. He mentally revivifies Susan in order to give her death the heart-wrenching grief it deserves, and he imagines the universe itself mimicking his behavior. The stars watch, pity, and mourn all the short-lived humans who stumble below, and because they have no voices, the trees speak for them, just as Wes speaks for Susan.

While some critics shy away from stylistic and structural criticism, McCarthy's novels seem to demand the reader's recognition of the integral relationship between form and content. The novels' intense stylistic resistance to revelations of interior life is meaningful only when that resistance is met by the few startling shifts into a character's consciousness. In an essay on the importance of formal analysis, Denis Donoghue claims that "form can not be evaded; it is the coherence of the work of art, 'however self-antagonistic and refracted, through which every work of art separates itself from the merely existing.' Form transfigures what otherwise merely exists, and by that transfiguration it maintains the validity of freedom" ("Teaching Literature" 13). The act of reading both the form and the thematic content of McCarthy's novels is an act that encourages readers to recognize the profound complexity of the human condition. The irreducible violence of these novels is both shocking and political. The regional and national history that gave birth to the scalpings, murders, and disfigurements plays out against a backdrop of consistent human depravity. The novels thus require their audience's recognition of their own immorality, in terms of their national history as well as of individual instincts. That fictional violence, however, is shot through with images of redemptive compassion and love, in a precarious narrative juggling act of bestiality and beauty. Although it is undeniably complex, the reader's experience of these novels need not end in a morass of ambiguity. An examination of McCarthy's narrative techniques demonstrates that the most violent characters are objectified and subject to judgment by being described through the long-distance lens of a removed narrator. Characters who practice empathy, however, are often depicted stylistically in a way that requires readers to empathetically engage with them. The novelistic technique of shifting between removed narration and subjective, interior narration is both political and ethical, a technique that demonstrates Donoghue's claim that "creative force is not a force alternative to form but itself the particular form of its erupting into being" ("Teaching Literature" 21).

In fact, a formal analysis of McCarthy's novels reinforces—and deepens—the instinctive reactions of many readers. In a personal-response essay reflecting on the impact of reading McCarthy's Border Trilogy, novelist Dagoberto Gilb writes that the men of these novels are "like John Wayne in his Old West movies [. . .] good—manly good" (115). Gilb seems to find the characters unproblematically good, albeit in a John Wayne sense—laconic, nonverbal, but deeply trustworthy. His assumption of morality in these novels is intriguing because literary critics of McCarthy's works are unlikely to find any of his characters possessing a soul of unconflicted "good," manly or otherwise. Clearly, McCarthy's works can be nothing less than deeply conflicted and deeply complex, but it is too simplistic to ignore luminous moments of heroism and hope, moments like the description of Billy's hand full of "God's plenty of signs and wonders," suggesting the possibility of recreative energy in an otherwise fundamentally dark place (COTP 291). There is a profound confidence in the human capacity to be moral in these novels, a confidence that Gilb recognizes and that an analysis of McCarthy's textual privileging of moral characters reinforces. In the end, all readers of these novels can identify a pervasive, if complicated, hope in the human race, personified by characters who heroically refuse to believe in a world where humanity has no value.

The complicated nature of this hope, of course, does not diminish its merit. On the contrary, McCarthy's theology of communal suffering seems to paint a picture in which hope is heroic only when it is practiced in the face of overwhelming despair. The "manly good" characters do demonstrate what seems initially to be a problematic and often morally tainted "goodness." They possess a disillusioned ethics, an uncertain and fragile belief in the worth of human life, transfixed between grief and love. However, a side remark White makes to Black suggests that these characters may be "manly good" precisely because of their conflicted hope (Gilb 115). White tells Black, "If you're just doing what you're supposed to then you dont get to be a hero." White makes this statement in order to suggest that, since Black apparently believes in a Jesus who sanctifies human life, his salvation of White is not moral but merely dutiful (*TSL* 4). Black, however, reminds White that his belief in a benevolent and meaning-granting deity hovers over a gulf of uncertainty. He says that "in this particular case" he acted out of a sense of brotherhood without any clear reason, only a strong and urgent need to act on the assumption that life is meaningful even without external evidence to support that belief (4–5). White's assumption is that heroism can only be classified as such if the term refers to actions carried out without any guarantee of their eventual success or of their inherent merit. The tragedy of the play's ending aptly demonstrates the failure of Black's quest, his inefficient actions based on an agnostic faith—qualities that, ironically, render his actions heroic in White's own estimation.

In McCarthy's novels, the flawed moral characters often face defeat, their attempts at morality fall short of any effective outcome, and they typically die in the end without any external evidence that their actions have a quantifiable merit. But by White's definition, all these characters who demonstrate acts of kindness or ethical awareness are heroes *because* they undergo epistemological crises and fail to act out the good they know they ought to do. And through narrative shifts into these characters' perspectives, readers are compelled to practice a literary empathy with these men. That literary empathy encourages readers to admit their own ethical obligations as they acknowledge the courage demonstrated by McCarthy's few broken men who struggle through a remarkably desolate world not with despair but with a fragile hope. Because of their empathetic encounters with these courageous characters, readers are then not permitted to find any excuse to relinquish their own hope or to cease the struggle to construct some sense of meaning in their lives. In the final analysis, McCarthy's blandishing descriptions of place depict this world as cold, vicious, and all but utterly destroyed. But, McCarthy suggests, as long as individuals capable of recognizing and acting upon their belief in the value of life and dignity still wander around, this apocalyptic waste is not entirely bereft of heroes. And if people are still capable of heroism, the world, though terribly damaged, cannot yet be doomed.

WORKS CITED

Arnold, Edwin T. "Naming, Knowing and Nothingness: McCarthy's Moral Parables." Arnold and Luce 41–67.
Arnold, Edwin T., and Diane C. Luce, eds. *Perspectives on Cormac McCarthy.* Jackson: UP of Mississippi, 1993.
Banfield, Ann. *Unspeakable Sentences: Narration and Representation in the Language of Fiction.* Boston: Routledge and Kegan Paul, 1982.
Bell, Vereen M. *The Achievement of Cormac McCarthy.* Baton Rouge: Louisiana State UP, 1988.
Bingham, Arthur. "Syntactic Complexity and Iconicity in Cormac McCarthy's *Blood Meridian.*" *Language and Literature* 20 (1995): 19–33.
Blakemore, Diane. *Relevance and Linguistic Meaning: The Semantics and Pragmatics of Discourse Markers.* Cambridge: Cambridge UP, 2002.
Boehme, Jacob. *The Way to Christ.* Trans. Peter Erb. New York: Paulist P, 1978.
Bowers, James. *Reading Cormac McCarthy's* Blood Meridian. Boise State University Western Writer's Series 139. Boise, ID: Boise State U, 1999.
Brickman, Barbara. "Imposition and Resistance in *The Orchard Keeper.*" Wallach, *Myth, Legend, Dust* 55–67.
Campbell, Joseph. *The Hero with a Thousand Faces.* Princeton, NJ: Princeton UP, 1972.
Cant, John. *Cormac McCarthy and the Myth of American Exceptionalism.* New York: Routledge, 2008.
Carr, Duane R. "The Dispossessed White as Naked Ape and Stereotyped Hillbilly in the Southern Novels of Cormac McCarthy." *Midwest Quarterly* 40.1 (Autumn 1998): 9–20.
Catechism of the Catholic Church (CCC). Libreria Editrice Vaticana. Mahwah, NJ: Paulist P, 1994.
Chamberlain, Samuel E. *My Confession.* New York: Harper, 1956.
Christman, Phil. "A Tabernacle in the Dark: On the Road with Cormac McCarthy." *Books and Culture: A Christian Review* 13.5 (Sept.–Oct. 2007): 40–42.
Cobb, William J. "*No Country for Old Men.*" *Houston Chronicle* 17 July 2005: 17.
Daugherty, Leo. "Gravers False and True: Blood Meridian as Gnostic Tragedy." Arnold and Luce 157–72.
Degh, Linda. "Folk Narrative." *Folklore and Folklife.* Ed. Richard M. Dorson. Chicago: U of Chicago P, 1972. 53–84.
Derrida, Jacques. *Writing and Difference.* Trans. Alan Bass. Chicago: U of Chicago P, 1978.
Donoghue, Denis. "Teaching *Blood Meridian.*" *The Practice of Reading.* New Haven: Yale UP, 1998. 258–77.

———. "Teaching Literature: The Force of Form." *New Literary History: A Journal of Theory and Interpretation* 30.1 (Winter 1999): 5–24.

Eaton, Mark A. "Dis(re)membered Bodies: Cormac McCarthy's Border Fiction." *Modern Fiction Studies* 49.1 (Spring 2003): 155–79.

Ellis, Jay. *No Place for Home: Spatial Constraint and Character Flight in the Novels of Cormac McCarthy.* New York: Routledge, 2006.

Fowler, Roger. *Linguistics and the Novel.* London: Methuen, 1977.

Frye, Steven. "Yeats' 'Sailing to Byzantium' and McCarthy's *No Country for Old Men*: Art and Artifice in the New Novel." *Cormac McCarthy Journal* 5.1 (2006): 27–41.

Gilb, Dagoberto. "The Border Trilogy by Cormac McCarthy." *Gritos.* Illus. Cesar A. Martinez. New York: Grove P, 2003. 114–21.

Giles, James R. "Teaching the Contemporary Naturalism of Cormac McCarthy's *Outer Dark*." *American Literary Naturalism Newsletter* 1.1 (2006): 2–7.

Grossman, Lev. "A Conversation between Cormac McCarthy and Joel and Ethan Coen." *Time* 29 Oct. 2007: 62–63.

Hillier, Russell M. "'In a Dark Parody' of John Bunyan's *The Pilgrim's Progress*: The Presence of Subversive Allegory in Cormac McCarthy's *Outer Dark*." *American Notes and Queries* 19.4 (2006): 52–59.

Holloway, David. *The Late Modernism of Cormac McCarthy.* Westport, CT: Greenwood P, 2002.

Irving, Washington. *The Legend of Sleepy Hollow and Other Stories [The Sketchbook of Geoffrey Crayon, Gent.].* New York: Penguin, 1978.

Iser, Wolfgang. *The Act of Reading: A Theory of Aesthetic Response.* Baltimore: Johns Hopkins UP, 1978.

Jarrett, Robert L. *Cormac McCarthy.* New York: Twayne, 1997.

———. "Genre, Voice and Ethos: McCarthy's Perverse 'Thriller.'" *Cormac McCarthy Journal* 5.1 (2005): 74–96.

Keen, Suzanne. *Empathy and the Novel.* Oxford: Oxford UP, 2007.

Kennedy, William. "Left Behind." *New York Times* 8 Oct. 2006. www.nytimes.com/2006/10/08/books/review/Kennedy.t.html.

Kirn, Walter. "*No Country for Old Men*: Texas Noir." *New York Times* 24 July 2005, late ed., Book Review sec.: 9.

Kreml, Nancy. "Stylistic Variations and Cognitive Restraint in *All the Pretty Horses*." *Sacred Violence: A Reader's Companion to Cormac McCarthy.* Vol. 2. Ed. Rick Wallach. El Paso: Texas Western P, 2002. 37–50.

Kuno, Susumu. *Functional Syntax: Anaphora, Discourse and Empathy.* Chicago: U of Chicago P, 1987.

Kushner, David. "Cormac McCarthy's Apocalypse." *Rolling Stone* 27 Dec. 2007. Online. DavidKushner.com.

Lanham, Richard A. *Analyzing Prose.* 2nd ed. London: Continuum P, 2003.

Luce, Dianne C. "Beyond the *Border*: Cormac McCarthy in the New Millenium." Paper presented at the conference "The Road Home: Cormac McCarthy's Imaginative Return to the South, 26–28 April 2007, Knoxville, TN. 1–11. www.lib.utk.edu/newfoundpress/pubs/mccarthy/dianneluceintroduction.pdf.

Martinez, Oscar J. *Troublesome Border*. Rev. ed. Tucson: U of Arizona P, 2006.

McCarthy, C. J. "A Drowning Incident." *Phoenix* Mar. 1960: 3–4.

———. "Wake for Susan." *Phoenix* Nov. 1959: 3–6.

McCarthy, Cormac. *All the Pretty Horses*. New York: Vintage International, 1992.

———. *Blood Meridian*. New York: Vintage International, 1992.

———. *Child of God*. New York: Vintage International, 1993.

———. *Cities of the Plain*. New York: Vintage International, 1999.

———. *The Crossing*. New York: Vintage International, 1995.

———. *No Country for Old Men*. New York: Knopf, 2005.

———. *The Orchard Keeper*. New York: Vintage International, 1993.

———. *Outer Dark*. New York: Vintage International, 1993.

———. *The Road*. New York: Knopf, 2006.

———. *The Stonemason: A Play in Five Acts*. New York: Vintage International, 1994.

———. *The Sunset Limited*. New York: Vintage International, 2006.

———. *Suttree*. New York: Random House, 1979.

McMurtry, Kim. "'Some Improvident God': Metaphysical Explorations in McCarthy's Border Trilogy." *Sacred Violence: A Reader's Companion to Cormac McCarthy*. Vol. 2. Ed. Rick Wallach. El Paso: Texas Western P, 2002. 143–57.

Metress, Christopher. "*Via Negativa:* The Way of Unknowing in Cormac McCarthy's *Outer Dark*." *Southern Review* 37.1 (Winter 2001): 147–54.

Morrison, Gail Moore "*All the Pretty Horses:* John Grady Cole's Expulsion from Paradise." Arnold and Luce 173–94.

Nafisi, Azar. *Reading Lolita in Tehran: A Memoir in Books*. New York: Random House, 2004.

No Country for Old Men. Dir. Ethan and Joel Coen. Vantage Paramount, 2007.

Nussbaum, Martha. *Poetic Justice: The Literary Imagination and Public Life*. Boston: Beacon P, 1995.

Palacas, Arthur L. "Parentheticals and Personal Voice." *Written Communication* 6.4 (Oct. 1989): 506–27.

Paredes, Americo. "The United States, Mexico, and Machismo." Trans. Marcy Steen. *Journal of the Folklore Institute* 8 (1957): 17–37.

Parrish, Tim. "The Killer Wears the Halo: Cormac McCarthy, Flannery O'Connor, and the American Religion." *Sacred Violence: A Reader's Companion to Cormac McCarthy*. Vol. 1. Ed. Wade Hall and Rick Wallach. 2nd ed. El Paso: Texas Western P, 2002. 35–49.

Pizer, Donald. *Realism and Naturalism in Nineteenth-Century American Fiction*. Rev. ed. Carbondale: Southern Illinois UP, 1984.

Propp, Vladimir. *Theory and History of Folklore*. Trans. Ariadna Y. Martin and Richard P. Martin. Ed. Anatoly Liberman. Minneapolis: U of Minnesota P, 1984.

Scoones, Jacqueline. "The World on Fire: Ethics and Evolution in Cormac McCarthy's Border Trilogy." *A Cormac McCarthy Companion: The Border Trilogy*. Ed. Edwin T. Arnold and Dianne C. Luce. Jackson: UP of Mississippi, 2001. 131–60.

Sepich, John Emil. "'What kind of Indians was them?': Some Historical Sources in Cormac McCarthy's *Blood Meridian*." Arnold and Luce 121–42.

Shaviro, Steven. "'The Very Life of the Darkness': A Reading of *Blood Meridian*." Arnold and Luce 143–56.

Spencer, William C. "Suttree, Linguistic Chameleon." *Publications of the Mississippi Philological Society* (2003): 18–24.

Stein, Edith. *On the Problem of Empathy*. 2nd ed. Trans. Waltraut Stein. The Hague: Martinus Nijhoff, 1970.

St. John, Edward B. "Review: Cormac McCarthy's *No Country for Old Men*." *Library Journal* 15 June 2005: 59.

Sullivan, Nell. "The Dead Girlfriend Motif in *Outer Dark* and *Child of God*." Wallach, *Myth, Legend, Dust* 68–77.

Toolan, Michael. *Language in Literature: An Introduction to Stylistics*. London: Arnold, 1998.

Wallace, Gary. "Meeting Cormac McCarthy." *Southern Quarterly* 30.4 (Summer 1992): 134–35.

Wallach, Rick, ed. *Myth, Legend, Dust: Critical Responses to Cormac McCarthy*. Manchester: Manchester UP, 2000.

———. "Prefiguring Cormac McCarthy: The Early Short Stories." Wallach, *Myth, Legend, Dust* 15–20.

Winfrey, Oprah. "The Exclusive Interview Begins." *Oprah's Book Club*. July 2007. www2.oprah.com/obc_classic/obc_main.jhtml.

Wood, James. "Red Planet: The Sanguinary Sublime of Cormac McCarthy." *New Yorker* 25 July 2005: 88–93.

Woodson, Linda. "'You are the battleground': Materiality, Moral Responsibility, and Determinism in *No Country for Old Men*." *Cormac McCarthy Journal* 5.1 (2005): 5–26.

Woodward, Richard B. "Cormac McCarthy's Venomous Fiction." *New York Times Magazine* 19 Apr. 1992: 28–31.

Yeats, William Butler. *The Yeats Reader*. Ed. Richard J. Finneran. New York: Scribner Poetry, 2002.

INDEX

apocalypse, 32, 134, 152
archetypes, 21
Arnold, Edwin T., 3, 77

Ballard, Lester, 12, 19–20, 41–50, 110
Beckett, Samuel, 4
Bell, Sheriff, 21, 111, 113–31
Bell, Vereen, 10, 25–27, 52
bildungsroman, 26, 54, 78
Bingham, Arthur, 10–11, 67
Black (from *The Sunset Limited*), 15, 25, 112, 152–53, 164–66, 172–73, 176
Blakemore, Diane, 166–67
Boehme, Jacob, 55, 73–74
Bowers, James, 2, 28–29, 41, 55, 67
Brickman, Barbara, 25, 27
Bruen, Ken, 117

camera angles, 9, 33, 38, 95, 174
cannibalism, 54, 156
Carr, Duane R., 51
Catechism of the Catholic Church, 55–57
Chamberlain, Samuel, 72–73
Chigurh, Anton, 17, 21, 110–31, 167–70
Christianity, 103
Christman, Phil, 134
Cobb, William J., 111
Coen, Ethan, 111, 117–18, 121
Coen, Joel, 111, 117–18, 121
confession, 21, 52–53, 55–66, 70, 74, 107; and anticonfession, 21, 57, 69–73; and penitence, 21, 53, 55–57, 62–66, 72–73

Daugherty, Leo, 99, 105
Degh, Linda, 119–21
deictics, 9, 34, 102
Derrida, Jacques, 106–07
dialect, 29–30, 113, 137–38, 169
discourse, 5–7, 12, 33, 107, 169; direct, 5, 9; indirect, 5, 35

Donoghue, Denis, 36, 66, 69, 74, 85, 114, 155–56, 174–75

Eaton, Mark A., 67
Ellis, Jay, 2, 4, 22, 54, 78, 113, 116–17, 161–63
Ellis, Uncle, 129–30
empathy, 2–5, 9, 16–21, 24, 40–57, 74, 78, 116, 144, 163–76; and confession, 53, 57; literary, 8, 17, 33, 56, 66, 162, 176; and sympathy, 17, 38, 65; theology of, 172
ethical philosophy, 107
ethics, 3–4, 19, 66–70, 75, 107, 130, 142, 159–63, 176; Christian, 96, 103; of empathy, 17
Eucharist, 54, 99, 105, 140

father, the, 1, 5, 19, 21, 29–30, 132–60, 163–64, 170–73
father figures, 13, 25, 33, 56
Faulkner, William, 11, 16, 110, 117
folklore, 118, 122, 127
Fowler, Roger, 68
Frye, Steven, 117, 151

genre, 128; confessional, 21, 56–58, 65; noir, 117, 128; Western, 55, 67, 76–78, 122, 128
Gilb, Dagoberto, 175–76
Giles, James R., 14, 37
Gnosticism, 65, 98–99
Grossman, Lev, 112, 118

Harrogate, Gene, 9–10, 13, 17–18, 58–63, 170
Hemingway, Ernest, 10, 124–25
heroism, 1–2, 22–23, 26–34, 40, 77–82, 106–08, 127, 133–37, 143–59, 175–77
hero's journey, 135–36. *See also* heroism
Hillier, Russell M., 128

Holden, Judge, 11–12, 54–73, 83, 110, 114, 118, 135, 164, 167–71
Holloway, David, 78, 87
Holme, Culla, 24–25, 36–40, 47–50, 84, 138, 154–57
Holme, Rinthy, 17–19, 36–51, 156

interiority, 2, 7, 11–27, 35–39, 45–48, 68, 84–102, 116, 139–42, 149
Irving, Washington, 119–20
Iser, Wolfgang, 4, 16–19, 165–66

Jarrett, Robert, 11, 128

Keen, Suzanne, 2–3, 16
Kennedy, William, 135, 157
kid, the, 7, 13, 25, 53–73, 78, 84, 96–101, 138, 167
Kirn, Walter, 111
Knoxville, Tenn., 42, 52, 61, 171
Kreml, Nancy, 10–11
Kuno, Susumu, 8, 33–34, 38, 44, 174
Kushner, David, 134

Lanham, Richard A., 124–25
linguistic worlds, 81

Mamet, David, 111–12
Manifest Destiny, 74
Martinez, Oscar J., 129
McCabe, Pat, 117
McCarthy, Cormac, 16–17, 54–55, 73, 111–12, 117, 133–34, 155, 158, 161, 171–72
—works: *All the Pretty Horses*, 10–11, 16–21, 28, 76–84, 133; *Blood Meridian*, 3, 6–7, 11–16, 25, 41, 53–75, 76–78, 83–85, 99–101, 110, 132–33, 145, 161, 168–71; *Child of God*, 12, 25–27, 40–50, 113, 137; *Cities of the Plain*, 18, 77–84, 94–109, 111, 155, 172; *The Crossing*, 19, 23, 28, 34, 76–84, 104–06; "A Drowning Incident," 14, 18–19, 26–27, 48, 156; *No Country for Old Men*, 12, 17, 23, 110–31, 137, 151, 167; *The Orchard Keeper*, 1, 25–40, 46–51, 78, 113, 133, 137; *Outer Dark*, 17, 24–27, 36–50, 84, 128, 132, 156, 172; *The Road*, 1, 5, 12–13, 29–30, 132–60, 163–64, 170–73; *The Stonemason*, 21, 79, 112–14; *The Sunset Limited*, 15, 22, 25, 112, 134, 152–59, 164–67; *Suttree*, 9–10, 12–13, 29–30, 52–66, 73–75, 137–38, 156, 171–73; "Wake for Susan," 5–7, 13, 19, 26, 46, 130, 174
McMurtry, Kim, 77
metarepresentation, 166–70. *See also* pragmatic linguistics
Metress, Christopher, 37
Mexico, 28, 78, 81–88, 96, 115, 129
morality plays, 50, 122, 128
Morrison, Gail Moore, 77
Moss, Llewellen, 111–23, 138, 167

naming, 45–51, 63, 98, 104
narrative perspective, 2–7, 12–15, 20–23, 38–39, 81–90, 137–38, 162, 173–74; close third person, 2, 8–13, 30, 58–64, 81, 137; first person, 2, 9, 12–13, 28–30, 57–65, 113, 136–46, 173; omniscient, 2–3, 8–13, 20, 30–41, 64–66, 77, 81–108, 110–24, 138–41. *See also* point of view
naturalism, 13–14, 37, 50–51
necrophilia, 19–20, 25
Nietzsche, Frederick, 66, 114, 155
nihilism, 94, 98, 133, 174
Nussbaum, Martha, 3–4, 20, 162, 169

O'Connor, Flannery, 25, 58
Ownby, Arthur, 28–35, 137–38

Palacas, Arthur, 80–81
Paredes, Americo, 127
parenthetical, 81, 87–93
Parham, Billy, 21, 28, 76–84, 95–108, 154–64, 172, 175
Parrish, Tim, 67, 159
personal voice, 81, 87, 92
Pizer, Donald, 14

point of view, 25–26, 31–44, 58, 113, 137, 143, 172–73; shifts in, 2, 7–9, 12, 30, 48. *See also* narrative perspective
pragmatic linguistics, 165–72. *See also* metarepresentation
prophet, 21, 152–53, 159; blind prophet, 24–25, 37, 42, 172; Chigurh as, 122–23; Ely, 133, 150; the father as, 133, 136, 139, 145–46; oracle, 136, 148; seer-prophet in *Cities of the Plain*, 103
Propp, Vladimir, 118
prose styles, 69, 88, 117, 131; "neuter austerity," 11, 66, 69; hypotaxis, 124–25; parataxis, 85, 124–25

Rattner, John Wesley, 1, 15, 25–36, 46
Rip Van Winkle, 119

sacraments, 54, 65, 74, 99, 108–09, 133–35, 140–54, 159
St. Augustine, 56
St. John, Edward, 111
Scoones, Jacqueline, 77
semantics, 31, 61, 88, 92–94, 99–100, 137, 141, 146, 167–70
Sepich, John Emil, 71–72
Sevierville, 42, 50
Shaviro, Steven, 66
Spencer, William C., 169–70
Stein, Edith, 57, 65

storyteller, 41, 69; and storytelling, 68, 111, 117, 131, 133–55
structural criticism, 174
Sullivan, Nell, 17–18
Suttree, Cornelius, 9–15, 18, 29–30, 52–66, 74, 99, 137, 154, 169–73
Sylder, Marion, 1, 15, 22–36
syntax, 9, 11–12, 64, 68–69, 82–88, 95, 101, 111, 124, 147. *See also* prose styles

Tennessee, 31, 54, 67, 132
Texas, 67, 129, 132
Texas-Mexico border, 119–22, 128
theology, 42–43, 172–73; theology of suffering, 173, 176
Tolstoy, Leo, 56
Toolan, Michael, 5, 145

Wallace, Gary, 155
Wallach, Rick, 2, 14
White (from *The Sunset Limited*), 15, 22, 25, 112, 134–35, 152, 154–59, 164–67, 172–76
Winfrey, Oprah, 134, 158, 171
Wood, James, 110–11, 131
Woodson, Linda, 128
Woodward, Richard B., 2, 37, 161

Yeats, William Butler, 117, 131, 151